The Arts of China

1450

Michael Sullivan

The Arts of China

with 235 illustrations, 14 in color,
and 34 diagrams and maps

University of California Press
Berkeley and Los Angeles

N
7340
.S92
1973

University of California Press
Berkeley and Los Angeles, California

© 1967 and © 1973 by Michael Sullivan. All rights reserved

This is a new and revised edition of *A Short History of Chinese Art*,
published by the University of California Press in 1967

Library of Congress Catalog Card Number: 73-78421

ISBN: 0-520-02496-6 (cloth)
         0-520-02548-2 (paper)

Printed and bound in Great Britain

Contents

To Khoan

Foreword and Acknowledgments

Since my *Introduction to Chinese Art* first appeared in 1961, discoveries and research have altered our picture of the history of Chinese art in some important respects. I tried to incorporate some of this new material in the revised *Short History of Chinese Art* which came out in 1967. At that time, the Cultural Revolution in China was at its chaotic and passionate climax. China had closed her doors, traditional culture was under attack, and publication of all the Chinese art and archaeology journals had ceased. It looked to the outside world as if all scholarly work had ended in China for good.

But in 1972 six years of silence were broken, when the sensational results of the archaeological work that had been quietly going on in China, even while the Cultural Revolution was at its height, were published and put on display in Peking. These events have made the *Short History* out of date. So I welcome this opportunity to produce a new and much revised edition, more generously illustrated, and incorporating the most important of the new discoveries and a more adequate assessment, in a new final chapter, of the state of the visual arts in China today.

Once again I should like to thank friends, colleagues and reviewers for their helpful comments on earlier versions of the book, and to express my appreciation to the private collectors and museum directors who have allowed me to reproduce works in their collections. I should like also to thank the staff of Thames and Hudson for making the production of this book such a pleasure.

As always, my wife Khoan and I have collaborated on the book at every stage, although the responsibility for its contents is entirely mine. We would like to record our thanks to Allen and Carmen Christensen for the generous support they have given, and continue to give, to our work.

Stanford University MICHAEL SULLIVAN
California
April 1973

Note. The diagrams and maps are not included in the numbered sequence of illustrations.

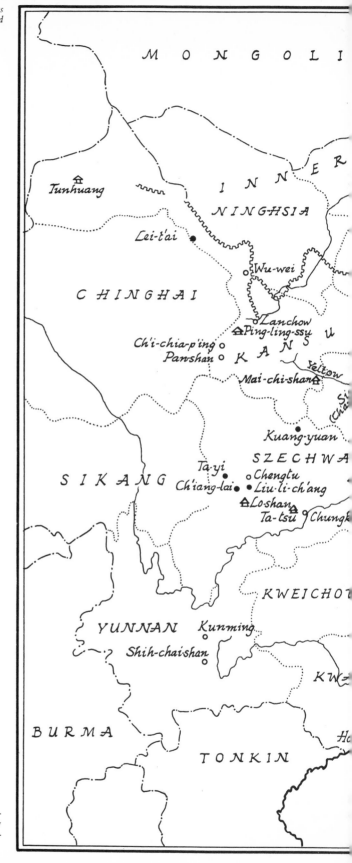

China, showing modern political divisions, chief pottery centres, and Buddhist monuments.

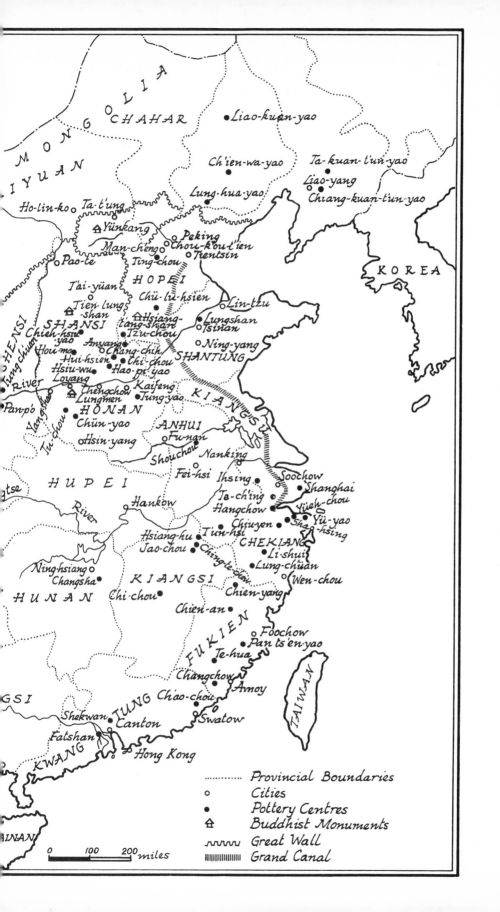

MONGOLIA

CHAHAR

• Liao-kuan-yao

SUIYUAN

• Ch'ien-wa-yao   • Ta-kuan-t'un-yao
                         ○ Liao-yang
Ho-lin-ko • Ta-t'ung   • Lung-hua-yao   • Chiang-kuan-t'un-yao

          ⛩ Yünkang   ○ Peking
     Man-ch'eng● ○○ Chou-k'ou-t'ien
• Pao-te   ● Ting-chou ○ Tientsin

     T'ai-yüan●   H O P E I
   ⛩ Tien-lung   • Chü-lu-hsien
       -shan   ○ Lin-tzu
SHENSI SHANSI ⛩ Hsiang- • Lungshan
  Chieh-hsu -t'ang-shan ○ Tsinan
Hou-ma● ● Anyang Tzu-chou●
  Hui-hsien● ● Chang-chih S H A N T U N G
Hsiu-wu● ● Chi-chou   ● Ning-yang
Loyang ● Hao-pi-yao

River   ● Kaifeng
  ⛩ Chengchow ● Tung-yao   K I A N G S U
   Lungmen
Pan-p'o● H O N A N
         Chün-yao●   A N H U I
     ○ Hsin-yang   ○ Fu-nan
              Shouchou   Nanking ○
                   Fei-hsi● Ihsing●   Soochow ○
H U P E I   Ta-ch'ing● ○ Shanghai
                    Hangchow ○ Yüeh-chou●
     ○ Hankow   Chiu-yen● Shao-hsing
          Hsiang-hu● ● T'un-hsi   ● Yü-yao
          Jao-chou● C H E K I A N G
               Ching-te-chen ● Li-shui
Ning-hsiang ○   K I A N G S I Lung-chüan●
Changsha●   Chi-chou●   Wen-chou●
H U N A N   Chi-chou●   Chien-yang●
                   Chien-an●
               F U K I E N
                    ○ Foochow
                  ● Pan-ts'en-yao
                  Te-hua●
             Changchow ●
         Chiao-chou● ○ Amoy
GSI Shekwan● Canton ○ Swatow●
  Fatshan●
KWANG ○ Hong Kong

AINAN

.... Provincial Boundaries
    ○   Cities
    ●   Pottery Centres
    ⛩   Buddhist Monuments
 ᨠᨠᨠ   Great Wall
 ||||||| Grand Canal

0   100   200 miles

KOREA

TAIWAN

TUNG

Yangtse River

Chronological Table

SHANG			*c.* 1550–*c.* 1030 BC

CHOU	Western Chou *c.* 1030–771	*c.* 1030–256
	Eastern Chou 770–256	
	'Spring and Autumn' period 722–481	
	Warring States period 480–222	

CH'IN	221–207

HAN	Former (Western) Han 202 BC–AD 9	202 BC–AD 220
	Hsin 9–23	
	Later (Eastern) Han 25–221	

THREE KINGDOMS	Shu (Han) 221–263	221–265
	Wei 220–265	
	Wu 222–280	

SOUTHERN (Six Dynasties)	Chin 265–316	265–581
	Eastern Chin 317–420	
	Liu Sung 420–479	
	Southern Ch'i 479–502	
	Liang 502–557	
	Ch'en 557–587	
and	Northern Wei (T'o-pa) 386–535	
NORTHERN DYNASTIES	Eastern Wei (T'o-pa) 534–543	
	Western Wei (T'o-pa) 535–554	
	Northern Ch'i 550–577	
	Northern Chou (Hsien-pi) 557–581	

SUI	581–618
T'ANG	618–906

FIVE DYNASTIES	Later Liang 907–923	907–960
	Later T'ang (Turkic) 923–937	
	Later Chin (Turkic) 937–946	
	Later Han (Turkic) 947–950	
	Later Chou 951–960	

Liao (Khitan Tartars)	907–1125
Hsi-hsia (Tangut Tibetan)	990–1227

SUNG	Northern Sung 960–1126	960–1279
	Southern Sung 1127–1279	

Chin (Jurchen Tartars)	1115–1234
YÜAN (Mongols)	1260–1368
MING	1368–1644
CH'ING (Manchus)	1644–1912
REPUBLIC	1912–1949
PEOPLE'S REPUBLIC	1949–

Reign Periods of the Ming and Ch'ing Dynasties

MING 1368–1644		CH'ING 1644–1912	
Hung-wu	1368–1398	Shun-chih	1644–1661
Chien-wen	1399–1402	K'ang-hsi	1662–1722
Yung-lo	1403–1424	Yung-cheng	1723–1735
Hung-hsi	1425	Ch'ien-lung	1736–1796
Hsüan-te	1426–1435	Chia-ch'ing	1796–1821
Cheng-t'ung	1436–1449	Tao-kuang	1821–1850
Ching-t'ai	1450–1457	Hsien-feng	1851–1861
T'ien-shun	1457–1464	T'ung-chih	1862–1873
Ch'eng-hua	1465–1487	Kuang-hsü	1874–1908
Hung-chih	1488–1505	Hsüan-t'ung	1909–1912
Cheng-te	1506–1521		
Chia-ching	1522–1566		
Lung-ch'ing	1567–1572		
Wan-li	1573–1620		
T'ai-ch'ang	1620		
T'ien-ch'i	1621–1627		
Ch'ung-chen	1628–1644		

NOTE

The earliest exactly known date in Chinese history is 841 BC. According to calculations made by a number of scholars on the basis of probable reign lengths, the date of the founding of the Shang Dynasty has been put between 1766 and 1523 BC, that of the Chou conquest between 1122 and 1018 BC.

1 Before the Dawn of History

In far-off times the Universe, according to a popular Chinese legend, was an enormous egg. One day the egg split open; its upper half became the sky, its lower half the earth, and from it emerged P'an Ku, primordial man. Every day he grew ten feet taller, the sky ten feet higher, the earth ten feet thicker. After eighteen thousand years P'an Ku died. His head split and became the sun and moon, while his blood filled the rivers and seas. His hair became the forests and meadows, his perspiration the rain, his breath the wind, his voice the thunder – and his fleas our ancestors.

A people's legends of its origins generally give a clue as to what they think most important. This one is no exception, for it expresses a typically Chinese viewpoint – namely, that man is not the culminating achievement of the creation, but a relatively insignificant part of the scheme of things; hardly more than an afterthought, in fact. By comparison with the beauty and splendour of the world itself, the mountains and valleys, the clouds and waterfalls, the trees and flowers, which are the visible manifestations of the workings of the *Tao*, he counts for very little. In no other civilization – unless it be, in far smaller compass, in that of Britain – do the forms and patterns of nature, and man's humble devotion and response to it, play so big a part. We can, moreover, trace the germs of this attitude back into the remote past, when in North China nature was a kinder master than she is now. Half a million years ago, in the time of Peking Man, that region was comparatively warm and wet; elephants' and rhinoceros roamed a more luxuriant countryside than today's barren hills and wind-swept plains. Within this till lately inhospitable area, forming the modern provinces of Honan, Hopei, Shensi and Shansi, was born a uniquely Chinese feeling of oneness with nature which, in course of time, was to find its highest expression in philosophy, poetry and painting. This sense of communion was not merely philosophical and artistic; it had a practical value as well. For the farmer's prosperity, and hence that of society as a whole, depended upon his knowing the seasons and attuning himself to the 'will of Heaven', as he called it. Agriculture in course of time became a ritual over which the emperor himself presided, and when at the spring sowing he ceremonially ploughed the first furrow, not only did he hope to ensure a good harvest thereby, but his office was itself further ennobled by this act of homage to the forces of nature.

13

This sense of 'attunement' is fundamental in Chinese thinking. Man must attune himself not only to nature but also to his fellow men, in ever-widening circles starting from his family and friends. Thus his highest ideal has always in the past been to discover the order of things and to act in accordance with it. As in the following pages the history of Chinese art unfolds, we will find that its characteristic and unique beauty lies in the fact that it is an expression of this very sense of attunement. Is that one reason why Westerners, often with no other interest in Chinese civilization, collect and admire Chinese art with such enthusiasm? Do they sense, perhaps, that the forms which the Chinese artist and craftsman have created are *natural* forms – forms which seem to have evolved inevitably by the movement of the maker's hand, in response to an intuitive awareness of a natural rhythm? Chinese art does not demand of us, as does Indian art, the effort to bridge what often seems an unbridgeable gulf between extremes of physical form and metaphysical content; nor will we find in it that preoccupation with formal and intellectual considerations which so often makes Western art difficult for the Asian mind to accept. The forms of Chinese art are beautiful because they are in the widest and deepest sense harmonious, and we can appreciate them because we too feel their rhythms all round us in nature, and instinctively respond to them. These rhythms, moreover, this sense of inner life expressed in line and contour, are present in Chinese art from its earliest beginnings.

CHINA IN THE STONE AGE Every lover of Chinese art today is familiar with the magnificent painted pottery of the Neolithic period, and we are apt to forget that little more than fifty years ago this stage in the evolution of Chinese civilization, and all that went before it, was completely unknown. It was not until 1921 that positive evidence was found that China had actually passed through a Stone Age at all. In that year the Swedish geologist J. Gunnar Andersson and his Chinese assistants made two discoveries of immense importance. The first was at Chou-k'ou-tien, south-west of Peking, where in a cleft in the hillside Andersson picked up a number of flint tools, indicating that it had been occupied by very early man. He himself did not excavate, but his find led to further excavations and to the eventual discovery by Dr P'ei Wen-chung of fossil bones which, with the exception of Late Java Man, *Pithecanthropus erectus*, were the oldest human remains yet discovered. The bones were those of a hominid, *Sinanthropus pekinensis*, who lived in the Middle Pleistocene period, about half a million years ago. The remains in the deep cleft, fifty metres thick, represent many thousands of years of occupation. Peking Man had tools of quartz, flint and limestone, made either from pebbles chipped to shape or from flakes struck off a large pebble. He was a cannibal who broke open the bones of his victims to suck out the marrow; he had fire, ate grain, and probably knew some very primitive form of speech. In 1964, in deposits on an open hillside in Lan-t'ien County, Shensi, palaeontologists discovered the skull-cap of a hominid believed, from related fossil remains, to be at least a hundred thousand years older than Peking Man, and so roughly the same age as Early Java Man, *Pithecanthropus robustus*.

Gradually, in the Late Pleistocene Age, the evolution of early man in China gathered pace. In recent years, remains of *Homo sapiens* have been found in many areas. 'Upper Cave Man' at Chou-k'ou-tien (20–10,000 B C) had a wider range of stone tools than his ancestors, he probably wore hides sewn together, and his wife adorned herself with stone beads, drilled and painted with hematite, the earliest known intentional decoration in the history of Chinese civilization. Finely fashioned microliths (very small stone implements) have been found in many desert sites in Ning-hsia and the Ordos region, different types of blades and flakes having been fashioned for different purposes. Further south, in the region of northern Honan that was to become the last seat of the Shang Dynasty, thousands of microliths were discovered in a habitation site in 1960; other rich remains have been found far to the south-west, in Szechwan, Yunnan and Kweichow. Although as yet the dating of these scattered sites and their relationship to each other are by no means clear, their distribution suggests that the Upper Palaeolithic culture, shading imperceptibly into the Meso-lithic, was spread very widely across ancient China.

These people were hunters and fishermen. The 'Neolithic Revolution' took place when they settled down, began to build villages and to learn the arts of farming and horti-culture. But even before the Neolithic culture had developed, the early Chinese were making pottery. A coarse cord-marked grey ware was produced by the primitive fishing folk living beside the rivers and lakes of Central and South China in Late Mesolithic times. No reliable dates for these wares have yet been published, but a Japanese archaeologist estimated an age of about twelve thousand years for pottery of this type which he found in Taiwan in 1966–67 – roughly contemporary with the earliest Japanese pottery of the Jōmon period, the dating of which has been firmly estab-lished by the Carbon 14 method.

The first definite evidence of the existence of a Neolithic culture in China was found in 1921 by Andersson and his assistants, who located at Yang-shao-ts'un in Honan an extensive deposit of Neolithic tools and beautiful red pottery painted with designs in black. Before long more sites had been discovered in Honan. In 1923 Andersson went to Kansu to attempt to trace the connecting links which he suspected existed between this painted pottery and that of the Near East, and there found more than fifty prehistoric sites representing a gradual development from about the third millennium B C to the Late Chou period. Some of the

NEOLITHIC CULTURE

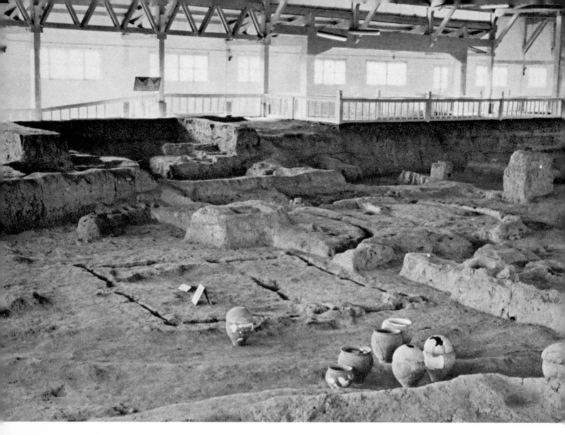

1 Pan-p'o, Shensi. Part of the Neolithic village after excavation, now a museum.

features of this Neolithic culture are common to all early civilizations and belong to a culture-complex that extends from the Nile Valley to Mesopotamia, from the Indus Valley to the Tarim Basin, linked to China by the 'Corridor of the Steppes', a natural migration-route. In all these areas there developed the use of polished stone tools and of the bow and arrow, and the domestication of animals. At first it was thought that in China this culture was concentrated in two areas only, Honan and Kansu, where Andersson made his finds; but more recent excavations by Chinese archaeologists – particularly those that have followed in the wake of the huge reconstruction schemes that have been in progress since 1950 – reveal that it was widely diffused throughout China.

For many years we had to visualize Chinese Neolithic culture in terms of the rather poor sites found by Andersson – notably the single grave at Pan-shan in Kansu, and the extensive but imprecise deposits at Yang-shao in Honan. This picture was dramatically revised in 1953 by the discovery of a group of Early Neolithic villages at Pan-p'o, east of Sian on the right bank of the Chan River. The villages cover two and a half acres; four separate layers of houses have been found in a cultural deposit three metres thick, representing many centuries of intermittent occupation between about 4000 and 2000 BC. The earliest inhabitants lived in round wattle-and-daub huts, each with reed roof and plaster floor and an oven in the centre, the design perhaps copied from an earlier tent or yurt. Their descendants built rectangular or square houses, each with a framework of wooden planking, sunk a metre below ground-level and approached by a flight of steps. The roof of one particularly large building, over twelve metres long, was supported on three rows of posts. In the village were found no less than six pottery kilns, of two types: a simple pocket-shaped pit with a perforated floor, and a cylindrical tunnel with forced draught, leading to a beehive-shaped chamber. In these kilns the Pan-p'o potters made both a coarse grey or red pottery and a fine red ware burnished and then painted in black with geometric designs and occasionally with fishes and human faces. They seem not to have known the potter's wheel, but made their vessels by coiling long strips of clay. From clay they also made spindle-whorls and even hairpins, but the finer objects, such as needles, fish-hooks, spoons and arrow-heads, were made of bone. Part of the village of Pan-p'o has been roofed over and preserved as a museum of Chinese Neolithic culture.

The painted pottery first discovered at Pan-shan in Kansu has not been matched in quality and beauty by any Neolithic wares discovered since. It consists chiefly of mortuary urns, wide and deep bowls and tall vases, often with loop-handles set low on the body. Though the walls are thin, the forms are robust, their generous contours beautifully enhanced by the decoration in black pigment which was clearly executed with a crude form of brush. Some of the designs are geometric, consisting of parallel bands or lozenges containing concentric squares, crosses or diamonds. The lower half of the body is always left undecorated, perhaps because it may have been set in the sandy ground to prevent it overturning. Many vessels are adorned with sweeping wave-like bands which gather into a kind of whirlpool; others make use of the stylized figures of men, frogs, fishes and birds, while a human face with some sort of ceremonial head-dress found at Pan-p'o perhaps represented a shaman. Shards found at Ma-chia-yao in Kansu reveal a quite sophisticated brush technique; in one case the artist depicted plants each of whose leaves ends in a sharp point, indicated with a flick of the brush – the same technique that was to be used by the Sung artist, three thousand years later, in painting bamboo. The naturalistic motifs however are rare, and the vast majority of vessels are decorated with geometric or stylized patterns whose significance is still a mystery. In point of technique, shape and even to some extent in the motifs themselves, the Yang-shao pottery may be remotely influenced by that of western Asia, for the very similar painted red ware found at Anau in Russian Turkestan is at least one thousand to two thousand years older (see figure). But the Kansu vases reveal in their lively, uplifted forms, and still more in the dynamic linear movement of their brush decoration, a quality that is uniquely Chinese. Moreover, in stratified deposits at Ma-chia-yao the local painted ware lies

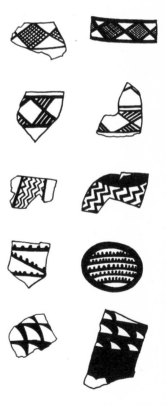

Neolithic painted pottery from Anau (*left*) and China (*right*) compared.

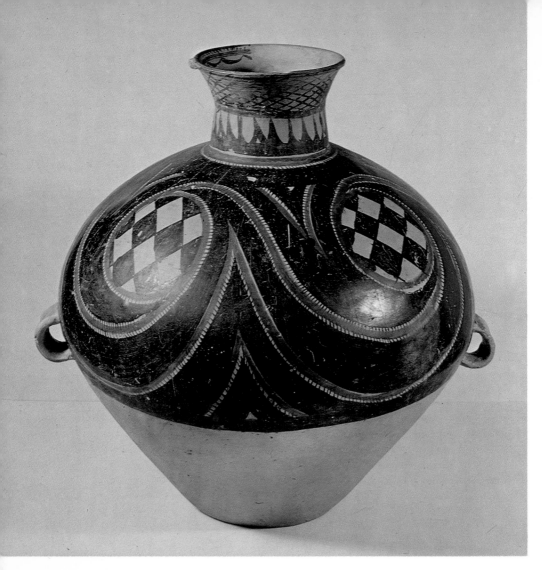

2 Funerary urn. Pottery decorated with slip pigments in red and black. Neolithic period.

above the Yang-shao type and is therefore later, indicating a westward movement of the Yang-shao culture from the Central Plain (Chung-yüan), rather than a movement into China of a western culture. But this is a controversial question that is by no means settled.

Until recently it was thought that the painted pottery Yang-shao culture was more or less directly superseded by a totally different culture centred on Shantung, and represented by the burnished black pottery of Lung-shan. But while the Lung-shan pottery is both distinctive in character and later in date than the Yang-shao, the precise relationship between the two 'cultures', if indeed they are distinct, is not yet clear. Since 1950, many stratified sites have been found in Central and eastern China containing both painted and black pottery in the same level, with a considerable proportion of cord-marked grey ware. This mixed culture was no mere transitional phase between Yang-shao and the 'classic' Lung-shan, but represents a major cultural period in prehistoric China, for which Chang Kwang-chih has coined the term 'Lungshanoid'.[1] Archaeologists in China also call it the 'Ch'i-chia-p'ing culture', after one of the sites in Hupeh. The classic Lung-shan may now be seen not as a separate uniquely north-eastern culture, but as a late and purely regional development from the mixed 'Lungshanoid' culture which succeeded the Yang-shao.

A curious example of this mixed culture is provided by the Pao-t'ou-ts'un site in Ning-yang-hsien, in Shantung. There the most conspicuous pottery is a highly burnished red Yang-shao-type ware painted with geometric motifs in black and white slip. This 'Ning-yang culture' is thought to be an offshoot of the Yang-shao and a precursor of the mature Lung-shan.

In 1928 Dr Wu Chin-ting of the Academia Sinica (Chinese Academy of Sciences) had discovered the first black pottery at Ch'eng-tzu-yai, near Lung-shan in western Shantung. It was made on the wheel of black clay fired in a reducing atmosphere, sometimes built up in thin sheets laminated together. Many of the shapes are elegant and somewhat metallic, while the decoration, consisting chiefly of raised bands, grooves and milled rings, gives it a rather machine-made look. Several of the Lung-shan shapes, notably the wide dish, beaker and dish on a tall stem, resemble vessels in use from one thousand to two thousand years earlier in western Asian sites such as Tepe Hissar, Anau and Susa; while in East Asia this type of pottery has been found in a

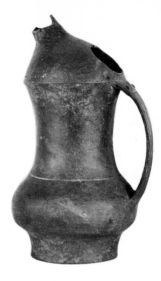

3 Ewer. Dark grey earthenware. From Ch'i-chia-p'ing, Kansu. Late Neolithic period.

4 Bowl. Pottery decorated with masks and other subjects in black slip. Excavated at Pan-p'o-ts'un, Shensi. Neolithic period.

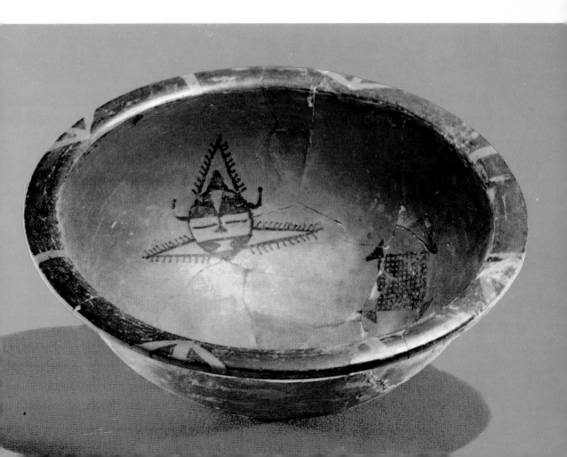

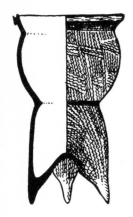

Hsien steamer from Chengchow.

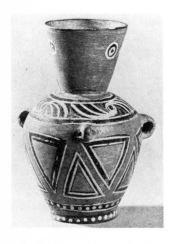

5 Jar. Earthenware decorated with black and white slip. From Pao-t'ou, Ning-yang District, Shantung. Late Neolithic period.

huge arc stretching from north-east China down to Thailand and northern Malaya. At some sites, such as Miao-ti-kou, it lies over a painted pottery stratum going back to about 3000 B C, while in its later phases, as at Hu-shu near Nanking, it continued down to about 500 B C, and hence well into the Late Bronze Age.

Among the black pottery types one vessel, the *li* tripod, was destined to have a special significance in early Chinese culture. This vessel, which is found also in the grey wares, appears to be derived from the joining together of three tall ovoid jars with pointed bottoms. Perhaps three such vessels had stood together over a fire, and some practical housewife had the idea of combining them into one, the hollow legs (whose mammiform shape cannot have been accidental) both supporting the body and presenting a greater surface to the fire. This shape, which in Kansu only appears in the latest Neolithic sites such as Hsin-tien, seems to be uniquely Chinese. It was transmitted into the bronze culture of the Shang Dynasty, where it gave the form to the most important and characteristic of the early ritual vessels. When supporting a pot with a perforated base, it becomes the *hsien* steamer, the pictograph for which meant 'to sacrifice'.

Some of the precision and symmetry of the black Lung-shan ware appears also in the thin, wheel-made grey pottery found by Andersson, and later by Dr Hsia Nai, at Ch'i-chia-p'ing in Kansu, and in sites in Ning-hsia and Inner Mongolia. The elegance of its vases and pitchers, with their long thin handles has suggested an origin in metal forms, but the first Carbon 14 dates published in China (see below) put the Ch'i-chia culture roughly contemporary with the Lung-shan. As yet there is no bronze, but the presence in several sites of almost pure copper ornaments and tools places Ch'i-chia on the threshold of the Bronze Age.

Neolithic culture persisted in outlying regions long after the beginning of the Bronze Age in North China. Painted pottery of Yang-shao type, for example, has been found in later sites in South China, Szechwan and Taiwan. Excavations in Anhui, Kiangsu and Kiangsi show that while the south-east borrowed from Yang-shao, and was more closely related to Lung-shan, it had distinctive characteristics of its own. Most notable is the technique of decorating pottery by stamping or impressing geometric designs in the clay before firing. This technique was remarkably persistent, and seems to have influenced not only the white pottery of Late Shang at Anyang but also the decoration of bronzes made in Kiangsu and Anhui during the Chou Dynasty.

Excavation in China since 1949 has proceeded at such a pace that no sooner is a statement – on Neolithic chronology, for example – made than it is rendered out of date by new discoveries. The Cultural Revolution put an abrupt end to their publication in 1966, and for several years it was widely thought abroad that all archaeological work had stopped. Late in 1971, however, reports began to appear of sensational discoveries made during the preceding five years, some of which are described in later chapters of this book, and in the spring of 1972 publication of two cultural and archaeological journals, *Wen Wu* and *Kaogu*, was resumed. The latter (Nos 1 and 5, 1972) contained the first brief reports on Carbon 14 dates established for Neolithic sites in China. Here are some of the results for sites mentioned in this chapter: Pan-p'o village, 4115 BC ± 110 years and 3890 BC ± 105 years; Ma-chia-yao (Kansu) 2185 BC ± 100 years; Pan-shan (Kansu) 2065 BC ± 100 years; Ch'i-chia-p'ing (Kansu), 1725 BC ± 95 years.

Some of the stone weapons and artefacts used in prehistoric China are common to all the Neolithic peoples of Asia; others are of purely Chinese origin. Among the latter we find a wide-bladed hoe and the *ko*-type dagger-axe (which was later to be translated into bronze and iron), and a broad rectangular chopping-knife bound to the handle by thongs passed through two holes bored in the upper part. Some of these tools are beautifully polished, the finest being made in jade, which, because of its hardness, fine texture and purity of colour, has been an object of special veneration from ancient times until today. In the Kansu hills, Andersson found beautifully worked jade axes, knives, ornaments and rings. The latter included the circle (*huan*) and flat disc (*pi*), while elsewhere was found a ring, square outside and circular inside, which was possibly the ancestor of the *tsung* (see page 48). By the Chou Dynasty the *pi* and the *tsung* had acquired an almost sacred place in court ritual as symbols of Heaven and of Earth. Whether or not these, or indeed any, symbolic meanings were already attached to them in the Late Neolithic period it is impossible to say.

Into this short chapter we have compressed half a million years of human history in China. Although the picture is enormously over-simplified (particularly with regard to the Neolithic period), it shows that before the dawn of recorded history there had already emerged many of those characteristics which we consider essentially Chinese: a highly organized social life centred on agriculture and bound together by ritual, high standards of craftmanship, the flexible brush as an instrument of artistic expression, the ceremonial use of jade, and preoccupation with man's fate after death. This primitive culture lingered on in South and West China long after the coming of bronze had opened a new and incomparably richer chapter in Chinese history.

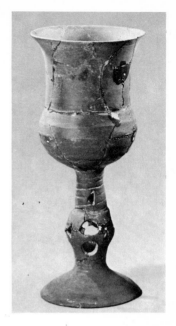

6 Stemcup. Black pottery. From An-chiu and Wei-fang, Shantung. Late Neolithic period.

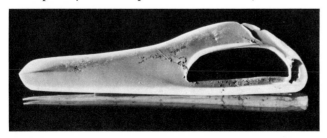

7 Scraper or dagger. Polished stone. From Pi-hsien, Kiangsu. Neolithic period.

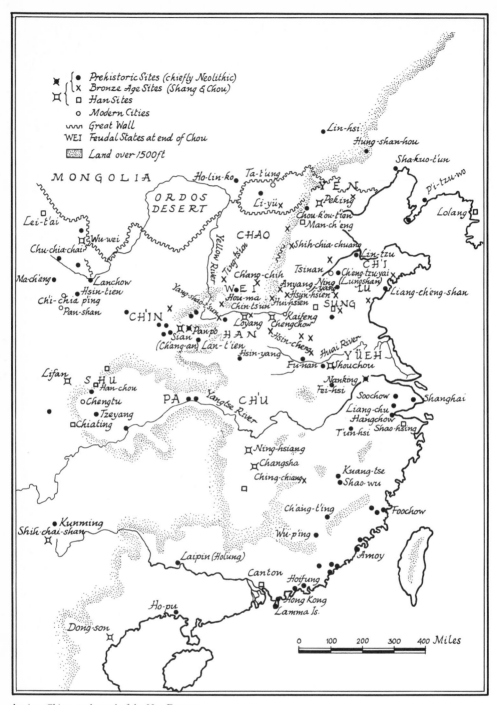

Legend:
- ● Prehistoric Sites (chiefly Neolithic)
- ✕ Bronze Age Sites (Shang & Chou)
- ☐ Han Sites
- ○ Modern Cities
- ⌇ Great Wall
- WEI Feudal States at end of Chou
- ▦ Land over 1500 ft

MONGOLIA

ORDOS DESERT

Lin-hsi
Hung-shan-hou
Sha-kuo-t'un
P'i-tzu-wo

Ho-lin-ko
Ta-t'ung
Li-yü
YEN
Peking
Lolang
Lei-t'ai
Chou-k'ou-t'ien
Man-ch'eng

CHAO

Wu-wei
Shih-chia-chuang
Lin-tzu
CH'I

Chu-chia-chai
Ch'ang-chih
Tsinan
Ch'eng-tzu-yai
(Lungshan)
LU
Liang-ch'eng-shan

Ma-ch'ang
Lanchow
Hsin-tien
WEI
Anyang
Ning-yang
Hsin-hsien
Chi-chia ping
Pan-shan
Yang-shao-ts'un
Hou-ma
Hui-hsien
SUNG
Chin-ts'un
CH'IN
Pan-p'o
Kaifeng
Chengchow
Loyang
Sian
(Ch'ang-an)
Lan-t'ien
HAN
Hsin-cheng
YÜEH
Lifan
Hsin-yang
Huai River
Fu-nan
Shouchou
SHU
Han-chou
Nanking
Fei-hsi
Chengtu
PA
Yangtse River
CH'U
Soochow
Shanghai
Tzeyang
Liang-chu
Chiating
Hangchow
T'un-hsi
Shao-hsing

Ning-hsiang
Changsha
Kuang-tse
Shao-wu
Ching-chiang

Ch'ang-t'ing
Foochow
Kunming
Shih-chai-shan
Wu-p'ing

Laipin (Holung)
Amoy

Canton
Hoifung

Ho-pu
Hong Kong
Lamma Is.

Dong-son

0 100 200 300 400 Miles

Ancient China, to the end of the Han Dynasty.

22

2 The Shang Dynasty

For centuries, farmers living in the village of Hsiao-t'un near Anyang in Honan have been picking up peculiar bones which they found lying in the fields after rain or while they were ploughing. Some were polished and shone like glass; most had rows of oval notches in their backs and T-shaped cracks; a few had marks on them that looked like primitive writing. The farmers would take these bones to apothecaries in Anyang and neighbouring towns, who often ground off the marks before selling them as 'dragon bones', a potent ingredient in restoratives. In 1899 some of the inscribed bones fell into the hands of the noted scholar and collector Liu Ngo, who recognized the writing as a still older form of the archaic script already known on the ritual bronzes of the Chou Dynasty. Soon other scholars, notably Lo Chen-yü and Wang Kuo-wei, took up the study of what were, in fact, fragments of the archives of the royal house of Shang, the actual existence of which had hitherto not been proved, though Chinese historians had never doubted it.

The bones were traced to Anyang. The farmers began to dig deeper, and before long there began to appear on the antique market in Peking and Shanghai magnificent bronze vessels, jades and other objects, whose exact place of origin was kept secret. For nearly thirty years the farmers and dealers' agents, working at night or during the idle winter months, continued their indiscriminate pillaging of Shang tombs. Finally, in 1928, the Chinese National Research Institute (Academia Sinica) began at Anyang an important series of excavations which were to provide the first definite archaeological evidence that the Shang Dynasty had actually existed and was not, as some Western writers had come to suspect, a pious fabrication of the backward-looking Chinese. By 1935 more than three hundred graves had been discovered, ten of which, of enormous size, were undoubtedly royal tombs.

These discoveries posed more problems than they solved. Who were the Shang people, and where did they come from? How was it that their earliest remains revealed a culture of such sophistication, particularly in their bronze techniques? If the Shang existed, then perhaps remains would be found of the even earlier Hsia Dynasty.

The Chinese traditionally believe that they are descended from Huang Ti, the Yellow Emperor, who lived for a hundred years. After him came Fu Hsi, who first drew the magical diagram *pa kua* (the 'eight trigrams') from which the art of writing is descended. Shen Nung, the Divine Farmer, invented agriculture and discovered the use of medicinal herbs. Then came Yao and the filial Shun, the ideal rulers, and finally Yü the Great, who founded the Hsia Dynasty. In these legendary figures the Chinese personified all that they held most sacred: agriculture, good government, filial piety, and the art of writing. Now it is believed that all these personages were invented or took on these roles at a much later date. Yü, Yao and Shun appeared first in Late Chou literature. Huang Ti was probably invented by the Taoists. As for the Hsia, although the character appears on the Shang oracle bones, it is never used there to refer to a dynasty, which may simply have been invented by the Chou people to legitimize their conquest of the Shang, whom they chose to consider as usurpers. Before the rise of the Shang there were, as we saw in the first chapter, many primitive communities, and one of those conquered by the first Shang ruler may have been called 'Hsia'. Such communities form a connecting link between the Late Neolithic and the full flowering of the Bronze Age.

As early Chinese culture coalesced it came to incorporate elements characteristic of several distinct regions. The people of North China practised shamanism and elaborate burial rites. Some authorities believe that they were originally matriarchal; they had timber houses partly sunk in the ground, and ate dry grains such as wheat and barley. By the second millennium B C they were being influenced by the north-western 'proto-turkic' peoples, who bridged the huge empty spaces between them and the cultures of Central and western Asia, and who brought to China itself a patriarchal nomadism, horses and horse-sacrifice, the worship of the heavenly bodies, tumulus graves and the use of earthen drums. At a somewhat later stage, and especially in the Chou period, North China felt the impact of the Yüeh group of peoples from the south-east and south, whose ethnic links were as much with South-east Asia and Oceania as with China proper. They lived by the sea and on the rivers, had longboats and fought naval battles, worshipped the forces of the rain and rivers in serpents and crocodiles ('dragons'), used bronze drums, tattooed themselves, perhaps lived in long-houses, cultivated wet rice, and decorated their pottery with stamped designs.

Until 1950 our knowledge of Shang culture was derived almost wholly from the ruins of the Shang capital at Anyang, founded by King P'an-keng between 1400 and 1300 B C, and finally conquered by the armies of the Chou at a date which most authorities on this highly controversial question put between 1122 and 1027 B C. At Anyang the bronze culture was at its height; the metal-workers were producing sacrificial vessels of a quality that has been equalled nowhere in the world – the culmination, clearly, of centuries of development. The oracle bones gave the names of eighteen kings before P'an-keng, and, according to tradition, the

Shang had moved their capital five times before finally settling at Anyang. If traces of these earlier capitals could be found, the gap between the Late Neolithic and the mature bronze culture of Anyang might be closed.

When the new régime came to power in 1949, there was some fear that the authorities would have no time or funds for archaeological excavation, and that the pioneer work of the Academia Sinica would be forgotten. Happily the position has, on the contrary, greatly improved. Popular education and the fostering of pride in China's cultural heritage have combined to arouse the interest of the poorest peasant, while the work of the Institute of Archaeology of the Chinese Academy of Sciences and of various regional organizations is rapidly altering the whole archaeological picture. One result of this activity has been that, since 1952, well over a hundred Shang sites have been discovered, in an area embracing the whole of Central and eastern China, from Shensi in the north-west to Kiangsi and Kiangsu in the south-east. Just how closely these areas were related to the centre of Shang power in Shansi and Honan is not yet clear, but the view that bronze culture began in Honan and spread outwards has now been abandoned in favour of a picture of primitive metal-working communities evolving in a number of centres more or less simultaneously.

The dawn of the historical Shang Dynasty broke in the Yen-shih district of Honan, lying between Loyang and Chengchow. One site, Kao-yai, is clearly stratified: Yang-shao–Lungshanoid–Lung-shan–Early Bronze Age; another, much richer, is Erh-li-t'ou on the Lo River near by. Here have been found the remains of a bronze-foundry, a bronze bell, turquoise, jade and shell ornaments, and new pottery shapes such as the *chia*, *ku* and *chüeh* (shortly to appear in bronze), some of which bear incised markings which may be a primitive form of script. It has been suggested that Erh-li-t'ou was the site of Po, capital of the first Shang monarch T'ang Wang.

The next big step in the development of Shang culture is represented by the remarkably rich finds in and around Chengchow. The lowest strata are typical Lung-shan, with no bronze, but the next stages, Lower and Upper Erh-li-kang, show a dramatic change. Remains of a city wall more than a mile square and sixty feet across at the base have been uncovered, together with what were probably sacrificial halls, houses, bronze-foundries, pottery kilns and a bone-workshop. Large graves were furnished with ritual bronze vessels, jade and ivory, while the pottery includes both glazed wares and the fine white ware first found at Anyang. All the evidence points to Chengchow having been the site of a great city, very probably Ao, capital of the tenth Shang ruler Chung-ting. The decline in quality of the remains in the last Shang phase at Chengchow, represented by the People's Park site to the north-west of the city, suggests that

THE EVOLUTION OF
SHANG CULTURE

by then the capital had already been moved to Anyang.

The inscriptions on the oracle bones tell much about the beliefs, social organization and activities of the Shang – or Yin, as the Chou people called them. Shang society was probably feudal, though this cannot be said as positively of the Shang as of the Chou. Successful generals, sons and even wives of the Shang rulers were enfeoffed, while small neighbouring 'states' paid regular tribute. Prominent among the officials was the *chen-jen* who, as a scribe, composed and probably wrote the inscriptions on the oracle bones, and, as a diviner, interpreted the cracks which appeared in them when a hot metal rod was applied to one of the holes bored into the back. These inscriptions were generally engraved, though a few were written with a brush and some sort of ink. About three thousand characters have been identified, rather less than half of which have been deciphered; they were written in vertical columns, moving either to the left or to the right, apparently according to the dictates of symmetry. In the early stages at Chengchow the oracle bones were mainly scapulae of pig, ox or sheep; in the final phase at Anyang tortoise-shells were used almost exclusively, fastened together with thongs passed through holes at each end, as is shown in the pictograph for a book, *ts'e* 冊. The inscriptions on the bones are either declarations of fact or of the ruler's intentions, or questions about the future which could be answered with a simple yes or no. They relate chiefly to agriculture, war and hunting, the weather, journeys and the all-important sacrifices by means of which the ruler attuned himself to the will of Heaven. They reveal that the Shang people had some knowledge of astronomy, knew precisely the length of the year, had invented the intercalary month, and divided the day into periods. Their religious belief centred in a supreme deity (Ti) who controlled the rain, wind and human affairs, and in lesser deities of the heavenly bodies, of the soil, of rivers, mountains and special places (the *genius loci*); special respect was paid to the ancestral spirits, who lived with Ti and could affect the destinies of men for good or ill, but whose benevolent concern in the affairs of their descendants could be ensured by elaborate sacrificial rites.

Many years' work at Anyang have given us a fairly clear picture of the later phases of Shang architecture. The Shang people built chiefly in wood and tamped earth. Remains have been found of several large buildings; one of them, over ninety feet long, was raised on a high plinth, its presumably thatched roof supported on rows of wooden pillars, of which the stone socles remain. Another was laid out axially with steps in the centre of the south side, and but for its roof would not have looked so very different from any large building in North China today. Some of the more important buildings were adorned with formalized animal heads carved in stone, and their beams were painted with designs similar to those on the ritual bronzes. The most popular method of construction – presumably because it was cheap and provided good protection against the piercing cold of the North China winter – was the *pan-chu* ('plank building') technique, in which the earth was stamped between vertical boards with a pole: the smaller the diameter of the pole, the stronger the wall. Chou texts relate that the common people lived in 'burrows and nests'. The 'nests' may refer to little huts raised, as in South-east Asia, several feet above the ground. The 'burrows' were either caves in the loess terraces, still inhabited today by millions of North China peasants, or dwellings sunk below the surface of the ground, a custom inherited from Neolithic times. Many of these dwelling-pits have been found at Anyang. They had plaster floors and walls, while, as in Neolithic times, rows of timber posts supported a thatched roof, probably with a hole in the centre through which the smoke from the central hearth escaped. Often a deep storage-pit was sunk in the floor of the house. We can imagine ancient Anyang as a cluster of these lowly dwellings, with here and there a large timber building raised on a platform, the whole city surrounded by a mud wall with gates at intervals surmounted by watch-towers.

The most spectacular of Shang remains, however, are not the buildings but the tombs. The Chinese belief that the spirit of the departed must be provided with all he possessed (or, indeed, would have liked to possess) in his earthly life led to immolation and human sacrifice on a gigantic scale. Later the more frightful practices were abandoned, but until the Ming Dynasty the custom persisted of placing in the tomb pottery models not only of furniture, farms and houses, but also of servants, guards and domestic animals. At the same time the corpse was decked out with the richest clothing, jewellery and jades that his family or the state could afford. Collectors are even known to have been buried with their favourite paintings. However much one may deplore this custom, it has ensured the preservation of many beautiful things that would otherwise have been irretrievably lost.

The Shang tombs throw a brilliant, even lurid, light upon early Chinese civilization. Some of them were of enormous size, and furnished with bronze vessels, jade objects and pottery. One royal personage, apparently an animal-lover, had his pets, including an elephant, buried near him in separate graves. The tomb excavated at Wu-kuan-ts'un had only two sloping ramps, north and south, but contained the remains of an elaborate canopy of painted leather, wood-bark and bamboo; here both the ramps and main chamber were crammed with the complete skeletons of no less than twenty-two men (one beneath the tomb-chamber) and twenty-four women, and in addition the skulls of a further fifty men were buried in adjacent pits. In some cases the bodies lie quietly with no signs of violence – the result, perhaps, of voluntary self-immolation by relations or

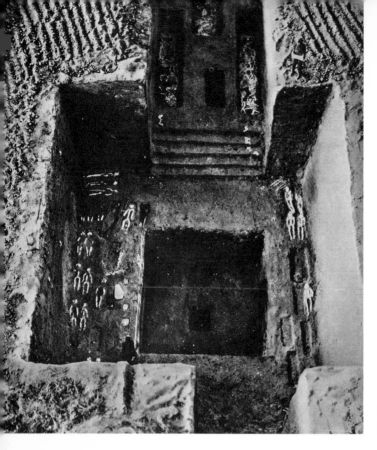

8 Tomb at Wu-kuan-ts'un, Anyang, Honan, after excavation. Late Shang period.

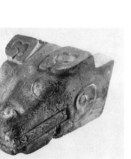

9 Ox-head. Marble sculpture. Excavated at Hou-chia-chuang, Anyang. Late Shang period.

retainers of the dead man – while the decapitated victims may have been slaves, criminals or prisoners of war. Other excavations at Hsiao-t'un and Ta-ssu-k'ung-ts'un have revealed chariot burials in which the complete chariot with horses and driver were buried in specially prepared pits with channels dug out for the wheels. The wood has of course perished, but impressions in the earth have made it possible to reconstruct the chariot itself, and thus to determine the position and function of many of its beautiful bronze fittings. It is disconcerting for us when we admire the marvellous refinement and craftsmanship of the ritual bronzes to be reminded of the ferocious rites with which they are associated. Mass immolation was not practised officially by the Chou, though it appears to have been revived from time to time, on a more modest scale, by later rulers.

One of the biggest surprises at Anyang was the discovery of Shang marble sculpture in the round, a notable example of which is the head of an ox illustrated here. Previously nothing of the sort earlier than the Han Dynasty was known, and even today only a handful of Chou stone-carvings have been unearthed, and those so small as hardly to deserve the name of sculpture. Other figures include tigers, buffaloes, birds, tortoises, a kneeling captive (or sacrificial victim) with his hands tied behind his back, two sitting figures, one headless and clasping his knees, the other complete, leaning back

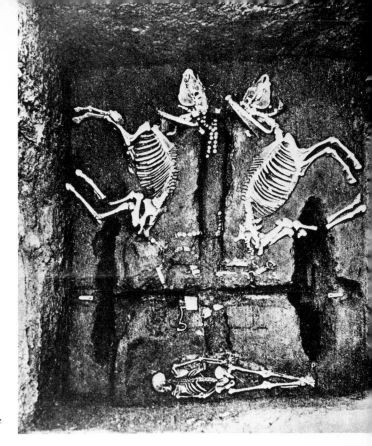

10 Chariot burial, Anyang, Honan, after excavation. Late Shang period.

on his arms, his head thrown back. A few of the larger pieces have slots in their backs, suggesting that they might have had some function in the structure and decoration of a building, perhaps in a sacrificial hall, for there is a close similarity in theme and style between many of these figures and those depicted on the ritual bronzes. They are carved four-square out of the block, rigidly frontal, and have something of the formality and compactness of Egyptian art. Their impressiveness derives from their solid, monumental feeling of weight, and from the engraved geometric and zoomorphic designs which play over their surface, ráther than from the tension over the surface itself which enlivens Egyptian sculpture.

Ceramics formed the backbone of early Chinese art, indispensable, ubiquitous, reflecting the needs and tastes of the highest and the lowest, lending its forms and decoration to the metal-worker and, less often, borrowing from him. In the Shang, the crudest is a grey earthenware, cord-marked, incised, or decorated with repeated stamped motifs ranging from squares and coils (the ancestor of the 'thunder pattern', *lei-wen*) to simple versions of the zoomorphic masks which appear on the bronzes. Pottery decorated by stamping or carving geometric designs in the wet clay has been found in a number of Neolithic sites in the south-east, notably in Fukien (Kuang-tse) and Kwangsi (Ch'ing-

SHANG POTTERY

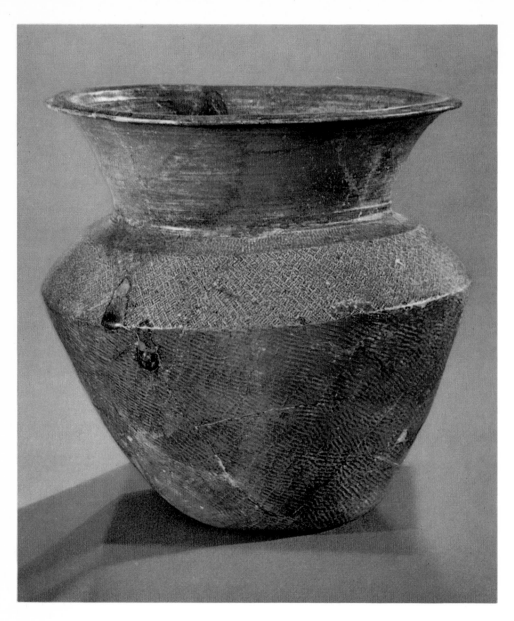

11 *Tsun* vase. Proto-porcelain, decorated with impressed design round shoulder under yellowish-brown glaze. From Chengchow, Honan. Middle Shang period.

chiang). In South China, this technique persisted into the Han Dynasty and was carried thence to South-east Asia – if, indeed, it had not originated there. It is very seldom found in the Neolithic pottery of North China, and its appearance on vessels at Chengchow and Anyang suggests that by the time of the Shang Dynasty the culture of the southern peoples was already beginning to make its influence felt.

The beautiful white Shang pottery is unique in the history of Chinese ceramics. So fine is it that it has been taken for porcelain, but it is in fact a very brittle ware made from almost pure kaolin, finished on the wheel, and fired at about 1,000° C. Many writers have remarked how closely its decoration echoes that of the bronzes, but there is no proof that this style in fact originated in bronze. As we have seen, south-east China had already evolved a technique for stamping designs in the wet clay, which in turn influenced bronze design; the white stoneware urn in the Freer Gallery, Washington, D.C., illustrated here is indeed very close in design and decoration to a bronze vessel in the Hellström Collection. The Chengchow finds suggest that some of the motifs decorating both the white ware and the bronzes originated in the earlier stamped grey pottery. The techniques and designs used in wood-carving suggest another possible source. Some of the grey and buff ware found in Shang sites in Honan is glazed. While in some cases the glaze was produced accidentally when wood-ash fell on the heated pottery in the kiln, in others it is a true felspathic glaze, generally reddish brown or greenish yellow, applied very thinly and evenly to both inner and outer surfaces of the vessel.

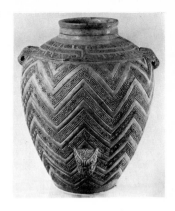

12 Jar. Carved white pottery. From Anyang. Late Shang period.

According to tradition, when the great Emperor Yü of the Hsia divided the Empire, he ordered nine *ting* tripods to be cast in metal brought as tribute from each of the nine provinces, and decorated with representations of the remarkable things characteristic of each region. These tripods were credited with magical powers; they could ward off noxious influences, for example, and cook food without fire. From dynasty to dynasty they were handed down as the palladia of empire, but at the end of the Chou they were lost. The unsuccessful efforts of the first Ch'in emperor, Shih-huang-ti, to recover one of them from the bed of a river are mocked in several delightfully humorous Han reliefs, though one of the Han emperors tried to accomplish the same thing by means of sacrifices and was just as unsuccessful. But so strong was the tradition of the nine tripods that as late as the T'ang Dynasty the Empress Wu caused a set to be cast in order to bolster up her own dubious claim to the throne.

Long before any archaeological evidence of the Shang Dynasty had been unearthed, the ritual bronzes bore witness to the power and vitality of this remote epoch in Chinese history. Bronze vessels have been treasured by Chinese connoisseurs for centuries: that great collector and savant, the Sung Emperor Hui-tsung, is even said to have sent agents to the Anyang region to search out specimens for his collection. These vessels which, as S. Howard Hansford has aptly observed, formed a kind of 'Communion plate', were made for the offerings of food and wine to ancestral spirits which formed the core of the sacrificial rites performed by the ruler and the aristocracy. Some of them bear very short inscriptions, generally consisting of two or three characters forming a clan-name. Often this inscription is enclosed within a square device known as the *ya-hsing*, from its resemblance to the character *ya*. A number of theories as to its meaning have been advanced. The recent discovery at Anyang of

THE RITUAL BRONZES

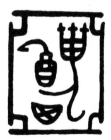

Yah-hsing with inscription.

31

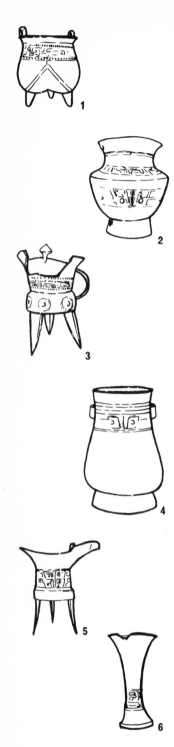

bronze seals leaving an impression of precisely this shape suggests that it was in some way connected with the clan-name.

Chemical analysis shows that the bronze vessels were composed of 5 to 30 per cent tin, and 2 to 3 per cent lead, the rest (apart from impurities) being copper. In course of time many of them have acquired a beautiful patina, much valued by connoisseurs, which ranges from malachite-green and kingfisher-blue to yellow or even red, according to the composition of the metal and the conditions under which the vessel was buried. Forgers have gone to enormous trouble to imitate these effects, and W. P. Yetts records the case of one family of which each generation buried fakes in specially treated soil, to be dug up and sold by the next generation but one. It was long thought that the Shang and Chou bronzes were made by the *cire-perdue* method; for how, it was argued, could such exquisite detail have been modelled except in wax? However, while the technique was probably used in the later periods, large numbers of outer and inner clay moulds and crucibles have been found at Anyang and Chengchow, and it is probable that most of the vessels were cast in such sectional moulds assembled round a solid central core, and that legs and handles were cast separately and soldered on. Many vessels still show ridges or rough places where two mould sections were imperfectly joined.

There are at least thirty main types of ritual vessels, which range in size from a few inches in height to a gigantic *ting*, unearthed at Anyang in 1939, which was cast by a Shang king in memory of his mother; it is over four feet high and weighs 1,950 lb. They can most simply be grouped according to their uses in the sacrifices. For cooking food (of which the essence only was extracted by the spirits, the participants later eating what they left behind), the chief vessels were the *li* tripod and the *yen* (or *hsien*) steamer, consisting of a *li* with a vessel having a perforated base resting on it. Both of these types, as we have seen, were common in Neolithic pottery and may already then have had a more-than-utilitarian function in some primitive rite. The *ting*, which has three or four straight legs, is a variant of the *li*, and like it generally has fairly large handles or 'ears' to enable it to be lifted off the fire. Vessels made for serving food included the two-handled *kuei* and the *yü* (basin). Among those for fluids (chiefly wine) were the *hu* (a vase or jar with a cover), the *yu* (similar but with a swing or chain handle and sometimes fitted with a spout), the *chih* (a cup with a bulbous body and spreading lip), the *ho* (kettle), the tall and elegant trumpet-mouthed *ku* for pouring libations, and its fatter variant, the *tsun* (both derived from pottery prototypes), the *chia* and the *chio* for pouring and probably also for heating wine, and the *kuang*, for mixing wine, shaped like a gravy-boat, generally with a cover and provided with a ladle. Other vessels, such as the *i* and *p'an*, were presumably made for ritual ablutions.

Ritual bronzes excavated at Chengchow: 1. *li*; 2. *tsun*; 3. *chia*; 4. *hu*; 5. *chüeh*; 6. *ku.*

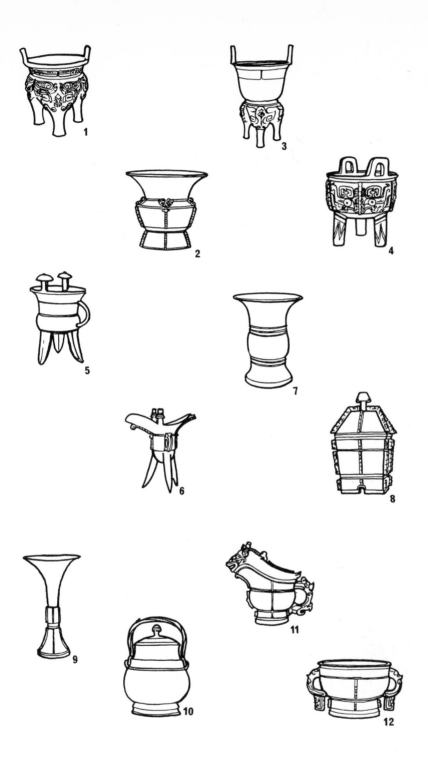

Ritual bronzes of the Late Shang and Early Chou Dynasties: 1. *li*; 2. *tsun*; 3. *hsien*; 4. *ting*; 5. *chia*; 6. *chüeh*; 7. *tsun*; 8. *fang-i*; 9. *ku*; 10. *yu*; 11. *kuang*; 12. *kuei*.

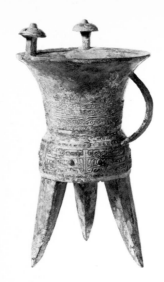

13 Ritual vessel, *chia*, Phase I.
Bronze. Middle Shang period.

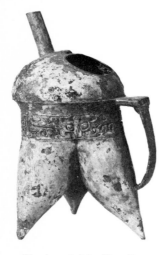

14 Ritual vessel, *li-ho*, Phase II.
Bronze. Middle Shang period.

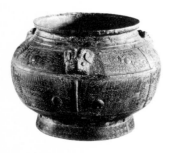

15 Ritual vessel, *p'ou*, Phase III.
Bronze. Shang Dynasty, Early
Anyang period.

During the fifteen hundred years that bronze-casting was a major art form in China, the style of decoration went through a series of changes which make it possible to date vessels to within a century or less. In 1953 Professor Max Loehr proposed five phases for the Shang which have since been largely confirmed by excavation. In Shang I, vessels have thin relief decoration, simple forms, and a light, airy effect. In Shang II, decoration is in ribbon relief and forms tend to be harsh and heavy. In Shang III, the designs are dense, fluent and curvilinear. (In fact, II and III are not always distinguishable, and may have been contemporaneous.) In Shang IV, main motifs and spiral background first become separated, though in the same plane. In Shang V, motifs rise in bold relief and background spirals may disappear altogether. Examples of phases I, II and III have been found at Chengchow; phases IV and V evolved after the move to Anyang.

The bronze vessels found in the early levels at Chengchow have not yet been adequately documented, but from the photographs available they appear to be much what one would expect – simpler, cruder versions of the magnificent bronzes of the Anyang period. The *chüeh* libation-cup, for example, which at Anyang is tall and elegant, with rounded bottom, gracefully curving spout, handle at one side and prominent 'horns', at Chengchow is squat and clumsy, with a flat bottom, no handle, and thinly cast in a poor-quality alloy. The decoration, which at Anyang is subtle and refined, is here crude and, with the exception of the protuberant eye, all in one plane of relief. These discoveries are sure to throw light on the vexed question of the connection between Shang China and the bronze cultures of southern Siberia, Russia and the Near East.

At Anyang, the bronze art is fully mature, the reflection of a stable and prosperous society. In the perfection of their craftsmanship and the immense power of their form and decoration, the Shang bronzes must rank as one of the great artistic triumphs of early civilization. The zoomorphic motifs which adorn them and give them their intense vitality may seem to be innumerable, but are for the most part variations on and combinations of the same few elements – notably the tiger, water-buffalo, elephant, hare, deer, owl, parrot, fish, cicada, and possibly the silkworm. Occasionally in a frieze round an otherwise plain vessel these creatures may be represented naturalistically, but far more often they are so stylized as to be barely recognizable: their bodies dissolve, their limbs break down or take on a life of their own, sprouting other creatures. The *k'uei* dragon, for example, may appear with gaping jaws, with a beak, with a trunk, wings or horns, or he may form the eyebrow of that most impressive and mysterious of all mythical creatures, the *t'ao-t'ieh*.

This formidable mask, which often appears to be split open on either side of a flange and laid out flat on the belly of the vessel, is the dominating element in the decoration of Shang bronzes. There has been much speculation as to precisely what it signified. Sung antiquarians named it *t'ao-t'ieh* in deference to a passage in a third-century BC text, the *Lü Shih Ch'un-ch'iu*, which runs, 'On the *ting* of the Chou there is applied the *t'ao-t'ieh*: having a head but no body he ate people, but before he had swallowed them, harm came to his body.' Thus by the end of Chou, the *t'ao-t'ieh* was considered as a monster; later it came to be called 'the glutton', and was interpreted as a warning against overeating. Modern scholars have claimed that it represents a tiger or a bull; sometimes it has the characteristics of the one, sometimes of the other. Mizuno has drawn attention to a passage in the *Ch'un-ch'iu Tso-chuan* describing the *t'ao-t'ieh* as one of the four devils driven away by the Emperor Shun, and subsequently made defenders of the land from evil spirits.[1] Like the grotesque characters who take part in the Tibetan 'devil dance', the more terrifying the *t'ao-t'ieh*, the greater his protective power.

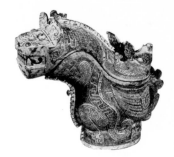

16 Ritual vessel, *kuang*, Phase IV. Bronze. Shang Dynasty, Anyang period.

Two examples will show how effectively the various elements can be combined and integrated with the shape of the vessel itself. The lid of the *kuang* which we have illustrated terminates in a tiger's head at one end and an owl's at the other; the tiger's legs can clearly be seen on the front of the vessel, the owl's wing at the back. Between them a serpent coils up on to the lid, ending in a dragon's head at the crown of the dorsal flange. The main decoration of the magnificent *chia* in Kansas City consists of *t'ao-t'ieh* masks divided down the centre by a low flange and standing out against a background of spirals, called *lei-wen* by Chinese antiquarians from their supposed resemblance to the archaic form of the character *lei*, 'thunder'. However, like the endless spirals painted on the Yang-shao pottery, their meaning (if any) is lost. The *t'ao-t'ieh* has large 'eyebrows' or horns; a frieze of long-tailed birds fills the upper zone while under

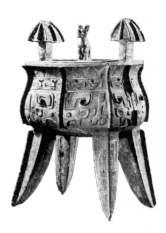

17 Ritual vessel, *chia*, Phase V. Bronze. Shang Dynasty, Anyang period.

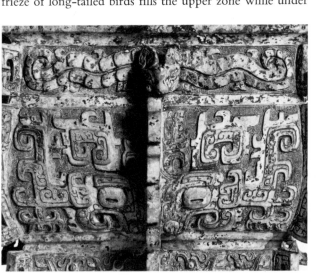

18 Detail of *t'ao-t'ieh* decoration on bronze *fang-i* (see Ill. 26).

35

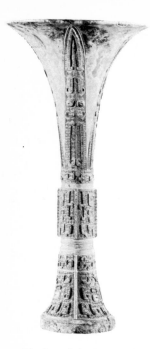

the lip is a continuous band of 'rising blades' containing the formalized bodies of the cicada, a common symbol of regeneration in Chinese art. The vessel is crowned with a squatting heraldic beast and two large knobs for lifting it off the fire with tongs, while the tapering legs are decorated with a complex system of antithetical *k'uei* dragons.

Several distinct bronze styles appear to have existed simultaneously.[2] The *ku* libation-vessel, for example, may be decorated all over, its motifs divided by high serrated vertical flanges which add considerably to its elegance; or the decoration may be confined to the 'collar' and the base, or, in the plainest example, to the collar alone. The *tsun* – a fatter and heavier relation to the *ku* – is often treated in the same way. In vessels of the *li* and *yu* types the zoomorphic designs may be confined to a narrow frieze below the lip, while the body of the *kuei* is generally rather severely treated with vertical flutings like a Georgian teapot, although its high handles, like those of most Shang bronzes, are vigorously modelled in the form of elephants, bulls, tigers, or more fabulous creatures. Occasionally the effect is too bizarre and extravagant to be altogether pleasing, but in the finest vessels the main decorative elements play over the surface like a dominant theme in music against a subtle 'ground bass' of *lei-wen*; indeed, to pursue the analogy further, these motifs seem to interpenetrate one another like the parts in a fugue, and at the same time to pulsate with a powerful rhythm. Already in the sweeping decoration of the Yang-shao painted pottery we saw a hint of that uniquely Chinese faculty of conveying formal energy through the medium of dynamic linear rhythms; here in the bronzes that faculty is even more powerfully evident, while many centuries later it was to find its supreme expression in the language of the brush.

The bronze weapons used by the Shang people show several aspects of this many-faceted culture. Most purely Chinese was a form of dagger-axe known as the *ko*, with pointed blade and a tang which was passed through a hole in the shaft and lashed to it, or, more rarely, shaped like a collar to fit round the shaft. The *ko* probably originates in a Neolithic weapon and seems to have had a ritual significance, for some of the most beautiful Shang specimens have blades of jade, while the handle is often inlaid with a mosaic of turquoise. The *ch'i* axe, which also originated in a stone tool,

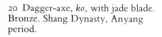

19 Ritual vessel, *ku*. Bronze. Shang Dynasty, Anyang period.

20 Dagger-axe, *ko*, with jade blade. Bronze. Shang Dynasty, Anyang period.

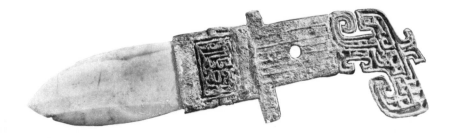

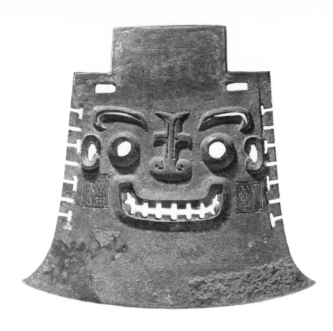

21 Axe, *ch'i*. Bronze. From I-tu, Shantung. Shang Dynasty.

has a broad curving blade like that of a medieval executioner's axe, while its flanged tang is generally decorated with *t'ao-t'ieh* and other motifs. I have illustrated a fine example of a *ch'i* axe, excavated in 1966 at I-tu in Shantung. On either side of the terrifying mask is a cartouche of *ya hsing* shape containing the figure of a man offering wine on an altar from a vessel with a ladle. Less exclusively Chinese are the bronze daggers and knives, simple forms of which have been found at Chengchow. At Anyang they become more elaborate, the handle often terminating in a ring, or in the head of a horse, ram, deer or elk. These have their counterpart in the 'animal style' of the Ordos Desert, Inner Mongolia and southern Siberia.

The problem as to whether China or Central Asia was the source of this style has long been debated. Much turns upon the date of the South Siberian sites, such as Karasuk, where it also appears, and until this is established the question of priority cannot be finally settled. It seems that an animal style existed simultaneously in western Asia (Luristan third phase), Siberia (Karasuk) and China (Anyang) roughly between 1500 and 1000 BC, and that China drew upon this style from her western neighbours and at the same time contributed to it from her own increasingly rich repertoire of animal forms. Elements of the animal style appear also in the bronze fittings made for chariots, furniture and weapons. Recent excavations at Anyang have made it possible to reconstruct the Shang chariot and to assign to their correct place such objects as hub-caps, jingles, pole-ends, awning-fittings and the V-shaped sheaths for horses' yokes.

The origin of the decoration on the bronzes represents a difficult problem. The most striking element in it is the

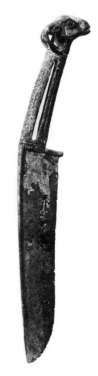

22 Knife. Bronze. From Anyang. Early Chou Dynasty.

profusion of animal motifs, not one of which appears in Chinese Neolithic art. The Shang people, the contents of whose tombs reveal this extraordinary passion for animals, had cultural affinities with the steppe and forest folk of Siberia and, more remotely, with the peoples of Alaska, British Columbia and Central America. The similarities between certain Shang designs and those, for example, in the art of the North-west Coast Indians of North America are too close to be accidental. Li Chi has suggested that the richly decorated, square-section bronze vessels with straight sides are a translation into metal of a northern wood-carving art, and Carl Hentze has amassed a considerable amount of evidence for the stylistic similarity between the decoration of these bronzes and the art of the northern nomadic peoples. On the other hand, the art of carving formalized animal masks on wood or gourd is native to South-east Asia and the Archipelago, and still practised today. Also surviving in South-east Asia is the technique of stamping designs in the wet clay, which survived in the Neolithic pottery of South China until well into the Iron Age, and may have contributed the repeated circles, spirals and volutes to bronze ornament. Clearly the sources of the decorative language of the Shang bronzes are more numerous and complex than was once supposed.

Whatever the origins of this language, we must not think of it as confined solely to the sacrificial bronzes. Only they have survived intact, but could we but transport ourselves to the home of some rich Anyang nobleman we would have seen *t'ao-t'ieh* and beaked dragons, cicadas and tigers, painted on the beams of his house and applied to hangings of leather and matting about his rooms, and, very probably, woven into his silk robes. This tends to reinforce the view that these motifs are not tied to the form or function of any individual bronze vessel, but belong to the whole repertoire, part decorative, part magical, of Shang art.

JADE Already in certain Neolithic sites we have encountered jade, selected, it appears, for objects of more than purely utilitarian purpose by virtue of its hardness, strength and purity. In the Shang Dynasty the craft of jade-carving progresses a further step forward, and we must briefly consider the sources of this stone, the technique of carving it and the unique place it occupies in early Chinese culture. Although early Chinese texts speak of jade from several places in China, for many centuries the chief source has been the river-beds of the Khotan region in Central Asia, and Western scholars had come to the conclusion that jade did not exist in its true state in China proper. Recent discoveries, however, seem to lend some support to the ancient texts, for a jadeitic stone used today by Peking jade-smiths has been traced to Nanyang in Honan. However, the true jade (*chen-yü*) prized throughout history by the Chinese is nephrite, a crystalline stone as hard as steel and of peculiar toughness. In theory it is pure white, but even small amounts of impurities will produce a wide range of colours from green and blue to brown, red, grey, yellow and even black. In the eighteenth century Chinese jade-carvers discovered in Burma a source of another mineral, jadeite, whose brilliant apple- and emerald-green have made it deservedly popular for jewellery both in China and abroad. Because of its unique qualities, jade has since ancient times been regarded by the Chinese with special reverence. In his great dictionary, the *Shuo-wen Chieh-tzu*, the Han scholar Hsü Shen described it in words now well known to every student of Chinese art. 'Jade is the fairest of stones,' he wrote. 'It is endowed with five virtues. Charity is typified by its lustre, bright yet warm; rectitude by its translucency, revealing the colour and markings within; wisdom by the purity and penetrating quality of its note when the stone is struck; courage, in that it may be broken, but cannot be bent; equity, in that it has sharp angles, which yet injure none.'[3]

The hardness and toughness of jade make it very difficult to carve. To work it, one must use an abrasive. Hansford has demonstrated that it is possible, given time, to drill a hole in a slab of jade using only a bamboo bow-drill and builder's sand. It has recently been suggested that metal tools were already employed at Anyang, and there is evidence that the Shang lapidary may also have used a drill-point harder than modern carborundum. Some small pieces carved in the round have been found in Shang sites, but the vast majority consist of weapons, ritual and decorative objects carved from thin slabs seldom more than half an inch thick. The jades from Chengchow include long, beautifully shaped knives and axe-blades (*ko*), circles, sections of discs, a figure of a tortoise, flat plaques in the shape of birds and other creatures pierced at each end for use as clothing ornaments or pendants. A particularly interesting type was a perforated disc called *hsüan-chi*, with groups of 'teeth' on the rim, which is believed to have been used together with a long sighting tube for astronomical observations.

The finds at Anyang have been incomparably richer in beauty, workmanship and range of types than those at Chengchow, and recent discoveries make it likely that the great numbers of jade objects labelled 'probably from Anyang' which have reached Western collections as a result of the indiscriminate digging of the last fifty years must have come from that site. The excavations at the Anyang village of Ta-ssu-k'ung-ts'un in 1953, for example, yielded plaques carved in the shapes of birds, fishes, silkworms and tigers; *pi* (discs), *tsung* (symbols of Earth), *yüan* (rings) and other ritual objects; beads, knife-handles and *ko* axes. The most impressive recent find at Anyang was a huge sonorous stone found on the floor of the grave-pit at Wu-kuan-ts'un; cut from a thin slab of marble thirty-three inches long and pierced for suspension, it is decorated on one side with a design of a tiger executed in thread relief.

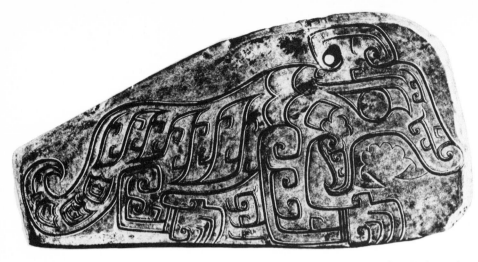

23 Chime, carved with tiger design. Stone. From tomb at Wu-kuan-ts'un, Anyang. Late Shang period.

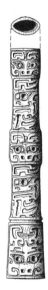

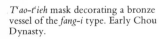

Carved bone handle from Hsiao-t'un.

Not all carving was done in such intractable materials as jade and marble. Some of the most beautiful of all Shang designs were carved in bone and ivory. Elephants roamed North China in prehistoric times and were probably still to be found north of the Yangtse during the Shang Dynasty. We know that at least one Shang emperor kept one as a pet, possibly sent as tribute from Yüeh, while a plentiful supply of ivory could be had from China's southern neighbours. On plaques of ivory and bone a few inches square, made presumably as ornaments for chariots, furniture or boxes, were carved *t'ao-t'ieh* and other designs of extraordinary intricacy and beauty, sometimes inlaid with turquoise. Like the bronzes, these bone and ivory carvings show striking similarities with the art of the North-west Coast Indians of North America. For years scholars have toyed with the fascinating possibilities that these similarities have opened up, but as yet no archaeological connecting links have been found to account for them.

T'ao-t'ieh mask decorating a bronze vessel of the *fang-i* type. Early Chou Dynasty.

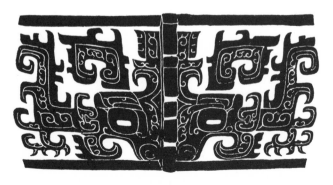

3 The Chou Dynasty

During the last years of the decline of Shang, the vassal State of Chou on her western frontier had grown so powerful that its ruler Wen was virtually in control of two-thirds of the Shang territories. Finally, in 1027 BC (Ch'en Meng-chia's chronology) Wen's son Wu, the Martial King, captured Anyang and the last Shang ruler committed suicide. Under Wu's young successor Ch'eng Wang, a powerful regent known to history as the Duke of Chou (Chou Kung) consolidated the Empire, set up feudal states and parcelled out the Shang domains among other vassals, though he took care to permit the descendants of Shang to rule in the little state of Sung so that they could keep up the hereditary sacrifices to their ancestral spirits. Chou Kung was the chief architect of a dynasty which was to have the longest rule in China's history, and even though its later centuries were clouded by incessant civil wars in which the royal house was crushed and finally engulfed, the Chou Dynasty, more than any other, gave to China her most characteristic and enduring institutions.

There was no abrupt break with Shang traditions; rather were many of them developed and perfected. Feudalism, court ritual and ancestor-worship became more elaborate and effective instruments in welding the state together – so effective, indeed, that from the time of confusion at the end of the dynasty many people, Confucius among them, came to look back upon the reigns of Wen, Wu and Duke Chou as a Golden Age. Religious life was still centred in worship of Shang Ti, though the concept of 'Heaven' (*T'ien*) now began to appear and eventually replaced the cruder notions embodied in Shang Ti. Bronze inscriptions and early texts indicate the beginnings of a moral code centred in adherence to the will of Heaven and in respect for *te* (virtue), both of which were to be fundamental in the teachings of Confucius. The Chou court became the focus of an elaborate ritual in which music, art, literature and pageantry all combined under the direction of the Master of Ceremonies (*pin-hsiang*) to give moral and aesthetic dignity to the concept of the state. The king held audiences at dawn and dusk (a custom that survived until 1912); orders for the day were written on bamboo slips, read out by the Court Historian and then handed out to officials for execution. From the time of Mu Wang (947–928 BC) onwards it became customary to preserve these orders by casting them on the bronze ritual vessels. These inscriptions, which became longer as time went on, are one of the main sources for the study of Early Chou history, the other chief documents being the *Book of Songs* (*Shih-ching*), an anthology of ancient court odes, ballads and love-songs said to have been compiled by Confucius, and the authentic chapters of the *Classic of History* (*Shu-ching*), which tell of the fall of Shang and the early years of the Chou. These documents bear witness to that sense of history which is one of the most striking features of Chinese civilization, and, as a corollary, to the almost sacred place held in Chinese life by the written word.

The first phase of Chou history ended in 771 with the death of Yu Wang and the shift of the capital eastwards from Shensi to Loyang. By this time the feudal States were growing more and more powerful, and P'ing Wang, the first ruler of Eastern Chou, was helped to power by two of them – Chin and Cheng. Before long the Chou state was declining still further, till eventually it became a mere shadow of its former self, kept artificially alive by the powerful states that surrounded it solely in order to maintain the prestige of the royal house, from which the 'mandate of Heaven' had not yet been withdrawn. The period from 722 to 481 is often known as the *Ch'un-ch'iu* (Spring and Autumn), because the events of the greater part of it are recorded in the *Spring and Autumn Annals* of the state of Lu; for the rest we have the stories in another classic, the *Tso-chuan*. The feudal chiefs spent their time, it appears, in making aggressive and defensive alliances with other states, in keeping the northern barbarians at bay, and in honouring the shrunken Chou, which survived, a pale shadow of its former glory, till its destruction in 256 BC at the hands of Ch'in.

CHOU CITIES At the moment, more is known about Shang architecture than about that of the Early Chou, for which we have to rely largely upon the evidence of the written word. One of the chief sources for the study of Chou institutions is the *Chou-li*, a manual of ritual and government compiled, it is believed, during the Former, or Western, Han Dynasty. Its authors, looking back through the mists of time to the remote Golden Age, present a somewhat idealized picture of Chou ritual and life, but the *Chou-li* is not without significance, for its descriptions were taken as canonical by later dynasts who strove always to follow the ancient institutions and forms as the *Chou-li* presented them. Writing of the ancient Chou city, the *Chou-li* says, 'The architects who laid out a capital made it a square nine *li* [about three miles] on a side, each side having three gateways. Within the capital there were nine lengthwise and nine crosswise avenues, each nine chariot tracks wide. On the left was the ancestral temple, on the right the Altar of the Soil; in front lay the Court of State, at the rear the market-place.'

Today, the work of the archaeologist has begun to fill out the picture of the Chou city given by the texts. At Chang-chia-p'o, west of Sian, the first Chou capital, Feng, is in process of excavation, while near by lie the remains of Hao, seat of twelve kings from Wu Wang to the end of Western Chou. The remains of over a score of Eastern Chou cities have been identified, the most important being Wang ch'eng, capital of Eastern Chou itself, discovered in the early 1950s when the Chung-chou road was constructed to connect Loyang with a new housing estate to the south-west. The capital of the state of Ch'i, in Lin-tzu-hsien, Shantung, was a mile from east to west and two and a half miles from north to south, surrounded by a wall of stamped earth over thirty feet high, with the palace area in the south-west corner; the capital of the state of Yen, located in I-hsien, Hopei, was even larger. Almost all that remain of these cities above ground today are traces of walls, and the thousands of roof-tiles with stamped designs which litter the fields.

A list of even the most important archaeological finds of the Chou period would severely try the reader's patience, so I will only mention three recent examples by way of illustration. A tomb of the reign of Mu Wang (947–928) has been found at P'u-tu-ts'un, Sian, containing bronzes with long inscriptions, jades and glazed pottery; a tomb rich in bronze vessels of a prince of the obscure state of Kuo, near the San-men Gorge dam site in Honan, must be earlier than 655 BC, when Kuo was absorbed by Ch'in; outside the west gate of Shou-hsien in Anhui an important tomb has been found of a Ts'ai prince, datable by its inscribed bronzes to between 518 and 491 BC. In addition to such scientifically conducted excavations great quantities of bronzes and jades have been dug up over a long period of years at Chin-ts'un and Hsin-cheng near Loyang, at Li-yü in Shansi, and at Shou-hsien (Anhui) and Changsha (Hunan), both in the ancient state of Ch'u. But we must not suppose that all of China had reached the same stage of a mature bronze culture. It is likely that in the Western Chou period the inhabitants of large areas of South and West China were still living in the Stone Age.

REMAINS OF CHOU CULTURE

The *Book of Songs* contains several vivid descriptions of ancestral halls and palaces. Here is part of one of them, translated by Arthur Waley:

ARCHITECTURE AND SCULPTURE

> To give continuance to foremothers and forefathers
> We build a house, many hundred cubits of wall;
> To south and east its doors.
> Here shall we live, here rest,
> Here laugh, here talk.
> We bind the frames, creak, creak;
> We hammer the mud, tap, tap,
> That it may be a place where wind and rain cannot enter,
> Nor birds and rats get in,
> But where our lord may dwell.
> As a halberd, even so plumed,
> As an arrow, even so sharp,
> As a bird, even so soaring,
> As wings, even so flying

Are the halls to which our lord ascends.
Well levelled is the courtyard,
Firm are the pillars,
Cheerful are the rooms by day,
Softly gloaming by night,
A place where our lord can be at peace.
Below, the rush-mats; over them the bamboo-mats.
Comfortably he sleeps,
He sleeps and wakes
And interprets his dreams. . . .[1]

In this and other ballads we get a picture of large buildings with rammed earth walls standing on a high platform, of strong timber pillars supporting a roof whose eaves, though not yet curving, spread like wings, of floors covered with thick matting like the Japanese *tatami*, of warmth, light and comfort. While the most monumental buildings were the ancestral halls, the palaces and private house were often large, and may well have had several successive courtyards as they do today. Chou texts are full of warnings against those who build too extravagantly, and above all against the usurper of royal prerogatives. Confucius, for example, rebuked a contemporary who kept a tortoise (presumably for divination) in a pavilion adorned with the hill pattern on its capitals and the duckweed pattern on its kingposts, insignia reserved exclusively for the emperor. Duke Chuang of Lu in 670 B C infringed the sumptuary laws by painting the pillars of his father's shrine bright red and carving his rafters. By comparison, the authors of these texts extol the simplicity of ancient times, when a virtuous ruler roofed his ancestral shrine with thatch, when King Ho-lu of Wu never 'sat on double mats. His apartments were not lofty . . . his palaces had no belvederes, and his boats and carriages were plain.'

The most conspicuous of Chou buildings, apart from palaces and ancestral halls, must have been the Ming-t'ang ('Bright Hall'), a ritual edifice of which detailed but conflicting accounts are given in early texts, and the towers (*t'ai*) constructed of timber on a high platform of rammed earth. Passages in the *Tso-chuan* show that the princes used them as fortresses, for feasting or simply as look-outs. Perhaps they survived in the tall storage and look-out towers that were, till recently, a feature of villages and farms in South China.

No trace of the kind of decorative stone sculpture that adorned Shang interiors has yet been discovered in Chou sites. But the Chou craftsmen were certainly capable of modelling a figure in the round and endowing it with extraordinary vitality, even when, as in the famous pair of tigers in the Freer Gallery, Washington, D.C., its limbs and features are stylized. Indeed, here the rhythmic movement of the semi-abstract decoration over the surface gives these creatures a curious animation different from, but no less intense than, that which a more naturalistic treatment would have

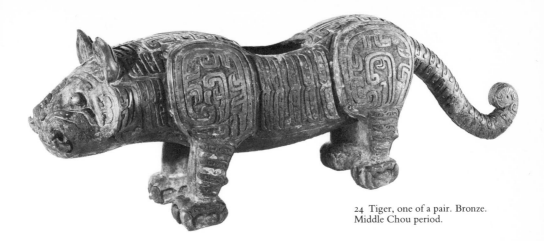

24 Tiger, one of a pair. Bronze. Middle Chou period.

achieved. Although they have been tentatively dated to as early as the tenth century B C, the coarseness of the modelling and the all-over 'baroque' decoration seem to herald the style of the Middle Chou period.

In the earliest Western Chou ritual bronzes the Shang tradition is carried on with little change, one of the more significant differences being in the inscriptions, which are no longer a simple record of ownership but become valuable historical documents, often setting out in some detail the circumstances in which that vessel was bestowed. A vessel of the reign of Ch'eng Wang (1024–1005), for instance, excavated in Tan-t'u, Kiangsu, had an inscription of 120 characters, that on a *ting* of the reign of his successor K'ang Wang runs to 291 characters. Later the inscriptions became even longer. The typical short Early Chou inscription on a *kuei* in the Alfred Pillsbury Collection shows the function of the vessel quite clearly. 'The King attacked Ch'i-yü and went out and attacked Nao-hei. When he came back, he made *liao*-sacrifice [burnt offering] in Tsung-chou and presented to me, Kuo Pao X, ten double strings of cowries. I presume in response to extol the King's grace, and so I have made my accomplished dead father's *kuei* vessel. May for a myriad years sons and grandsons for ever treasure and use it.'[2]

For perhaps a century after the Chou conquest Shang bronze styles survived, though increasingly modified by the taste of the Chou invaders from the west. By the tenth century the *ku*, *chüeh*, *kuang*, *yu* and square *i* had disappeared, along with such ubiquitous Shang motifs as the *t'ao-t'ieh*, cicada, 'rising blades', and long-tailed bird. The *ting* had become a wide, shallow bowl on three cabriole legs, and the *li*, when it appears at all, has a curiously arched contour. The *p'an*, a wide flat dish, has become more common, while the *kuei* may have two or, more rarely, four handles and stand

THE RITUAL BRONZES

45

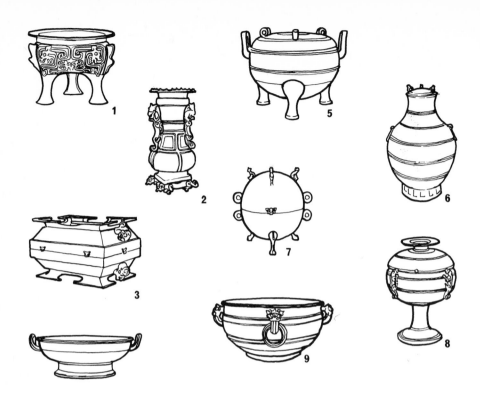

(*Left*) Ritual bronzes of the Middle Chou period: 1. *li*; 2. *hu*; 3. *fu*; 4. *p'an*. (*Right*) Ritual bronzes of the Warring States period: 5. *ting*; 6. *hu*; 7. *t'ui*; 8. *tou*; 9. *chien*.

on a square base. Bronzes of this period generally show a certain exaggeration and coarseness of modelling, while shapes become increasingly slack and sagging. Flanges tend to be large and spiky, and new creatures make their appearance, among them the gaping monster with spiral tail and a bird with head turned back and frills of quill-like feathers along its body. By the ninth century birds and beasts are dissolving into a variety of vertical and horizontal scales, and broad, flat meander patterns that cover the whole surface. The bronzes of Late Western Chou, often called the 'Middle Chou style' (Yetts's 'Second Phase', ninth and eighth centuries), have none of the dynamic tension and unity of design that mark the vessels of Late Shang and the first decades of the Chou; instead, we find an increasing variety of regional styles as each of the feudal rulers assumed the right to cast his own ritual vessels.

The stylistic change was given a further impetus in the eighth and seventh centuries, first by foreign ideas and techniques brought back by the Chou kings from their northern campaigns, and later by increasing pressure from the northern barbarians themselves. The most striking new feature which this contact introduced was the art of inter-

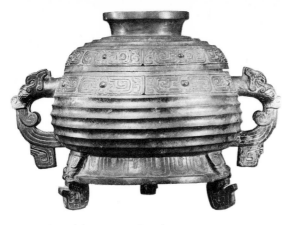

25 Ritual vessel, *kuei*. Bronze. Dated
by inscription to 825 BC. Middle
Chou period.

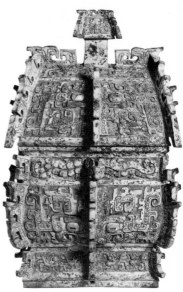

26 Ritual vessel, *fang-* (square) *i*.
Bronze. Long dedicatory inscription
of the Court Annalist, Ling. Early
Western Chou period.

27 Ritual vessel, *hu*. Bronze.
Inscription dated equivalent to 862
or 853 BC.: 'It was in the 26th year,
10th moon, first quarter, in the day
chi-mao, when Fan Chü Sheng had
this bridal *hu* cast as a bridal gift for
his first child, Meng Fei Kuai. May
sons and grandsons for ever treasure
and use it.'

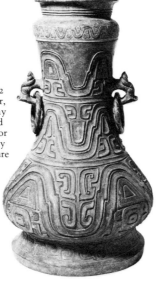

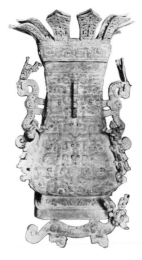

28 Ritual vessel, *hu*. Bronze. Middle
Chou period, about the sixth
century BC.

lacing animal forms into intricate patterns. This first appears
in Chinese art in the bronzes excavated from seventh-
century graves at Hsin-cheng and Shang-ts'un-ling in
Honan. A more highly developed example is the Hsin-
cheng *hu*, datable to about 650 BC, which I have illustrated.
It stands on two tigers; two more tigers with huge horns and
twisting bodies curl up the sides to form handles, while
smaller tigers play at their feet. The body is covered with an
all-over pattern of flat, rope-like interlaced dragons. The
lid is surrounded with flaring leaf-shaped flanges, while in
the centre a crane with spreading wings seems about to take
flight. Gone is the wonderfully integrated quality of the

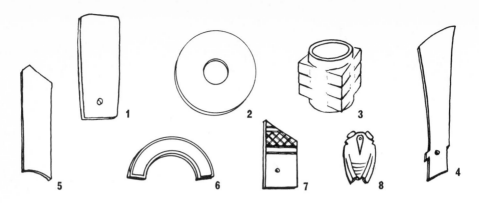

Ritual and funerary jades. 1. *kuei*; 2. *pi*; 3. *tsung*; 4. *ya-chang*; 5. *yen-kuei*; 6. *huang*; 7. *chang*; 8. *han*.

early bronzes, in which so perfect a fusion of form and decoration was achieved. Gone too is the coarse but imposing strength of the early Middle Chou. These Hsin-cheng bronzes represent a restless period of transition before the flowering of the refined art of the Warring States.

JADE

Reliable archaeological evidence on the jade of the Early and Middle Chou is scanty, but constantly increasing with new finds. Before the Second World War archaeologists working at Hsin-ts'un in Hsün-hsien (Honan) discovered a number of jade objects which were for the most part rather cruder versions of Shang types, with the relief carving often confined to shallow incisions on a flat surface. Since 1950 excavations of graves at Loyang and at P'u-tu-ts'un, near Sian, have tended to confirm the impression that there was a decline in the craft in the Early Western Chou. But the Chou jades excavated under controlled conditions still represent a minute proportion of the total number; this, combined with the likelihood that the traditional forms must have persisted for long periods without change, and that when buried, jades may already have been treasured antiques, makes the dating of individual pieces extremely difficult.

There is less doubt, fortunately, about the meaning and function of the ritual and funerary jades. According to the *Chou-li*, certain shapes were appropriate to particular ranks. The king in audience, for example, held a *chen-kuei*, a broad, flat, perforated sceptre; a duke held a *huan* (ridged sceptre); a prince a *hsin* (elongated sceptre); an earl a *kung* (curved sceptre); while the lower ranks of viscount and baron held *pi* discs decorated with the little bosses known as the 'grain pattern'. Proclamations were issued with jade objects to indicate the royal authority – as for instance the *ya-chang* (a long knife) for mobilizing the imperial garrison, a *hu* (tiger) in two halves for transmitting military secrets, a *yen-kuei* (sceptre with concave butt) for protecting official envoys, and so on. Equally specific were the jades used to

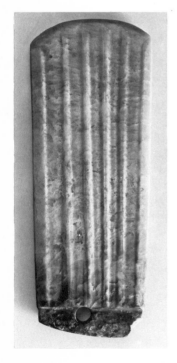

29 Ceremonial axe. Jade. Excavated at Anyang.

protect the body at burial, numbers of which have been found in their original positions in the grave. Generally the corpse lay on his back (a change from Shang practice). On his chest was placed a *pi* disc (symbol of Heaven); beneath his body a *tsung* (symbol of Earth); to the east of the body was placed a *kuei* sceptre, to the west a tiger, to the north (at his feet) a *huang* (half circle), to the south a *chang* (a short stubby *kuei*); the seven orifices of the body were sealed with jade plugs, while a flat plaque, *han*, generally in the shape of a cicada, was placed in the mouth. Thus was the body protected from all harm without, and sealed lest any evil influences should escape from within.

An extreme instance of the belief in the preserving power of jade was the jade burial-suit, long known from references in early literature, but never seen (except in fragments) until the accidental discovery of the tombs of a Han prince and princess at Man-ch'eng in Hopei in 1968. The corpses of Liu Sheng (died 113 BC) and of his wife Tou Wan were completely encased in head-mask, jacket and trousers, each made of over 2,000 thin jade plaques sewn together with gold thread (Ill. 47). Each suit, it has been calculated, would have taken an expert jade-smith ten years to make. In addition to mortuary jades, the Early Chou lapidaries carved many kinds of pendants and ornaments, as during the Shang Dynasty, but as these were to be far more beautiful and refined in the Late Chou period we will defer discussion of them to the next chapter.

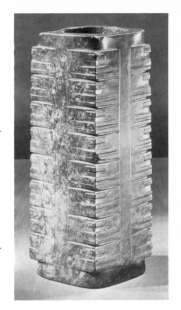

30 Ritual tube, *tsung*. Jade.

By comparison with the bronzes, the pottery of Western and Early Eastern Chou is sober stuff. Many of the finest pieces are crude imitations of bronze vessels, though generally only the shape is copied, such bronze-like decoration as there is being confined to bulls' heads or *t'ao-t'ieh* masks attached to the sides. Although a few specimens of plain red ware have been found, most Western Chou pottery consists of a coarse grey ware, the most popular purely ceramic shape being a round-bottomed, wide-mouthed storage jar which is often cord-marked.

CERAMICS

Recent discoveries show that in addition to this mass of unglazed wares a much more sophisticated ceramic art was beginning to develop. Dr Hsia Nai has gone so far as to say that very early in the Chou Dynasty period pottery 'had been perfected almost to the level of proto-porcelain by high-temperature firing',[2] a statement supported by the discovery of vessels described as 'proto-porcelain' in Western Chou tombs at Pei-yao-ts'un in suburban Loyang. The important tomb of the reign of Mu Wang (947–928) at P'u-tu-ts'un near Sian contained vessels decorated with horizontal grooves and covered with a thin bluish-green glaze quite different from the blackish or yellowish Shang glazes. Other glazed wares, datable by bronze inscriptions to the eleventh and tenth centuries, have been found in graves in Honan, Kiangsu and Anhui.

4 The Period of the Warring States

A map of China in the sixth century BC would show a tiny and impotent state of Chou, somewhat like modern Canberra, surrounded by powerful principalities constantly forming and breaking alliances and attacking each other, condescending to consult the royal house only on matters of legitimacy and inheritance. In the north, Chin kept the desert hordes at bay until she was destroyed in 403 and parcelled out among the three states of Chao, Han and Wei. At one time these three states formed an alliance with Yen and Ch'i in the north-east against the power of the semi-barbarian Ch'in, now looming dangerously on the western horizon. The smaller states of Sung and Lu, which occupied the Lower Yellow River Valley, were not militarily powerful, though they are famous in Chinese history as the home of the great philosophers. In the region of modern Kiangsu and Chekiang, Wu and Yüeh were emerging into the full light of Chinese culture, while a huge area of Central China was under the domination of the southward-looking and only partly sinicized state of Ch'u. Gradually Ch'u and Ch'in grew stronger. In 473 Wu fell to Yüeh, then Yüeh to Ch'u. Ch'in was even more successful. In 256 she obliterated the pathetic remnant of the great state of Chou; thirty-three years later she defeated her great rival Ch'u, simultaneously turning on the remaining states of Wei, Chao and Yen. In 221 BC she defeated Ch'i, and all China lay prostrate at her feet.

As often happens in history, these centuries of ever-increasing political chaos were accompanied by social and economic reform, intellectual ferment and great achievement in the arts. Iron tools and weapons were coming into use. Now for the first time private individuals could own land, and trade was developing, much aided by the invention of currency – bronze 'spade' money in Central China, knife-shaped coins in the north and east. This was the age of the 'Hundred Schools', when roving philosophers known as *Shui-k'e* ('persuading guests') offered their counsel to any ruler who would listen to them. The most enlightened patronage was that offered by King Hsüan of Ch'i, who welcomed brilliant scholars and philosophers of every school to his 'Academy of the Chi Gate'. But this was exceptional. Confucius, the greatest of them, was ill used in the state of Lu, for in those chaotic times few rulers saw any immediate advantage in the Sage's emphasis upon the moral and social virtues, upon *jen* ('human-heartedness'), or upon the value of knowledge and self-cultivation. Wanting power at home and victory over their enemies abroad, they were often more attracted by the Machiavellian doctrines of Lord Shang and the Legalists, which were to find their ultimate justification in the rise of the totalitarian state of Ch'in.

Against the social commitment of Confucius and his follower Mencius on the one hand and the amoral doctrines of the Legalists on the other, the Taoists offered a third solution – a submission not to society or the state but to the universal principle, *Tao*. Lao Tzu taught that discipline and control only distort or repress one's natural instinct to flow with the stream of existence. In part this was a reaction against the rigidity of the other schools, but it was also a way of escape from the hazards and uncertainties of the times into the world of the imagination. It was, in fact, through Taoism, with its intuitive awareness of things that cannot be measured or learned out of books, that the Chinese poets and painters were to rise to the highest imaginative flights. The state of Ch'u was the heart of this new liberating movement. The great mystical philosopher-poet Chuang Tzu (*c.* 350–275) belonged in fact to the neighbouring state of Sung, but, as Fung Yu-lan has observed, his thought is closer to that of Ch'u, while Ch'ü Yüan and Sung Yü, who in their rhapsodic poems known as *sao* poured out a flood of such passionate feeling, were both natives of Ch'u. It is perhaps no accident that not only the finest poetry of this period, but also the earliest surviving paintings on silk, should have been produced within its boundaries.[1]

During the Early Warring States period, however, the Chung-yüan, or Central Plain, of southern Shensi and northern Honan was still the heart of Chinese civilization, protected by the defensive walls which were being constructed at intervals along China's northern frontiers. The most ancient section of wall was built about 353 B C across modern Shensi, not only to keep the marauding nomads out, but equally to keep the Chinese in, and to attempt to prevent that 'desinicization' which during the Six Dynasties was to accompany the foreign occupation of much of North China.

Until recently archaeologists had given much less attention to the remains of the Chou Dynasty than had been devoted to the Shang. Before the Second World War, only one important Late Chou site had been scientifically excavated, at Hsin-cheng in Honan, where were found tombs containing bronzes that span the years from the 'baroque' extravagances of Middle Chou to the simpler forms and more intricate decoration of the Early Warring States period. At the same time the local farmers living between Loyang and Chengchow had for some years been robbing tombs at Chin-ts'un. Bronzes believed to have come from these tombs range in style from late, and rather subdued, versions of the Hsin-cheng manner to magnificent examples of the mature style of the fourth and third centuries B C.

Since 1950, however, controlled excavations have been carried out extensively in the region of Hui-hsien, which, like Chin-ts'un, lay within the state of Wei. At Liu-li-ko, just outside Hui-hsien, a pit was found containing nineteen chariots, with the horses buried separately – a late survival of the Shang custom. At Ku-wei-ts'un tomb-pits have been found containing magnificent bronzes inlaid with gold and silver, jades and other precious objects; while a tomb at Chao-ku-chen yielded a number of copper and bronze vessels, one of which bears an engraved picture of a house – perhaps the earliest representation of architecture yet found in China. All these Hui-hsien sites may be dated to the late fourth or early third century BC.

Excavations have also been proceeding continuously at Loyang, the Late Chou capital. Between 1950 and 1954 it was reported that over six hundred tombs (of various periods) had been opened, yielding over ten thousand objects. It would be very surprising if all of them had received the attention of trained archaeologists, and in fact very few of them have yet been published. Just how widely Late Chou culture was diffused is shown by recent important discoveries not only in Central China but also in northern Shansi, Shantung, Anhui, Chekiang, Kiangsu and Szechwan. All reflect in varying degrees the artistic developments that were taking place in the Loyang-Hui-hsien region, although they also show, particularly in the finds from south-east China, quite distinct local characteristics.

CHANGES IN BRONZE STYLE Already in the seventh century a change is beginning to become apparent in the bronze style. The huge extravagance of the Middle Chou decoration seems to have exhausted itself. Ungainly excrescences are shorn off, the surface is smoothed away to produce an unbroken, almost severe silhouette. The decoration becomes even more strictly confined and is often sunk below the surface, or inlaid in gold or silver. Hints of archaism appear in the emphasis upon the *ting* tripod and in the discreet application of *t'ao-t'ieh* masks, which now make their reappearance as the clasps for ring-handles. But this stylistic revolution was not accomplished all at once. In vessels unearthed in 1923 at Li-yü, and more recently in the much more prosperous and important area of Ch'ang-chih in Central Shansi, the décor of flat interlocking bands of dragons looks forward to the restless, intricate decoration of the mature Huai style; but in their robust forms, in the tiger masks which top their legs and the realistic birds and other creatures which adorn their lids, these vessels recall the vigour of an earlier age.

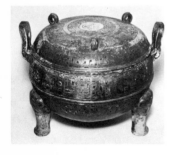

31 Ritual vessel, *li*, with reversible cover. Bronze. 'Li-yü style.' Eastern Chou period, sixth to fifth century BC.

This 'decrescendo' from the coarse vigour of the Middle Chou style continues in the later bronzes from Hsin-cheng and in the new style associated with Chin-ts'un and Li-yü. The typical broad three-legged *ting* from Li-yü and Ch'ang-chih, for example, is decorated with bands of interlocked dragons separated by plait-like fillets. The tendency to imitate other materials is carried even further in a *hu* from Li-yü on which knotted cords are modelled in relief in the bronze – perhaps reproducing the flask carried by the northern nomads. Another flask from Chin-ts'un is flat with a circular silhouette, the surface covered with plain bars imitating leather straps, between which the intricate pattern which Karlgren has called 'teeming hooks' seems to suggest, perhaps accidentally, some coarse stuff or animal pelt.

The earliest of the vessels found at Chin-ts'un are soberly decorated, though their ungainly flanged lids are clearly a survival from Middle Chou. However, in a square *lien* now in Toronto we can see a further stage: the main body has an all-over pattern in which the interlaced dragons have almost completely broken down into 'teeming hooks', typical of the sixth century B C, but the upper part is decorated with a flat band of geometric decoration inlaid with malachite and gold. As time goes on this motif, which at first consists of modest rectangular elements divided diagonally and set about with small curls and volutes, gradually grows until it dominates the decoration not only of bronzes but also of lacquer and jade. The final evolution of this tradition can be seen in the beautiful bronzes from the later phase at Chin-ts'un. The simple shapes recall pottery; except for the masks and ring-handles the surface is flat, giving full play to the inlaid decoration which is sometimes geometric, and sometimes sweeps in great curves over the contour of the vessel. Gold had been used at Anyang, but now the goldsmith's art comes into its own, and in form, decoration and

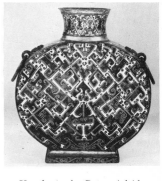

32 Vessel, *pien-hu*. Bronze inlaid with silver. Warring States period.

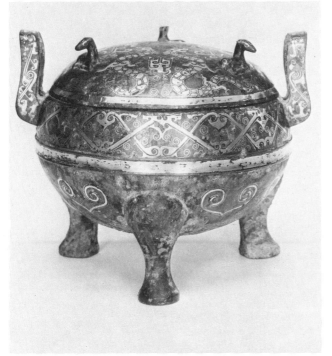

33 Ritual vessel, *ting*. Bronze with silver. Probably from Chin-ts'un, Loyang. Late Warring States period, fourth to third century BC.

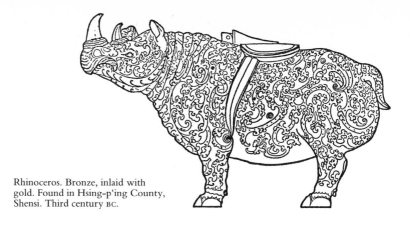

Rhinoceros. Bronze, inlaid with
gold. Found in Hsing-p'ing County,
Shensi. Third century BC.

craftsmanship the finest of the Warring States inlaid bronzes
from the Loyang region are unsurpassed.

With the decline of the ancient ritual and the emergence of
a wealthy upper middle class, the metal-worker's art was
diverted, so to speak, from 'Communion plate' to 'family
plate'. A rich man would give his daughter inlaid vessels as
part of her dowry, while for himself he could adorn his
furniture and carriages with bronze fittings inlaid with gold,
silver and malachite, and when he died, take them with him
into the next world. If anyone criticized him for his extravagance, he might well quote in self-defence this advice from
the philosophical and economical treatise *Kuan Tzu*, much
of which was probably written at about this time: 'Lengthen
the mourning period so as to occupy people's time, and
elaborate the funeral so as to spend their money. . . . To have
large pits for burial is to provide work for poor people; to
have magnificent tombs is to provide work for artisans. To
have inner and outer coffins is to encourage carpenters, and
to have many pieces for the enshrouding is to encourage
seamstresses.'

The value of music as a moral force in society was recognized by Confucius as it was by his contemporary Pythagoras.
Ballads were sung at the feudal courts not merely as entertainment but as admonition and example; the stately measure
of the classical modes was an aid to right thinking and
harmonious action, and it is not surprising that some of the
finest of the bronzes of the Ch'un-ch'iu and Late Chou
should be the bells (*chung*) made in sets, either with a loop
for suspension (*po*) from a wooden frame, or with a long
handle. The rubbing from a relief in a third-century tomb in
Shantung, which we have illustrated, shows how the
performer struck these bells with a heavy wooden beam
suspended from the ceiling. Bells of the *po* type, decorated
on the side with magnificent *t'ao-t'ieh* masks, have recently
been unearthed at Anyang, together with hand-bells (*chih-
chung*) and harness-jingles. In the Western Chou period
chung bells became larger and more elaborate. Oval in
section, the lower part was decorated with an animal mask

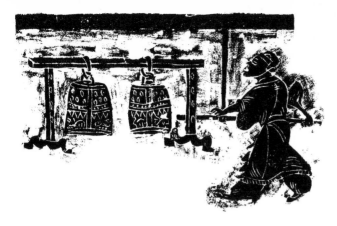

Striking the bells. From a rubbing of a third-century stone relief in a tomb at I-nan, Shantung, illustrated on page 72.

or interlaced dragons; the upper part consisted of three bands of projecting knobs alternating with a dragon or *k'uei* motif on either side of a vertical panel which often contained an inscription. In the Warring States period these knobs were flattened into serpent coils with feline heads, and the loop-handle was often beautifully modelled in the form of back-to-back creatures, real or fabulous. In the tombs at Chin-ts'un nearly fifty bells were found from thirteen different sets, one of which, according to its inscriptions, was made for the Piao clan in 404 B C.

While the aristocracy of metropolitan China were indulging in music, dancing and other delights in the comfort and security of their great houses, the inhabitants of less fortunate

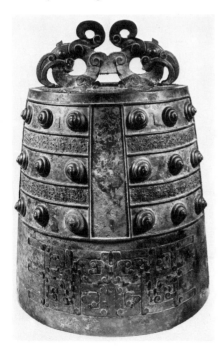

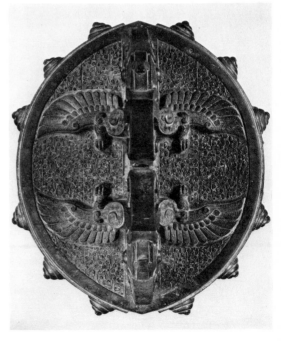

34 Bell, *chung*. Bronze. Warring States period.

35 Bell, *chung*. Bronze. Detail of decoration on top.

55

areas were fighting a desperate battle against the savage tribes who harried the northern frontiers. Mounted on horseback and using the compound bow, the nomads were more than a match for the Chinese troops, who were finally forced to abandon the chariot and copy both the methods and the weapons of their attackers. The influence of the nomads on the Chinese did not end with warfare. Their arts were few but vigorous. For centuries they and their western neighbours of the Central Asiatic Steppe had been decorating their knives, daggers and harness with animal carvings – first in wood, and later in bronze cast for them, it is believed, by slaves and prisoners of war. This 'animal style', as it is called, was totally unlike the abstract yet fanciful style of the Chinese bronzes. Sometimes the modelling is realistic, but more often it is crudely formalized and without the typical Chinese elegance of line. With barbaric vigour the nomads of the Ordos Desert and the wild regions to the north and west of it fashioned elk and reindeer, oxen and horses; they liked also to depict with compact savagery a tiger or eagle pouncing on to the back of some terrified game-beast – a scene they often witnessed, and the representation of which was probably intended to bring success to their own hunting expeditions. Hints of this animal style appeared, as we have seen, on some of the knives at Anyang. During the Late Chou and Han, when the impact on China of the Hsien-yün, the Hsiung-nu and other northern tribes was at its height, the influence of the Ordos style can be seen in the design of some of the inlaid bronzes, on which hunting scenes are modelled with a curiously un-Chinese angularity and harshness of form.

The widest variety of animal designs is found on the bronze garment- or belt-hooks. Many of these hooks, indeed, are purely Chinese in style, being fashioned in the exquisite inlaid technique of Chin-ts'un and Shouchou, Anhui. Court dancers wore them, as we know from the poem entitled *Chao Hun* ('The Summons to the Soul'):

> Two rows of eight, in perfect time, perform a dance of
> Cheng;
> Their *hsi-pi* buckles of Chin workmanship glitter like
> bright suns. . . .[2]

The beautiful specimen which I have illustrated is fashioned in gilt-bronze, inlaid with a dragon in jade and multicoloured balls of glass. Some, representing the creatures of the steppes singly or in mortal combat, are almost purely 'Ordos' in style. Yet others are in a mixed style: a magnificent garment-hook recently excavated at Hui-hsien, for example, is decorated with three penannular jade rings in a setting formed of two intertwined dragons in silver overlaid with gold. The dragons are Chinese, but the sweeping angular planes in which they are modelled come from the northern steppes.

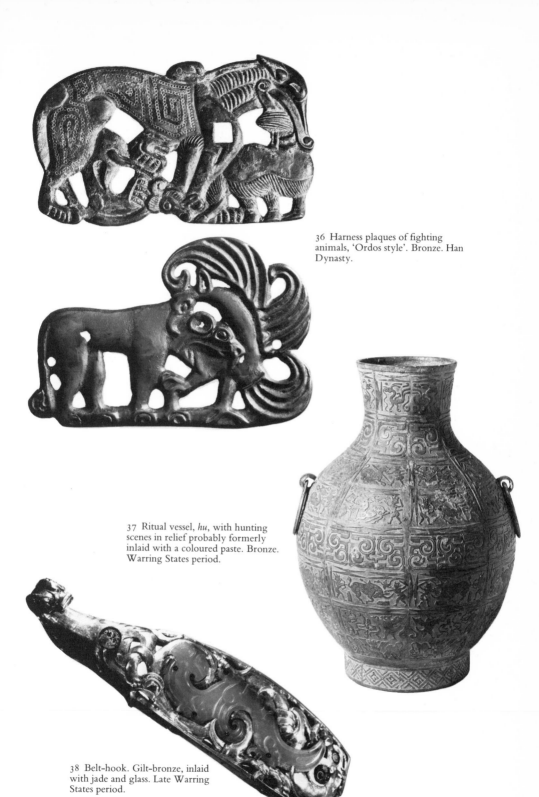

36 Harness plaques of fighting
animals, 'Ordos style'. Bronze. Han
Dynasty.

37 Ritual vessel, *hu*, with hunting
scenes in relief probably formerly
inlaid with a coloured paste. Bronze.
Warring States period.

38 Belt-hook. Gilt-bronze, inlaid
with jade and glass. Late Warring
States period.

No such barbarian influences appear in the pottery of North China at this time: the nomads, indeed, had little use for pottery and no facilities for making it. The grey tradition continues, but the coarse cord-marked wares of the Early Chou have been left behind. Shapes become more elegant, often imitating bronze, the most popular forms being the *tsun*, the three-legged *ting*, the tall covered *tou* (stem-cup) and an egg-shaped covered *tui* on three feet. Generally they are heavy and plain; but some of those found at Chin-ts'un bear animals and hunting scenes stamped or incised with great verve in the wet clay before firing. Sometimes the potter even attempted to imitate the original metal by giving his vessel a lustrous black surface. Some of the most remarkable vessels were found in the big graves at Ku-wei-ts'un, Hui-hsien. Obviously intended as substitutes for bronzes, they are painted in bright colours either with slightly stylized birds and animals, or with geometric designs in rather clumsy imitation of the later Chin-ts'un style.

During the early 1940s a group of miniature pottery vessels and figurines, said to have come from Late Chou tombs in the Hui-hsien region, began to appear on the Peking antique-market. Very heavily potted and beautifully finished, the vessels included miniature *hu*, covered *ting*, *p'an*, and a garment-hook and mirror, on the burnished black surfaces of which the inlaid geometric decoration of the Chin-ts'un bronzes was imitated in red pigment. Among the animals depicted were a tiger, an owl and several horses. The figurines were, however, the most striking; simply and compactly modelled with flat, schematic faces, they nevertheless convey a remarkable feeling of life and movement by the way in which their twisting bodies and wide-flung arms express the movements of the dance. These are indications that many, if not all, of these pieces are modern forgeries. It seems hardly possible that a forger could have completely invented this type, however, and excavations have in fact produced two possible sources of inspiration for them. Small pottery figurines, with simplified bodies, incised features and red pigment, were discovered in 1954 in a small tomb at Ch'ang-chih in South Shansi (as works of art they are in every way inferior to the 'Hui-hsien' pieces); while as a possible model for the ritual vessels we have a group of rather similar miniature pottery vessels unearthed in 1959 in a tomb of the Warring States period at Ch'ang-p'ing near Peking, three of which I have illustrated.[3]

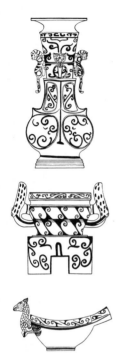

Miniature pottery vessels excavated at Ch'ang-p'ing, near Peking. Warring States period.

THE ARTS OF CH'U
While what might be called the 'classical' tradition was developing in the Honan-Shensi region, a quite different style of art was maturing in the large area of Central China dominated by the state of Ch'u. It is not known precisely how widely her boundaries extended (particularly in a southward direction), but they included the city of Shouchou on the Huai River in modern Anhui, while the influence of the art of Ch'u can be traced in the bronzes of Hui-hsien,

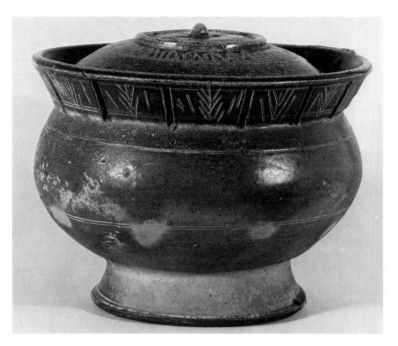

39 Covered bowl. Grey stoneware with olive-green glaze. Probably from Shouchou. Late Warring States period.

Honan and even northern Hopei. Until Ch'in rose menacing in the west, Ch'u had been secure, and in the lush valleys of the Yangtse and its tributaries had developed a rich culture in which poetry and the visual arts flourished exceedingly. So vigorous, indeed, was Ch'u culture that even after Ch'in sacked the last Ch'u capital, Shouchou, in 223 B C, it survived to become a significant element of Chinese civilization during the Han Dynasty.

In the late sixth century B C Shouchou was still under the state of Ts'ai. A grave of this period recently excavated in the district contained bronzes most of which were rather restrained versions of the Hsin-cheng style, and the art of Shouchou, even after its absorption into the expanding state of Ch'u, always retained some of its northern flavour. It must also have been an important ceramic centre at this time, if we are to judge by the beauty and vigour of the pottery excavated there. The body of this type is of grey stoneware with incised decoration under a thin olive-green glaze, the immediate predecessor of the Yüeh-type wares of the Han Dynasty, and the ancestor of the celadons of the Sung.

It is only in recent years that archaeological excavation in the Changsha region has revealed both the wealth and the essentially southern character of Ch'u art. Indeed, it is interesting to speculate on the course that Chinese culture would have taken if the victory in 223 B C had gone, not to the Ch'in savages from the western marches, but to this sophisticated and enlightened people.

Since the replanning of Changsha started in 1950 many large tombs have been brought to light. The coffin – or,

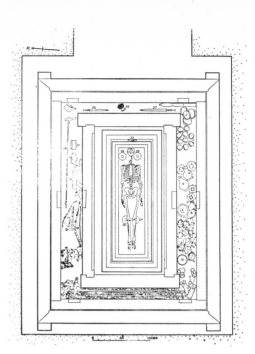

Sketch of a reconstructed tomb of the Warring States period at Changsha, showing the *ming-ch'i* crammed between the inner and outer coffins.

rather, multi-layered coffins, such as the *Kuan Tzu* recommended as giving employment to worthy artisans – was placed at the bottom of a deep shaft, and often surrounded by a layer of charcoal and a much thicker layer of white clay, which has in some mysterious way preserved the contents in spite of the fact that many of the tombs have been waterlogged for more than two thousand years. The space between the outer coffin and the chamber wall is often crammed with funerary furniture (*ming-ch'i*). Sometimes the body lay on a long wooden plank carved with exquisite pierced scroll patterns, while about it were set discs of jade, stone and glass (excavations have yielded glass beads as early as Western Chou), bronze weapons and vessels, pottery and lacquer-ware. The filter of white clay and charcoal has even preserved fragments of silk and linen, documents written with a brush on slips of bamboo, beautifully painted shields of lacquered leather, and musical instruments.

Here for the first time we find large numbers of wooden figurines of attendants and slaves. Confucius is said to have condemned the practice of carving these, as he thought it would lead people on, or back, to burying the living with the dead. He thought straw figures were safer. During the succeeding Han Dynasty pottery cast in moulds was found to be both cheaper and more enduring than wood, and perhaps more acceptable to Confucians. The Changsha figures, carved and painted, give useful information about Late Chou costume. More spectacular are the cult objects, consisting of grotesque monster heads, sometimes sprouting antlers and a long tongue, and the drum- or gong-stands formed of birds standing back-to-back on tigers or entwined serpents, decorated in yellow, red and black lacquer. The gong-stand found in 1957 in a tomb in the Ch'u city of Hsin-yang in Honan reflects the contacts of Ch'u with the south: similar stands are engraved on a number of bronze vessels from Ch'u sites, while bronze drums found in the Dongson region of northern Indo-China also bear snake and bird designs, believed to be connected with rain-magic.

A remarkable offshoot of the Ch'u culture has been unearthed at Shih-chai-shan, about twenty miles south of Kunming, capital of Yunnan. A score of tombs have been opened there, containing a wealth of bronze weapons and ritual objects, and gold and jade ornaments. Most extraordinary are the bronze drums and drum-shaped containers filled with cowrie-shells, the top of one of which I have illustrated. The figures who crowd it are evidently taking part in some sacrificial rite. Prominent are the ceremonial drums, some of which seem to be of enormous size, while a set of smaller drums stands on a platform under a wagon roof of a type still common in South-east Asia today.

From Chinese sources we know that these are the tombs of the rulers of the state of Tien, which had been conquered by a Ch'u general in the third century B C, and continued to flourish in remote independence well into the Han Dynasty. As would seem natural from its geographical position, the Shih-chai-shan culture contains elements of Chinese and Dongson art, and of the animal style of the western nomads. Struck by its extraordinary vigour, a recent Chinese writer has suggested that Dongson is the debtor, and, in fact, 'no more than a pale reflection of the high bronze culture of the Tien people in ancient Yunnan'. The unadulterated realism of Shih-chai-shan art, however, hardly justifies such a conclusion. Indeed, its very 'stylelessness' suggests that it

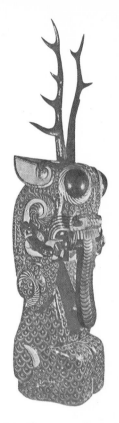

40 Cult object or guardian in the form of a horned, long-tongued creature eating a snake. Carved and lacquered wood. Excavated in Hsin-yang District, Honan. Late Warring States period.

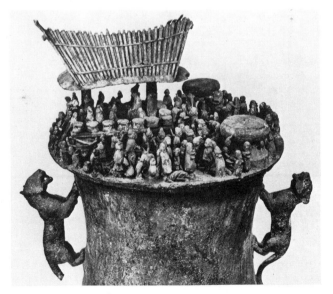

41 Drum-shaped container decorated with modelled sacrificial scene. Bronze. Late Warring States or Early Han Dynasty, third to second century BC.

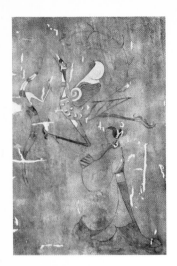

42 Woman, with dragon and phoenix. Painting on silk. Excavated at Changsha, Hunan. Late Warring States period.

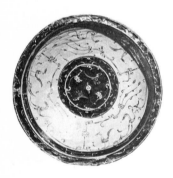

43 Bowl. Painted lacquer. Late Warring States period.

was produced in almost total isolation from the main stream of Chinese culture.

Whether it be the accident of preservation or that the Ch'u people actually did develop pictorial art at an earlier stage than North China is an open question, but it is the Changsha graves that have yielded the oldest painting on silk yet discovered. Swiftly sketched with deft strokes of the brush, it shows a woman in a full-skirted dress tied with a sash at the waist, standing in profile attended by a strutting phoenix and a sinuous dragon, whose reptilian origin is vividly suggested. A bamboo brush with rabbit's fur tip has also been found at Changsha, together with other writing and painting materials. Much of the most beautiful painting, however, appears on the lacquer-ware for which Ch'u was famous – the lacquer bowls, dishes, toilet-boxes, trays and low tables which, though made for daily use, in due course were placed in their owner's tomb. In black lacquer on a red ground, or red on glossy black, the swirling volutes may transform themselves into tigers, phoenixes or dragons. Common vessels were lacquered over a core of wood or woven bamboo, but the finest were built up of alternate layers of cloth and lacquer without a wood core, and are of incredible lightness and delicacy.

Also to be classed with the pictorial arts are the lively scenes cast on the surface of a remarkable bronze *hu* in the Palace Museum, Peking. In separate panels we see an attack on a city wall, a fight between longboats, people shooting wild duck with arrows on the end of long cords, mulberry-picking and other domestic arts, all carried out in silhouette with extraordinary vitality, elegance and humour. The free treatment of this and other engraved and inlaid vessels, considered together with the miniature lacquer-paintings, suggests that the source of the pictorial naturalism of Han art is to be found as much in Changsha and Shouchou as in metropolitan Loyang and Ch'ang-an.

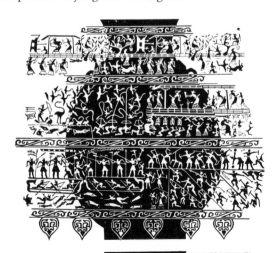

Designs engraved on an inlaid bronze *hu*. Peking. Late Warring States period.

Large numbers of bronze mirrors have been found both in the north and within the confines of Ch'u state. At first, and always to some degree, their purpose was not to reflect one's face only, but one's very heart and soul. An entry in the *Tso-chuan* under the year 658 BC, for instance, says of a certain individual, 'Heaven has robbed him of his mirror' – that is, made him blind to his own faults. The mirror, too, is that in which all knowledge is reflected, as it was to the medieval encyclopaedist St Vincent of Beauvais. 'The heart of the sage is quiet,' wrote Chuang Tzu, 'it is a mirror of Heaven and Earth, a mirror of all things.' The mirror also holds and reflects the rays of the sun, warding off evil and lighting the eternal darkness of the tomb.

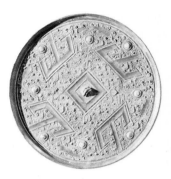

44 Mirror, Shouchou type. Bronze. Late Warring States period, third century BC.

A bronze disc with a loop-handle and dragon and snake decoration, believed to be a mirror, was found in a Shang tomb at Anyang. Perhaps the earliest true mirrors are those of the Ch'un-ch'iu period from Shang-ts'un-ling in Honan. Thereafter they are plentiful at Loyang. The face is polished, all decoration being confined to the back. Round the central loop (for the tassel) a mass of *lei-wen* or dragon-like creatures writhe within a confining border of ropes or twisted cowrie strings. A slightly later group (sixth–fifth centuries BC), most of which come from the Chin-ts'un tombs, are decorated with *t'ao-t'ieh* masks within a broad flat rim. The earliest mirrors from Ch'u were nearly all found in the Shouchou region. The boss rises from a bare ring of bronze; over a background of comma patterns appear either quatrefoil petals or large staggered ⅛-shaped motifs resembling the later form of the character *shan* ('mountain'), or swirling dragons or other semi-stylized creatures reminiscent of those on the lacquer vessels. Some of the most beautiful of all were made in the Loyang region in the fourth and third centuries BC. Upon an intricate interlocked geometric or lozenge design, borrowed from textile patterns, superb creatures stride or whirl round the plain central ring. The contrast in texture between the background and the dynamic yet simple forms of the dragons makes these mirrors a triumph of design.

This power to unite in one object the most intricate refinement of detail with a dynamic rhythm and boldness of silhouette is present also in the carved jades of the Late Chou period, which must surely be among the great achievements of the Chinese craftsman. Now jade was no longer reserved for worship of Heaven and Earth or for the use of the dead; it became at last a source of delight for the living. Indeed, as the ritual objects such as the *pi* and *tsung* lost their original symbolic power they too became ornaments, while jade was now used for sword-fittings, hairpins, pendants, garment-hooks – in fact, wherever its qualities could show to best advantage. Until recently very few jades had been found in controlled excavations, and dating on purely stylistic grounds is often, in view of the Chinese love of copying the antique, extremely unreliable. But the jade objects found in

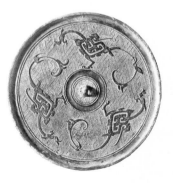

45 Mirror, Loyang type. Bronze. Late Warring States period, third century BC.

1953 in a tomb at Yang-tzu-shan outside Chengtu confirm the impression that at this time the quality of carving rises to new heights; the stones are chosen for their rich, unctuous texture; the cutting is flawless and the finish beautiful. A chain of four discs in the British Museum, London, connected by links and carved from a single pebble less than nine inches long, is a technical *tour-de-force* which suggests that the iron drill and cutting disc were already in use. Few of the *pi* of the period are left plain; their surface is generally decorated with a row of spirals, either engraved or raised to form the popular 'grain pattern', and sometimes confined within an outer geometric border. Flat plaques in the form of dragons, tigers, birds and fishes combine an arresting silhouette with a surface treatment of extraordinary delicacy. One of the most beautiful early Chinese jades yet discovered is the celebrated disc in the Nelson Gallery, Kansas City, ornamented with heraldic dragons: two on the outer rim, a third crawling round a small inner disc in the centre.

As we survey the inlaid bronzes of Chin-ts'un, the mirrors of Shouchou, the marvellous lacquer-ware of Changsha, the jades and the minor arts, we become aware that the period between 500 and 200 BC was one of the great epochs in the history of Chinese art. Moreover, the forms perfected during these restless years, the vocabulary and syntax, as it were, of Chinese decorative art, were to remain the characteristic modes of artistic expression throughout her later history.

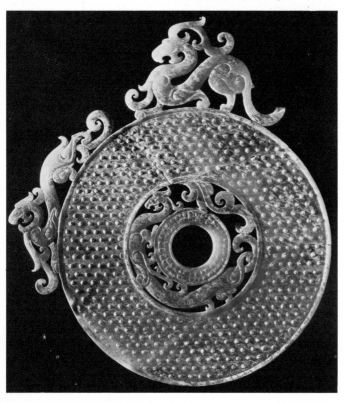

46 *Pi* disc. Jade. Late Warring States period.

5 The Ch'in and Han Dynasties

By 221 BC the inexorable steamroller of the Ch'in armies had crushed the remnants of the ancient feudal order. Now all China was united under the iron rule of King Cheng, who set up his capital in Hsien-yang and proclaimed himself Ch'in Shih-huang-ti – First Emperor of the Ch'in Dynasty. Aided by his Minister Li Ssu, an ardent Legalist, he proceeded to consolidate the new state. He strengthened the northern frontiers against the Huns and, at the cost of a million lives, linked up the sections of wall built by the previous kings of Chao and Yen into a continuous rampart fourteen hundred miles long. The boundaries of the Empire were greatly extended, bringing South China and Tonkin for the first time under Chinese rule. The feudal aristocracy were dispossessed and forcibly moved in tens of thousands to Shensi; rigid standardization of the written language, of weights and measures and of wagon axles (important in the soft loess roads of North China) was enforced, and over it all Shih-huang-ti set a centralized bureaucracy controlled by the watchful eye of the censors. All that recalled the ancient glory of Chou was to be obliterated from men's minds; copies of the classical texts were burned, and the death penalty was imposed on anyone found reading or even discussing the *Book of Songs* or the *Classic of History*. Many scholars were martyred for attempting to protest. But while these measures imposed an intolerable burden on the educated minority, they unified the scattered tribes and principalities, and now for the first time we can speak of China as a political and cultural entity. This unity survived and was consolidated on more humane lines during the Han Dynasty, so that the Chinese of today still look back on this epoch with pride and call themselves 'men of Han.'

The megalomania of the First Emperor drove him to build at Hsien-yang vast palaces the like of which had never been seen before. In one series, ranged along the riverside, he copied the apartments of each of the feudal lords whom he had defeated. The climax was the O-p'ang or O-fang Kung; he never lived to complete it, and it was destroyed in the holocaust which, in the manner so frequent in Chinese history, marked the fall of his dynasty. The Emperor lived in constant fear of assassination, and the roads connecting his many palaces were protected by high walls. So great was his dread of even a natural death, that he was for ever seeking through Taoist practitioners the secret of immortality. In his search for the elixir, tradition has it that he sent a company

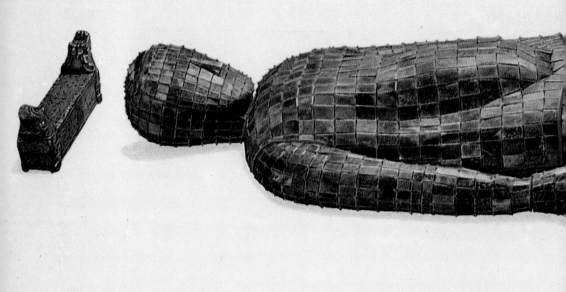

of aristocratic youths and girls across the Eastern Sea to
where the fabulous Mount P'eng-lai rises amid the waves –
ever receding as one approaches it. They never returned, and
it was later thought that they might have reached the shores
of Japan.

Shih–huang–ti died in 210 B C. The reign of his son Hu Hai
was short and bitter. His assassination in 207 was the signal
for a rebellion led by Hsiang Yü, a general of Ch'u, and
Liu Pang, who had started his life as a bandit. In 206 the
Ch'in capital was sacked; Hsiang Yü proclaimed himself
King of Ch'u, while Liu Pang took the crown of Han. For
four years the two rival kings fought for supremacy, till
finally in 202, when defeat seemed inevitable, Hsiang Yü
committed suicide and Liu Pang, after the customary
refusals, accepted the title of Emperor of the Han with the
reign name Kao-tsu. He established his capital at Ch'ang-an,
and there inaugurated one of the longest dynasties in Chinese
history.

So sharp was the popular reaction against the despotism of
the Ch'in that the Former, or Western, Han rulers were
content to adopt a policy of *laissez-faire* in domestic matters
and even restored the old feudal order in a limited way. At
first there was chaos and disunion, but Wen Ti (179–157)
brought the scattered Empire together and began to revive
classical learning and to restore to court life some of the
dignity and order that had attended it under the Chou. The
Early Han emperors were constantly either fighting or

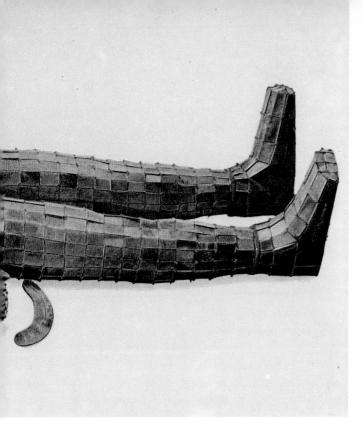

47 Burial suit. Jade plaques, sewn together with gold thread. From the tomb of Liu Sheng (died 113 BC), Man-ch'eng, Hopei. Eastern Han period.

bribing the Hsiung-nu, who had taken advantage of the fall of Ch'in to drive their arch-enemy the Yüeh-chih westwards across the deserts of Central Asia and invade North China. Finally, in 138 BC the Emperor Wu (140–87) sent out a mission under General Chang Ch'ien to make contact with the Yüeh-chih and form an alliance with them against Hsiung-nu. The Yüeh-chih were no longer interested in their old and now distant enemy and the mission failed; but Chang Ch'ien spent twelve years in the western regions, where he found Chinese silk and bamboo, brought there, he was told, by way of India. He returned to Ch'ang-an with a report which must have stirred the public imagination as did the travels of Marco Polo or Vasco da Gama. Henceforth, China's eyes were turned westwards. Further expeditions, sent into distant Ferghana to obtain the famous 'blood-sweating' horses for the imperial stables, opened up a trade-route which was to carry Chinese silk and lacquer to Rome, Egypt and Bactria. Travellers told of great snow-capped ranges reaching to the clouds, of fierce nomadic tribes and of the excitement of hunting wild game among the mountains. Somewhere beyond the horizon lay Mount K'un-lun, the axis of the world and home of Hsi Wang Mu, Queen Mother of the West, and the counterpart of the foam-washed P'eng-lai on which dwelt Tung Wang Kung, the immortal King of the East.

During these first two centuries of the Han, indeed, the popular mind, from the Emperor down, was filled with fantastic lore, much of which is preserved in pseudo-classical texts such as the *Huai Nan Tzu* and *Shan-hai-ching* ('Classic of Hills and Seas'), which are useful sources for the interpretation of the more fabulous themes in Han art. With the unification of the Empire many of these cults and superstitions found their way to the capital, where were to be found shamans, magicians and oracles from all over China. Meanwhile, the 'Taoists' were roaming the hillsides in search of the magical *ling-chih* (spirit-fungus) which, if properly gathered and prepared, would guarantee one immortality, or at least a span of five hundred years. Yet, at the same time, Confucian ceremonies had been intro-duced at court, scholars and encyclopaedists had reinstated the classical texts, and Wu Ti, in spite of his private leanings towards Taoism, deliberately gave Confucian scholars precedence in his entourage. It is these diverse elements in Han culture – native and foreign, Confucian and Taoist, courtly and popular – that give to Han art both its vigour and the immense variety of its styles and subject-matter.

When Wu Ti died, China was at one of the highest points of power in her history. The Empire was secure; her arms were feared across the northern steppes; Chinese colonies were flourishing in Tonkin, Manchuria, Korea and Central Asia. But Wu Ti's successors were weak and the administra-tion was crippled by palace intrigues and the power of the eunuchs, a new force in Chinese politics. In AD 9 a usurper named Wang Mang seized the throne and under the cloak of Confucian orthodoxy embarked upon a series of radical reforms which, had he been served by an honest and loyal administration, might have achieved a revolution in Chinese social and economic life. But by antagonizing the privileged class Wang Mang ensured his own downfall. He was murdered by a merchant and his brief Hsin Dynasty came to an end in AD 25. The Han house was restored and at once began the task of reconstruction. From their capital at Loyang the Later, or Eastern, Han reached out once more into Central Asia, consolidated their hold on Annam and Tonkin, and for the first time made contact with Japan. By the end of the century so great was their prestige that for a time even the distant Yüeh-chih, now established as the Kushan Dynasty in Afghanistan and North-west India, paid them tribute.

The Kushan brought Indian culture and religion into Central Asia. This region became a melting-pot of Indian, Persian and provincial Roman art and culture, which in turn travelled eastwards to China by way of the oases to north and south of the Tarim Basin. Buddhism may have been known by repute at least in the Former Han – the mythical Mount K'un-lun was very likely a Chinese version of the Buddhist Meru, or the Hindu Kailas, the axis of the universe – but now it began to take root in Chinese soil. The well-known story of the Emperor Ming, who in AD 67 dreamed of a 'golden man' (that is, a Buddhist image) in the far west and sent emissaries to fetch it, is a late fabrication, but already two years earlier a certain Liu Ying, Prince of Ch'u, had held a great feast for monks (*śramana*) and lay brethren, which indicates that at least one monastic community was in existence in Central China by that date, while there are several references to Buddhism in the *Hsi-ching-fu*, 'Rhapsody (or 'Rhyme-prose') on the Western Capital' (Ch'ang-an), by Chang Heng (78–139). During the second century there was also a flourishing Buddhist community in Katigara (modern Tonkin), whence the new faith gradually spread northwards into South China and Szechwan.

Until the time of troubles that accompanied the downfall of the Han, however, Buddhism was merely one among many popular cults. Officially, Confucianism still reigned supreme, and the Later Han saw the enormous expansion of a scholarly and official class nurtured in the Confucian doctrines. Many of these men had been trained in the Imperial Academy, founded by Wu Ti in 136 BC. From its graduates, selected by competitive examination in the Classics, were drawn recruits for that remarkable civil service which was to rule China for the next two thousand years. Unswerving loyalty to the Emperor, respect for scholarship and a rigid conservatism which sought for every measure the sanction of antiquity – these became the guiding principles of Chinese social and political life. Such ideals, however, offer no stimulus to the imagination, and it was not until Confucianism was enriched by Buddhist metaphysics during the Sung Dynasty that it became a source of the highest inspiration to painters and poets.

Already during the Former Han period, those who possessed skills useful to the Emperor were organized under a bureau known as the Yellow Gate (*huang-men*), which was based on the somewhat idealized picture of Chou institutions set out in the *Chou-li*. The highest ranks in this professional hierarchy were known as *tai-chao*, officials in attendance on the Emperor. These included not only painters, Confucian scholars and astrologers, but also jugglers, wrestlers and fire-swallowers, who might be called upon at any time to display their various skills in the imperial presence. The lower ranks of artists and artisans, such as those who made and decorated furniture and utensils for court use were known as *hua-kung*. This organization was not confined to the court, however; each commandery – in theory – had its own agency (*kung-kuan*) for the production and decoration of such things as ritual vessels, robes, weapons and lacquer-ware, for which latter Ch'u and Shu (Szechwan) were especially famous. Gradually, however, this system was relaxed. Under the Later Han, the emergence of the scholar-official class, the decline of the rigid Confucian order at court, and the corresponding rise of Taoist individualism, all combined to reduce the importance and activity of these largely anonymous professionals. By the end of the dynasty there had come into being a gulf between the intellectual aristocracy

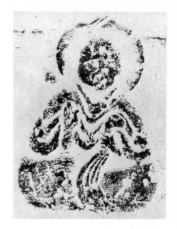

Seated Buddha in *abhaya-mudrā*. Rubbing of a relief in a shaft of the Later Han period at Chiating, Szechwan.

on the one hand and the unlettered craftsmen on the other which was to have a profound influence on the character of later Chinese art.

The wonders of Ch'ang-an and Loyang are vividly described in the *fu* rhapsodies on the Han capitals by Chang Heng and Ssu-ma Hsiang-ju, and though their beauties may have been somewhat exaggerated, some idea of the scale of the palace and government buildings can be gauged from the fact that the audience hall of the Wei-yang Palace at Ch'ang-an was over four hundred feet long – considerably longer than the T'ai-ho-tien, its counterpart in latter-day Peking. To the west of the capital Han Wu Ti built a pleasure palace, linked to the Wei-yang Palace within the city by a covered two-storeyed gallery ten miles long. At Loyang the palace lay in the centre of the city with a park behind it, built up with artificial lakes and hills into a fairy landscape in which the Emperor could indulge his Taoist fancies. Other parks further from the capital and likewise landscaped on a colossal scale were stocked with all manner of game-birds and beasts, some brought as tribute from remote corners of the Empire. From time to time a vast imperial hunt, or rather slaughter, was organized, followed by lavish feasting and entertainments. The *fu* poems describe these extraordinary spectacles, in which by some Leonardesque device the mountains P'eng-lai and K'un-lun, with wild animals fighting on their slopes, might be made to appear out of a cloud of smoke while attendants in galleries overhead crashed great stones together to simulate thunder. These hunts among mountains and the wild extravagant orgies that followed them were to become favourite subjects in Han art.

ARCHITECTURE

The gateways of the palace were marked by pairs of tall watch-towers (*ch'üeh*), while within its precincts stood multi-storeyed pavilions (*lou*) or towers (*t'ai*) which were used for entertainment, for admiring the view or simply for storage. When Loyang was burned in AD 185 the Cloud Tower (Yün-t'ai) went up in flames, and with it a huge collection of paintings, books, records and *objets d'art* – to say nothing of the portraits of thirty-two distinguished generals which Wu Ti had had painted on the walls of the tower itself. This was but one of the many occasions in Chinese history when the art treasures accumulated through a whole dynasty were destroyed in a few hours. Palaces, mansions and ancestral halls were built of timber, their tiled roofs supported by a simple system of brackets resting on wooden pillars. Their timberwork was picked out in rich colours and their inner walls, like those of the Yün-t'ai, were often decorated with wall-paintings.

These great mansions come vividly before our eyes as we read such poems as the *Chao Hun*, a passionate appeal addressed by an unknown Han author to the soul of a king which, in his illness, has left his body and gone wandering to

the edge of the world. To lure it back, the poet describes the
delights that await it in the palace:

> O soul, come back! Return to your old abode.
> All the quarters of the world are full of harm and evil.
> Hear while I describe for you your quiet and reposeful
>   home.
> High halls and deep chambers, with railings and tiered
>   balconies;
> Stepped terraces, storeyed pavilions, whose tops look on
>   the high mountains;
> Lattice doors with scarlet interstices, and carving on the
>   square lintels;
> Draughtless rooms for winter; galleries cool in summer;
> Streams and gullies wind in and out, purling prettily;
> A warm breeze bends the melilotus and sets the tall orchids
>   swaying.
> Crossing the hall into the apartments, the ceilings and
>   floors are vermilion,
> The chambers of polished stone, with kingfisher hangings
>   on jasper hooks;
> Bedspreads of kingfisher seeded with pearls, all dazzling in
>   brightness;
> Arras of fine silk covers the walls; damask canopies stretch
>   overhead,
> Braids and ribbons, brocades and satins, fastened with rings
>   of precious stone,
> Many a rare and precious thing is to be seen in the
>   furnishings of the chamber.
> Bright candles of orchid-perfumed fat light up flower-like
>   faces that await you;
> Twice eight handmaids to serve your bed, each night
>   alternating in duty,
> The lovely daughters of noble families, far excelling
>   common maidens. . . .
> O soul, come back![1]

Much of our knowledge of Han architecture is derived from
the reliefs and engravings or the stone slabs lining tombs and
tomb-shrines. In crude perspective, these show two-storeyed
gateways flanked with towers and often surmounted by a
strutting phoenix, symbol of peace and of the south. The
reliefs from the Wu family shrines in Shantung show a two-
storeyed house in whose kitchens on the ground floor a
banquet is in preparation, while the host entertains his guests
on the *piano nobile* above. The humbler dwellings – farm-
houses, granaries, even pig-sties and watchmen's huts –
survive in the rough and lively pottery models made to be
placed in the tombs.

Never in Chinese history, indeed, was so much care
lavished on the tomb and its contents as during the Han
Dynasty. Huge numbers of tombs have survived and every
day more are revealed. They are interesting not only for
their contents but also for their structure, which varies
considerably in different areas and provides us with almost
the only surviving remains of Han architecture. They are
not, of course, representative of Han building as a whole,
nearly all of which was carried out in timber; the more
adventurous techniques of the dome and vault in brick or

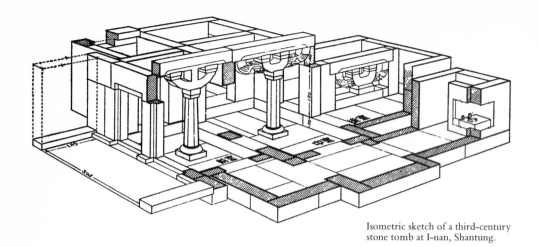

Isometric sketch of a third-century
stone tomb at I-nan, Shantung.

stone were reserved almost exclusively for the permanent
mansions of the dead. In the Chinese colonies in Korea and
Manchuria tombs were square or rectangular with flat roofs
of stone slabs supported on stone pillars, or shaped like
clusters of beehives with corbelled brick vaults. Tombs in
Shantung were also of stone, sunk in the ground, while
before them stood stone shrines, *tz'u*, for offerings to the
spirits of the departed. I have illustrated an elaborate example
of a Shantung tomb discovered at I-nan. At Nanyang in
southern Honan they were brick-vaulted, long and narrow,
lined with stone panels carved in relief. Sometimes the walls
were plastered and painted. In Szechwan most of the tombs
are small barrel-vaulted structures built of bricks on the
inner face of which a lively scene was stamped in relief,
though at Chiating deep tomb-shafts were cut into the cliffs
in groups, with a common vestibule carved out to suggest a
timber building. The tombs of the Ch'u people of Central
China, whose culture underwent a considerable revival
during the Han, were either deep pits containing layered
timber coffins, or rectangular chambers sometimes vaulted
in brick.

Elaborate as some of these tombs were, they were insignificant in comparison with the tombs of the Ch'in and Han
emperors, whose stone passages and vaults were enclosed in
the heart of an enormous artificial hill, approached by a
'spirit way' lined with colossal guardian figures carved in
stone, and guarded by booby-traps. It has long been thought
that all the tombs of the Han royal house were desecrated at
the fall of the dynasty. But the accidental finding in 1968 of
the huge concealed rock-cut tombs of Han Wu Ti's elder
brother Liu Sheng (died 113 BC) and his wife, clad in the
jade suits described in an earlier chapter, suggests that this
was not the case and that, hidden Tutankhamun-like in the
cliffs and valleys of Central China, there may be more great
tombs still intact, awaiting discovery.

It is during the Han Dynasty that we encounter the earliest monumental sculpture in stone. Its appearance at a time when China was highly receptive to Western ideas and forms, combined with the style of the sculpture itself, are more than suggestive of foreign origins. Near Hsien-yang in Shensi is a mound believed to be the grave of General Ho Ch'ü-ping, who died in 117 BC after a brief and brilliant career of campaigning against the Hsiung-nu. Before the tomb the life-size stone figure of a horse stands with majestic indifference over a fallen barbarian soldier who is attempting to kill him with his bow. The modelling is massive but shallow, giving the impression more of two reliefs back to back than of carving in the round, and indeed in its heavy, flat and somewhat coarse treatment this piece is from the technical point of view more reminiscent of the Sasanian rock-cut reliefs at Taq-i Bustan in Iran than of anything in early Chinese art. Many writers have pointed out how appropriate such a monument would be to a Chinese general whose victories over the western nomads were due to the very horses which China had acquired from their enemy and used so effectively against them.

Clearly, however, the Chinese sculptors had not yet mastered the art of carving in the round on a big scale. Indeed, carving is not the technique in which the Chinese craftsman feels happiest. He was to become more and more

48 Horse trampling on barbarian archer. Stone sculpture which formerly stood before the reputed tomb of Ho Ch'ü-ping (died 117 BC), Hsing-p'ing District, Shensi. Western Han period.

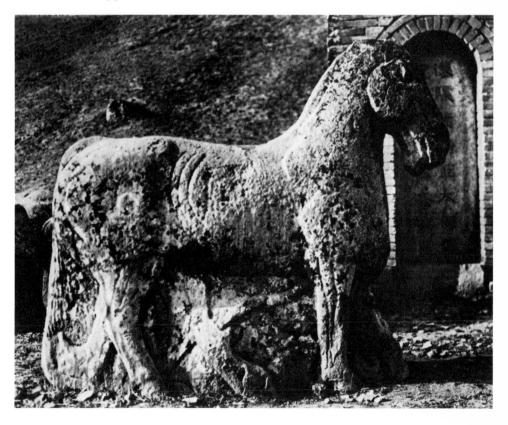

at home in modelling, and his most expressive plastic forms are modelled in clay or cast in bronze from clay or wax moulds, a very beautiful example being the gilt-bronze lamp, held by a kneeling girl, found in the tomb of Tou Wan at Man-ch'eng. Arresting in quite a different way is the bronze horse from a Western Han tomb in Kansu, discovered in 1969. He is poised as if flying, and one of his hoofs rests lightly on a swallow with wings outstretched, suggesting in a beautiful and imaginative way the almost divine power which the Chinese at this time believed the horse to possess.

While the idea of executing stone sculpture in relief was probably derived from western Asia, it had been thoroughly assimilated by the Later Han. Stone reliefs have been found in almost every part of China. The most truly sculptural are the animals and figures carved on a pair of funerary pillars standing before the tomb of an official named Shen, who was buried at Ch'ü-hsien in Szechwan during the second century AD. The pillars themselves are timber towers translated into stone. In high relief between the beam-ends is a monster like a gargoyle; at the corners crouching Atlantean figures – perhaps representing barbarian prisoners – support the beams, while above on each main face stand a

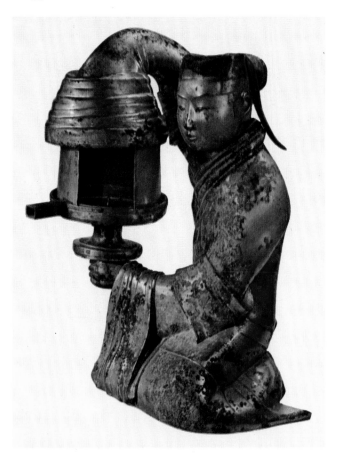

49 Lamp held by a kneeling servant-girl. Gilt-bronze. From the tomb of Tou Wan (died c. 120–100 BC), Man-ch'eng, Hopei. Western Han period.

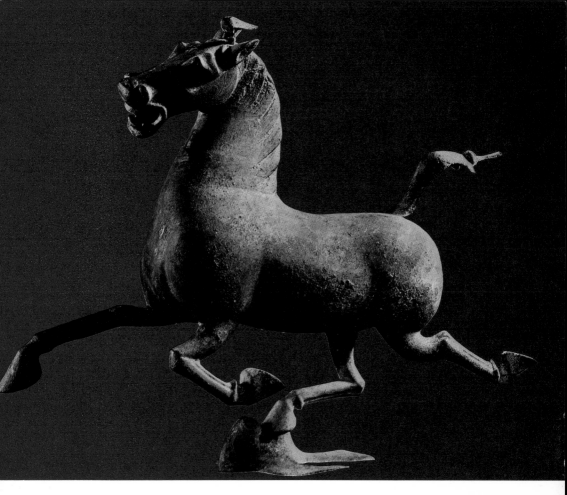

beautifully modelled deer and rider. The only figures in flat
relief are the directional symbols: on the east the dragon, on
the west the tiger, to the north the 'dark warrior' (snake and
tortoise), to the south the phoenix.

Nearly all of what passes for 'relief sculpture' in the Han
period, however, is not really sculpture at all, so much as
engraving in the flat surface of a stone slab, or flat relief with
the background cut back and striated to give a contrasting
texture. These slabs preserve the subject-matter – and
something even of the composition – of the lost mural
paintings of the Han Dynasty. They not only give a vivid
picture of daily life in this far-off time, but also show clear
regional differences in style, so that we can without much
difficulty identify the elegant dignity of some of the
Shantung reliefs, the luxuriance of the stones from Nanyang
in Honan, the wild, extravagant manner of the reliefs from
distant Szechwan. After the Han Dynasty China became
ever more of a single cultural entity, and these regional styles
very largely disappeared.

The stone shrines standing before the tombs were often
decorated with engraved designs, the best-known series
being those at the Hsiao-t'ang-shan (Hill of the Hall of
Filial Piety) near Fei-ch'eng in Shantung, and the slabs from

50 Horse, poised on a swallow with
wings outstretched. Bronze. From a
tomb at Lei-t'ai, Kansu. Western
Han period.

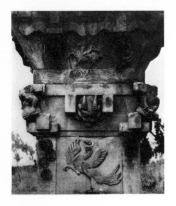

51 Top of memorial pillar (*ch'üeh*) for a number of the Shen family. Stone. Ch'ü-hsien, Szechwan. Han Dynasty.

four now-demolished shrines of the Wu family near Chia-hsiang in south-western Shantung, which are dated by their inscriptions between A D 145 and 168. The scenes, which are left in silhouette on the flat surface of the stone while the background is cut away, give a remarkable picture of the syncretic nature of Han art, in which Confucian ideals, historical events (real and legendary), and 'Taoist' mythology and folklore are all brought together. On the shallow end gables of two of the shrines to east and west, we find the legendary rulers Tung Wang Kung and Hsi Wang Mu respectively. Below we see the equally legendary meeting of Confucius and Lao Tzu, or ancient kings, filial sons and virtuous women. The attempted assassination of Ch'in Shih-huang-ti, and his effort to raise one of the tripods of the Emperor Yü, are favourite themes. The central recess and most of the remaining space is devoted to a banqueting scene. Below, all the preparations for the feast are shown with great precision and no little humour, while above, the host (presumably the deceased) welcomes his guests in a pavilion flanked by towers. We see the ponderous officials in their voluminous robes, the short deep-chested horses of Central Asian stock who trot with high-stepping precision while the air above them is filled with swirling clouds and loud with the clamour of a fantastic assortment of winged creatures come to do honour to the dead. In this fabulous setting, the soul of the deceased can pass easily from the world of men to the world of the spirits.

PAINTING AND LACQUER-WORK

There can be little doubt that both the style and the subject-matter of the tomb reliefs owe much to the great cycles of wall-paintings in halls and palaces, all traces of which have long since disappeared. Only a few miles away from the Wu family tombs lay the Ling-kuang Palace, built by a brother of Han Wu Ti. The fame of its wall-paintings is celebrated

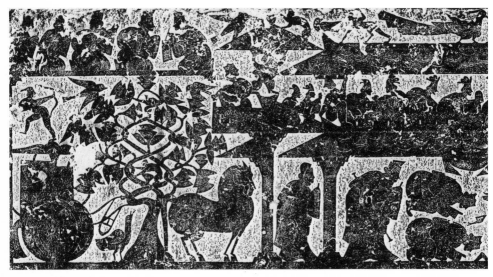

52 The Archer Yi; the Fu-sang Tree and a Mansion. Detail of rubbing from stone relief from tomb-shrine of Wu Liang, Shantung Province. Han Dynasty.

in a poem by Wang Yen-shou, written a few years before the Wu family shrines were erected, which exactly describes the subject-matter of their reliefs:

Upon the great walls
Flickering in a dim semblance glint and hover
The Spirits of the Dead.
And here all Heaven and Earth is painted, all living things
And their tribes, and all wild marryings
Of sort with sort; strange spirits of the sea,
Gods of the hills. To all their thousand guises
Had the painter formed
His reds and blues, and all the wonders of life
Had he shaped truthfully and coloured after their
    kinds. . . .[2]

By contrast with these lost wall-paintings, the reliefs from vaulted brick tombs in distant Szechwan show an easy naturalism far in advance of the pictorial art of the rest of China at this period. One of these moulded panels depicts salt-mines set in a landscape of wooden hills, with towers for hoists, pipe-lines of bamboo carrying the brine to the evaporating-pans – methods still in use in Szechwan in the twentieth century. Another, divided horizontally, shows in the lower half men harvesting and threshing in the rice-fields, while another man brings their lunch; above, two hunters kneel at the shore of a lake, shooting up at the rising ducks with arrows trailing long cords.

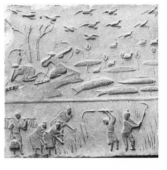

53 Shooting birds on a lake-shore and harvesting scene. Moulded pottery tile. From Kuang-han, Szechwan. Han Dynasty.

The reliefs on the Wu family shrines are in one plane, the only concession to the third dimension being to twist a chariot slightly sideways to show both wheels, while its three horses are drawn in echelon as on an early Greek vase. A more advanced treatment of architecture is seen in the I-nan reliefs, where buildings are boldly placed on a diagonal and we are able to see over roofs and into court-yards. It is in Szechwan, however, that we first encounter a convincing landscape in three dimensions. In the hunting scene, for example, the border of the lake winds back, seeming almost to lose itself in the mist, while behind the hunters stand two bare trees. On the surface of the water are fishes and lotus flowers, and ducks swimming away towards the upper border of the panel as fast as they can go. It shows that already in the Later Han period artists in Szechwan – perhaps because it was furthest removed from the formal 'court style' of Honan and Shantung – were beginning to solve the problem of *continuous* recession in depth which, three hundred years later, was still to defeat the engraver of the famous sarcophagus in the Nelson Gallery, Kansas City.

Landscape must, however, have played a very subordinate part in the great fresco cycles which decorated the palaces and ancestral halls. The themes were most often Confucian, as illustrated by a passage from the *Han-shu*: 'The Mother of Jih Ti in teaching her sons had very high standards: the Emperor [Wu Ti] heard of it and was pleased. When she fell ill and died, he ordered her portrait to be painted on [the walls of] the Kan-ch'üan Palace [in Shensi]. . . . Every time

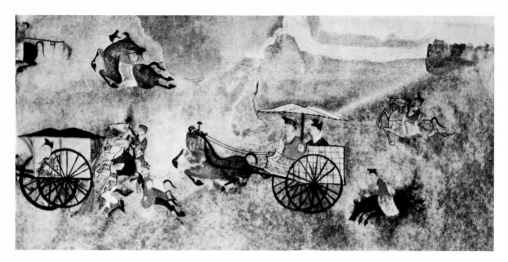

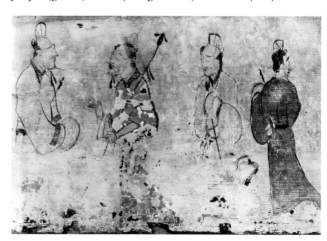

54 Guests arriving for the funeral feast. Detail of a wall-painting. From a tomb in Liao-yang, north-east China. Han Dynasty.

Jih Ti saw the portrait he did obeisance to it and wept before he passed on.' A rough provincial echo of this kind of painting survives in the large figures of civil and military officials paying their respects to the deceased, painted on the walls of a tomb at Wang-tu in Hopei. Other passages in the *Han-shu* bear witness to the Taoist predilections of the Han emperors. Wu Ti, for example, had a tower in the Kan-ch'üan Palace where were depicted 'the demons and deities of Heaven, Earth, and the Supreme Unity. Sacrificial utensils were set out, by which the divine beings were to be addressed.'

The finest Han wall-paintings yet discovered line the plastered walls of a stone tomb at Liao-yang in Manchuria. Their theme is the most popular one in Han funerary art – an entertainment given by the deceased for his friends and fellow officials. We find him ensconced in a pavilion, receiving two guests, while beneath a three-storeyed tower the entertainment is in progress, with feasting, juggling, acrobatic feats, a dance round a great revolving drum, and a group of four girl musicians seated on a mat, with clappers, *p'i-p'a* (guitar), *hsiao* (straight flute) and *ch'in* (lute). On one

55 Detail of a tile from a tomb-shrine. Painted pottery. Han Dynasty.

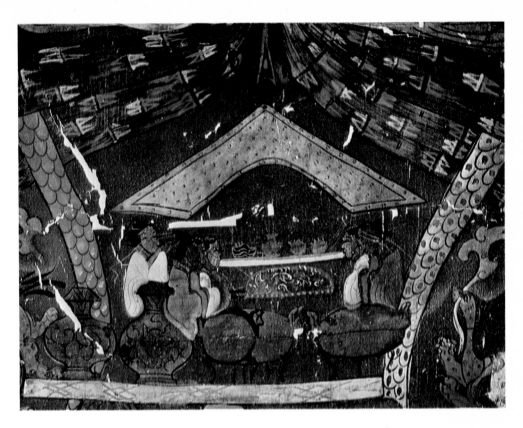

wall gentlemen in covered carriages pass across the scene at a smart pace, accompanied by others on horseback. These, too, are stock subjects in Han funerary art. The only deliberate perspective device is the placing of the carriages at a slight angle so that the dashboard, both occupants, both wheels and horses are clearly visible. Other horsemen gallop along near the top of the panel, one partly concealed by his horse's head which is turned right back to see who is following. There is no ground, no hint of any setting, and yet we seem to be looking down from above on a rolling plain across which these horsemen are dashing with tremendous speed. These wall-paintings show that the lateral movement from right to left, and the open composition which seems to extend beyond the picture area, both characteristic of later scroll-painting, were already mastered by painters during the Han Dynasty.

This subtle sense of space appears too in the relationship between the figures painted on a celebrated series of tiles from the gable of a tomb-shrine now in the Boston Museum of Fine Arts. One scene depicts an animal combat; another may represent, as Laurence Sickman has suggested, an incident in the life of the virtuous Princess Chiang of the ninth century BC, who took off her jewels and demanded to be incarcerated in the gaol for court ladies as a protest against the Emperor's dissipation – a threat which soon brought him

56 Painted banner. Silk. Detail; see also larger detail below. Ma-wang-tui, Changsha, Hunan. Western Han period, c. 180 BC.

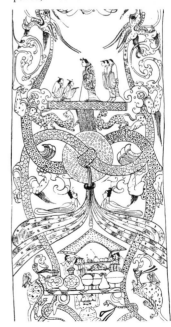

79

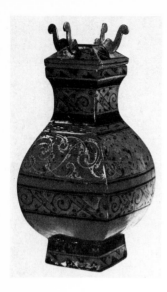

to his senses. The figures, drawn in long sweeping lines with a sensitive, pliant brush, stand and move with wonderful ease and grace; the men discuss the affair in dignified agitation, while the women, elegant and playful, seem to find the whole incident rather amusing. Happy the man whose tomb was adorned with such charming figures!

The power of the Chinese craftsman to impart life and movement to his subjects is vividly shown in the decoration of the lacquer objects for which Szechwan province was especially famous. That the output of her factories – especially those of Shu and Kuang-han – must have been considerable we know from the first-century *Discourses on Salt and Iron*, whose author protests that the rich were spending five million copper cash annually on lacquer alone. A number of Szechwan lacquer bowls, cups and boxes, bearing dates between 85 BC and AD 71, have been found in tombs in the vicinity of Pyongyang in North Korea. Most famous, though undated, is the 'painted basket' (actually a box) found in a tomb at Lolang.

Round the top under the fitted lid are ninety-four figures of filial sons, virtuous and wicked rulers and ancient worthies. All are sitting on the floor, but monotony is avoided by the skill and inventiveness with which they turn to one side or the other, gesticulate or engage in lively conversation. Even in this crowded space we find the same sense of individuality, of interval and psychological relationship between the figures, that we encountered on the tiles in the Boston Museum of Fine Arts. Other lacquer objects, such as bowls and trays, of which many beautiful examples have been preserved in the waterlogged soil of Changsha, are adorned with sweeping scrolls and volutes evolved out of the decoration of the lacquers and inlaid bronzes of the

57 Covered square-section jar, *fang-hu*. Lacquered wood. From a tomb at Ma-wang-tui, Changsha, Hunan. Western Han period, about 180 BC.

58 Paragons of filial piety. Lacquer painting on basket-work box. Lo-lang, Korea. Eastern Han period.

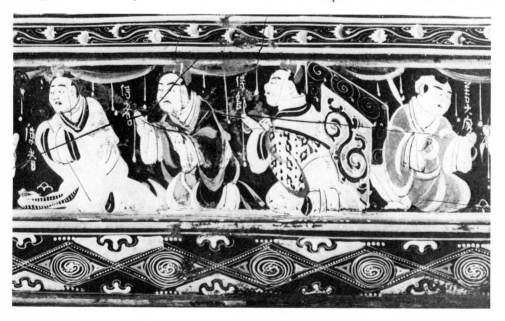

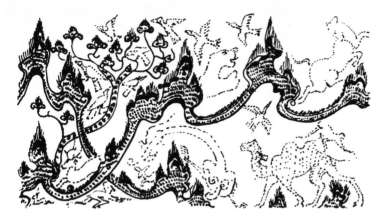

Warring States period. Now, however, these whirls erupt into flame-like tongues. The presence of a flying phoenix turns these tongues into clouds; when set about with tigers, deer and hunters they are magically transformed into hills; sometimes the transformation is aided – as on a beautiful inlaid bronze tube in the Hosokawa Collection – by vertical striations suggesting grass, or by little trees which grow from the volutes on some of the painted pottery *hu* (wine-jars). There is no attempt to depict a real landscape; rather has the craftsman taken the sweeping volute as the essential form common to all things in nature, and by means of a few accessories transformed it into clouds, waves or mountains, without robbing it of any of its rhythmic force. Because its forms follow the natural sweep and movement of the artist's hand they express the rhythms of nature itself.

From the kind of pictorial art that I have been describing, rough and provincial as most of it is, we may imagine what the finest Han paintings must have been like. Although a 'quasi-paper' made from pounded refuse silk was in use in the Former Han period, and possibly even earlier, real paper made from vegetable fibres was the invention of a eunuch in charge of the Shang-fang (imperial workshop) named Ts'ai Lun, who presented his formula to the Emperor in AD 105. Paper, however, was probably not used by artists for some time, and paintings continued to be executed on rolls of silk. Figure subjects included illustrations to the Classics and Histories, and more fanciful works such as the *Huai Nan Tzu* and *Shan-hai-ching*, while for landscape there were illustrations to the *fu* rhapsodies describing the capitals, palaces and royal hunting-parks.

It has long been thought that the hanging scroll was introduced with Buddhism from India, because the earliest known pictures in this form were the Buddhist banners of the T'ang Dynasty discovered at Tunhuang. However, a remarkable discovery has recently been made, in a Former Han tomb at Ma-wang-tui in the suburbs of Changsha, of a silk banner painting that is a thousand years older than all known Chinese hanging scrolls, and leaves no doubt that this format is native to China. The T-shaped banner, six feet high and nearly three feet wide across the top, depicts beings of the nether world, the world of men, and of the heavens; it is fitted with tassels and a cord for suspension very like that of the familiar hanging scroll.

Some of the most interesting attempts at landscape must have been the pictorial maps made for strategic purposes or for flood control, óf which the most ambitious was probably the huge sectional relief map of China made by the cartographer Hsieh Chuang in the fifth century. Not one of these paintings has survived, however. Most of the imperial collection was destroyed in the sack of the capital in AD 190. Seventy cartloads – all that remained – were sent westwards for safety, but half was lost on the way, and remnants were used by the soldiers to patch their tents.

BRONZE

With the fall of the Chou the traditional rituals were forgotten, and consequently Han bronzes, while many were no doubt used in domestic rites of various sorts, are generally more utilitarian or decorative than those of Shang and Chou. Shapes are simple and functional, the commonest being the deep dish and the wine-jar (*hu*) which were often decorated with inlaid designs in gold or silver. One object with definite ritual associations was the *Po-shan hsiang-lu*, a censer in the shape of a fairy mountain, often covered with animals, hunters and trees modelled in relief. Its base is lapped by the waves of the Eastern Sea, while a hole behind each little peak emits the incense smoke symbolizing the cloud-vapour (*yün-ch'i*) which is the exhalation of the fairy mountain – and, indeed, of all mountains, for, according to traditional Chinese belief, all nature is alive and 'breathing'. The beautiful hill-censer inlaid with gold and silver which I have illustrated was found in the Western Han tomb of Liu Sheng, the jade-clad brother of the Emperor Wu.

In Han tombs there have been found great quantities of bronze objects, including harness- and carriage-fittings, swords and knives, utensils and belt-buckles, many of which are inlaid with gold or silver, turquoise or jade. Even the trigger mechanism of a crossbow was often so cunningly inlaid as to make it a thing of beauty. Some of these objects show the powerful impact of the 'animal style' of the Ordos Desert, which in turn was influenced by that curious mixture of stylization and brutal realism characteristic of the art of the northern steppes.

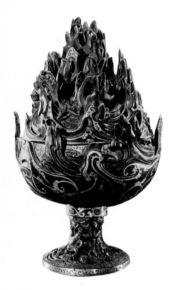

59 Fairy mountain incense-burner, *Po-shan hsiang-lu*. Bronze inlaid with gold. From the tomb of Liu Sheng (died 113 BC) at Man-ch'eng, Hopei. Western Han period.

BRONZE MIRRORS

The bronze mirrors of the Han Dynasty continue the traditions developed at Loyang and Shouchou during the Warring States period. The Shouchou coiled dragon design becomes more complex and crowded, the dragon's body being drawn in double or triple lines, while the background is generally cross-hatched. Another group, also chiefly from Shouchou, has an all-over design of spirals on which a scalloped many-pointed device is sometimes superimposed;

its significance may be astronomical. Most interesting and most pregnant with symbolic meaning are the so-called 'TLV' mirrors, of which the finest were produced in the Loyang region between 100 BC and AD 100, although the design was already being used on mirror-backs in the second century BC.

A typical TLV mirror has a large central boss surrounded by a square panel with twelve smaller bosses separating the characters of the twelve Earthly Branches. The Ts, Ls and Vs protrude into a circular zone adorned with four-directional animals, which, with the fifth, central zone, symbolizes the five elements, a system of cosmology first set down by Tsou Yen (c. 350–270) and very popular in Han times. According to this system, the great ultimate (t'ai-chi) produces the positive-negative dualism of yang and yin, the interaction of which in turn gives birth to the five elements (wu-hsing) from which all events and objects are derived. The way in which the five elements work upon each other and are symbolized is as follows:

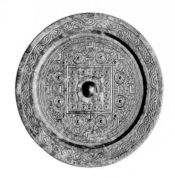

60 'TLV'-type mirror. Bronze. Han Dynasty.

element	function	colour	direction	season	symbol
WATER	puts out fire	black	north	winter	'black warrior' (snake and tortoise)
FIRE	melts metal	red	south	summer	bird (phoenix)
METAL	destroys wood	white	west	autumn	tiger
WOOD	overcomes earth	green	east	spring	dragon
EARTH	absorbs water	yellow	centre		tsung

On the TLV mirror, the central circle within a square represents the earth symbol, tsung, while the four directions, seasons and colours are symbolized by their animals in the appropriate quarters. Many bear inscriptions which clearly set out the meaning and purpose of the design, such as this one on a mirror in the Museum of Far Eastern Antiquities, Stockholm: 'The Imperial mirror of the Shang-fang [imperial workshop]', it runs, 'is truly without blemish; a skilled artisan has engraved it and achieved a decoration; to the left the Dragon and to the right the Tiger eliminate what is baleful; the Red Bird and Black Warrior conform to the yin and yang forces; may your sons and grandsons be complete in number and be in the centre; on it are Immortals such as are customary [on mirrors]; may you long preserve your two parents; may your joy and wealth be splendid; may your longevity outstrip that of metal and stone; may you be like a prince or a king.'[3]

The TLV design was primarily an auspicious cosmological diagram combining celestial and terrestrial symbols; its terrestrial elements made up the board for playing liu-po, a popular game in Han times which is represented on a number of Han reliefs and in clay models. The object of this game, which Professor Yang Lien-sheng has reconstructed from ancient texts, is to capture your opponent's men or

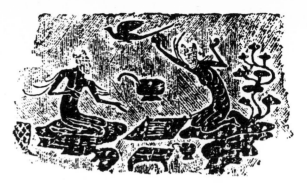

Immortals playing *liu-po*. Rubbing from stone relief from tomb at Hsin-chin, Szechwan. Han Dynasty.

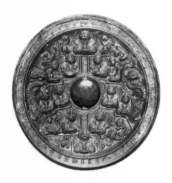

61 Mirror. Bronze. Late Eastern Han period, second to third century AD.

JADE

drive them into the 'benders' (presumably the Ls on the outer edge), in order to attain the centre, or, as Schuyler Cammann has put it, 'to establish an axis for symbolic control of the Universe'. In Han mythology *liu-po* was a favourite game of Tung Wang Kung, and of ambitious human heroes who sought to pitch their skill against that of the gods and, by defeating them, to acquire magic powers.

To judge by the mirror designs, the game seems to have gone out of fashion towards the end of the Han Dynasty. The mirror-backs of Late Han and the Three Kingdoms often preserve the directional symbolism, but now become crowded with figures fully modelled in relief; for the most part these are Taoist fairies and immortals, but after AD 300 Buddhist themes begin to appear as well.

In jade-carving the main technical advance at the end of the Chou Dynasty and the beginning of the Han was in the introduction of iron cutting tools. The iron drill made it possible to cut deep into the stone, while the rotary cutting disc enabled the lapidary to hollow out quite large pebbles into the form of toilet-boxes and bowls such as the *yü-shang* ('winged cup'), a small oval bowl with flanges on the long sides, made for eating and drinking and for offerings in the tombs. They have been found sometimes in sets standing on a tray, not only in jade but also in pottery, silver and lacquer. This new technical freedom made the lapidary more adventurous, inspiring him to carve, in three dimensions, figurines and animals, of which perhaps the most beautiful specimen is the famous horse in the Victoria and Albert Museum, London. He no longer rejects the flawed stone, but begins to exploit the discolorations: the brown stain, for instance, becomes a dragon on a white cloud. Jade has by this time begun to lose its ritual significance; it now becomes instead the delight of the scholar and the gentleman, for whom its ancient associations and beauty of colour and texture will become a source of the profoundest intellectual and sensual pleasure. Henceforward he will be able to enjoy his pendants and garment-hooks, his seals and the other playthings on his desk, in the confident knowledge that in them aesthetic and moral beauty are united. This, however, can hardly be said of the jade burial suits described above

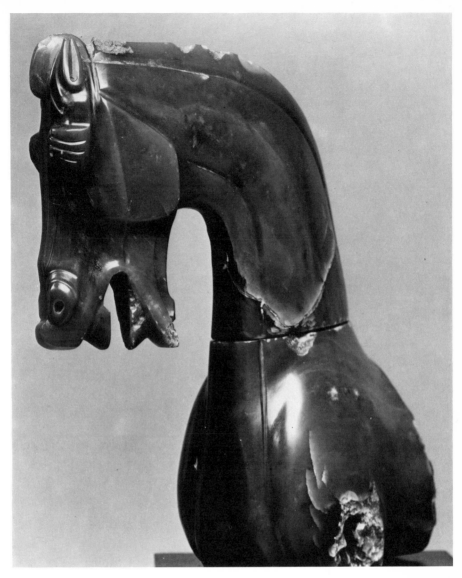

on page 49, which were made at enormous cost in human travail for members of the Han imperial family. After the fall of the Han there was a reaction against this sort of extravagance, and most graves of the ensuing period (that of the Six Dynasties) are simply furnished.

Under the Han Dynasty, the customs and amenities which in Shang and Chou had been confined to a minute privileged aristocracy in a small region now spread over a much wider area and a much larger segment of society. Chinese handicrafts of the period have been found far beyond China's own frontiers – in Indochina and Siberia, Korea and Afghanistan. The ruins of a Chinese-style palace recently discovered in southern Siberia contained Chinese bronze fittings, coins,

62 Head and shoulders of a horse. Jade. Han Dynasty.

TEXTILES

85

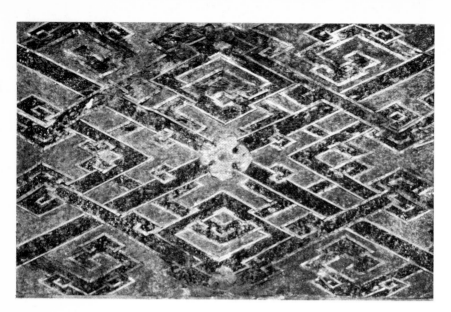

63 Woven silk textile. From the tomb at Ma-wang-tui, Changsha Hunan. Han Dynasty.

tiles and pottery house models, the last presumably made locally by Chinese potters. Chinese archaeologists have suggested that this might have been the palace of the daughter of Madame Wen-chi, who had been married to a chieftain of the Hsiung-nu in AD 195 but eventually was forced to return to China, leaving her devoted husband and children behind.

Chinese textiles, too, reached the limits of the civilized world. The Greek word *Seres*, 'the Silk People', was probably first used not of the Chinese themselves – of whom the Greeks had no direct knowledge – but of the western Asiatic tribes who traded in this precious commodity. Direct intercourse with China came only after Chang Ch'ien's expedition, and the establishment of the 'Silk Road' across Central Asia. This great caravan-route, leaving China at the Jade Gate in modern Kansu, crossed Central Asia to both north and south of the Taklamakan Desert, reuniting in the region of Kashgar, whence one branch led westwards across Persia to the Mediterranean world while the other struck south into Gandhāra and India. Chinese stuffs have been found in the Crimea, in Afghanistan, Palmyra and Egypt, while in Rome in the time of Augustus there was a special market for imported Chinese silk in Vicus Tuscus. According to legend, it was the consort of the Yellow Emperor herself who first taught the Chinese people the cultivation of the mulberry on which the silkworms feed, the spinning, dyeing and weaving of the threads. So important has the industry been to China that, until the Revolution of 1911, the Empress sacrificed to the spirit of the Yellow Emperor's consort every year in her own temple in Peking. Evidence of the art of weaving was found in the Neolithic village of Pan-p'o in Shensi; the Shang people at Anyang had tailored clothing of silk and hemp, while a number of passages in the

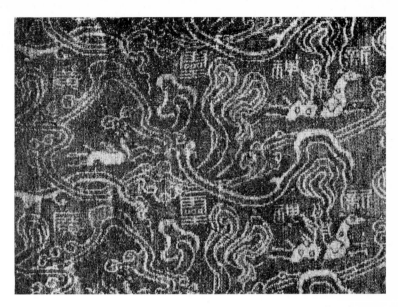

Book of Songs refer to coloured woven silk. Silk panels with
painted designs have been found in Late Chou graves at
Changsha; but the most remarkable finds of early Chinese
textiles were made in Central Asia, notably in the tumulus
graves at Noin-Ula in southern Siberia, excavated by the
Koslóv expedition in 1924–25, and in the sand-buried sites
of Turfan and Khotan, explored first by Sir Aurel Stein early
in this century and more recently by Chinese archaeologists.
The grave in Changsha that yielded the silk banner which I
have illustrated was also crammed with rolls of silk. The
techniques included moiré, damask, gauze, quilting and
embroidery, and the designs were chiefly of three kinds:
pictorial, generally representing fierce animal combats such
as appear also on the Ordos bronzes; diapered, with geo-
metrical motifs repeated over the whole surface; or, thirdly,
composed of those endless rhythmic cloud-volutes which we
have already encountered on the inlaid bronzes, set about
with horsemen, deer, tigers and more fabulous creatures.
The silk panel from Noin-Ula which I have illustrated is a
kind of 'Taoist' landscape composed of giant spirit-fungus
(*ling-chih*) alternating with rocky crags topped by phoenixes
and adorned with formalized trees, executed in a mixed
Chinese-Western style which suggests that Chinese weavers
were already designing for the export market.

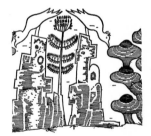

Silk panel from Noin Ula.

Han ceramics vary enormously in quality, from unglazed
and roughly modelled earthenware to a high-fired, glazed
stoneware verging on porcelain. The character *tz'u*, which
already in the Han dictionary *Shuo-wen* denoted 'earthenware', probably did not come to mean true porcelain until
the sixth century AD; during the Six Dynasties it referred to
a hard fine stoneware, or 'proto-porcelain', which rang
when struck. Most of the grave goods, however, were in

CERAMICS FOR USE AND
FOR BURIAL

87

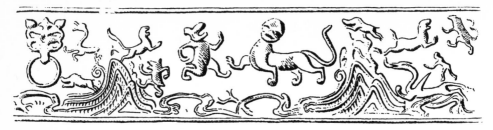

The hunt among the mountains. Relief on the shoulder of a pottery *hu*.

coarse pottery, generally covered with a lead glaze which easily oxidizes, producing that silvery-green iridescence which is so attractive a feature of this class of Han wares. The technique of lead-glazing was known in the Mediterranean world before the Han, and if not discovered independently may have been introduced by way of Central Asia. The finest of these lead-glazed wares are the jars (*hu*) for grain or wine; one labelled 'for white wine' has recently been found in a tomb in Wen-teng-hsien, Shantung. Their shapes are simple and robust, the imitation of bronze being aided by very precise finish and the application of *t'ao-t'ieh* masks in relief, while incised lines or geometric motifs round the shoulder enhance the beauty of their form. Sometimes they are decorated with a frieze, depicting, in relief under the glaze, a 'hunt among mountains', in which all manner of creatures, real and imaginary, chase each other round and round – as on those extraordinary full-scale models of Mount P'eng-lai which were made to appear at

65 Jar, *hu*. Stoneware, decorated with relief designs under a dark-green glaze. Han Dynasty.

66 Watch-tower. Green glazed pottery. Han Dynasty.

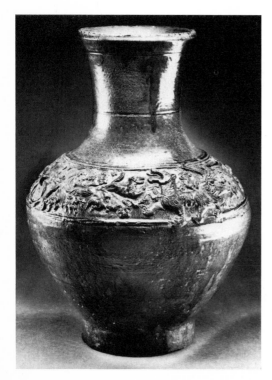

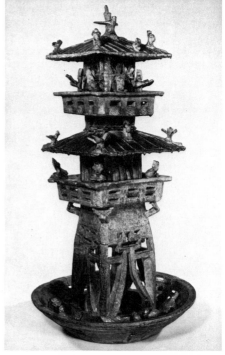

the hunting-feasts of the Han emperors. These reliefs, in which we often find towering ranges of hills, may well preserve the designs of Han scroll-paintings on silk.

In Han times, many people believed that on quitting this world one who had the secret of immortality could take with him to Heaven his family, servants, personal possessions, domestic animals, and even his house. As these could not actually accompany him, models (*ming-ch'i*) were placed in the tomb, and the custom persisted long after belief in immortality died out. Thus we find in the Han tombs a retinue of servants and guards, farmhands, musicians and jugglers such as its occupant probably never enjoyed in his lifetime. There were barns with fowl modelled in relief on the top. There were tall watch-towers in several storeys, their wooden beams and transoms either indicated by incisions in the clay or painted red. A celebrated three-storeyed house in the Nelson Gallery, Kansas City, has its structural parts picked out in colour while the magical *fu-sang* tree, with its crows, emblems of the sun and of the south, are painted in panels on its walls – possibly to counteract the effects of an inauspicious orientation of the tomb. The houses and barns of the South China tombs are raised on stilts, like those in South-east Asia today. Farm animals are modelled with uncanny realism; watch-dogs from Szechwan graves are squat and menacing; those from Changsha, with heads erect and muzzles quivering, look so alert that one can almost hear them sniffing. These figurines are a useful source of information for the daily life, beliefs and economy of Han China. The delightful tableau excavated in 1969 from a

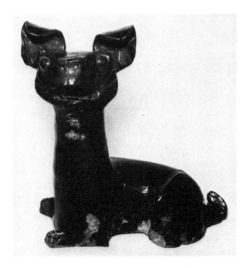

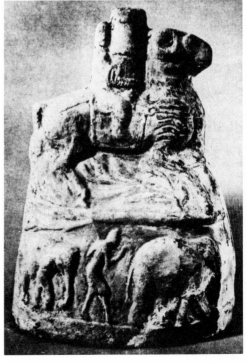

67 Dog. Pottery covered with reddish-brown glaze. From Changsha, Hunan.

68 Coin-tree or lamp-stand. Pottery. From a tomb at Nei-chiang, Szechwan. Han Dynasty.

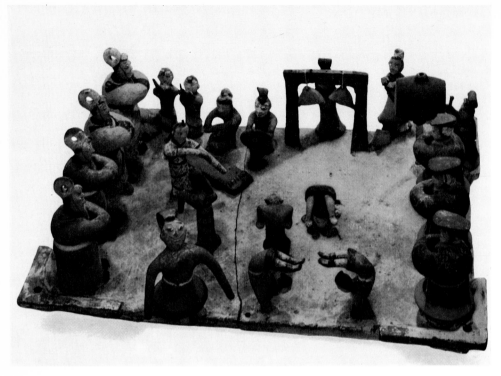

69 Tray with figures of acrobats, dancers, musicians and spectators or attendants. Painted pottery. From a tomb at Tsinan, Shantung. Western Han period, second to first century BC.

Western Han tomb at Tsinan in Shantung depicts the kind of entertainment, with music, tumblers and dancers, that was often represented on the walls of tombs and tomb-shrines. The figurines illustrate, too, the extent of China's foreign contacts at this time. The pottery stand for a bronze 'coin-tree' found in a grave in Szechwan, for example, is decorated with a frieze of elephants in relief, modelled with a lively naturalism that has no counterpart in other Han reliefs but at once calls to mind the animals of the Four Quarters carved on the capital of the Aśokan column at Sarnath.

Some of the Han figurines were individually modelled, but the majority of the smaller pieces were mass-produced in moulds: though the forms are reduced to essentials, none of their vitality and character is lost. At Changsha, where the clay was often poor and glazes were apt to flake off, the *ming-ch'i* were generally made of painted wood, which, like the silk and lacquer found in the Changsha tombs, has miraculously survived the ravages of time.

Of quite a different kind was the fine-quality felspathic stoneware, which was made in a number of centres in Chekiang. This ancestor of the Sung celadons has a hard body and thin glaze ranging in colour from grey through olive-green to brown. It is often called Yüeh ware because the type-site is at Chiu-yen near Shao-hsing, the old name of which is Yüeh-chou. Recent Chinese writers confine the term 'Yüeh ware' to the porcellanous celadon made for the court of Wu-Yüeh in the tenth century, calling all earlier celadons simply *ch'ing tz'u* ('green porcelain'). However, in translation this is misleading, as some of it can hardly be called green, and none of it is true porcelain. In this book, therefore, the term 'Yüeh' ware is retained to cover the whole huge family of pre-Sung Chekiang celadons.[4]

The Chiu-yen kilns were in operation at least from the first century A D, those at Te-ch'ing, north of Hangchow, perhaps even earlier. Many of their products, found in dated tombs in the Nanking region, are imitations of bronze vessels, even to the loop-handles and *t'ao-t'ieh* masks that adorn them. Some are stamped with geometric or diaper designs under the glaze, preserving an ancient tradition of Central and South China which spread not only northwards but also into the Nan-hai, the peninsula and islands of Southeast Asia. Gradually, however, true ceramic forms began to emerge, aided by a rich, luminous and even luscious glaze. The Chiu-yen kilns seem to have closed down in the sixth century, after which the Yüeh tradition was carried on in many parts of Chekiang, the chief factories being round the shores of Shang-lin Hu in Yü-yao-hsien, where the remains of more than twenty celadon kilns have so far been discovered.

70 Basin. Stoneware with modelled and incised decoration under a grey-green glaze, Yüeh ware. Third or fourth century AD.

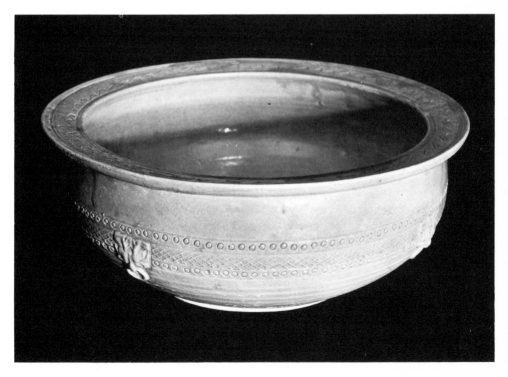

6 The Six Dynasties

During the four hundred years between the fall of the Han Dynasty and the rise of the T'ang, China went through a period of political, social and intellectual ferment comparable to that of modern Europe. No less than thirty dynasties and lesser kingdoms passed across the scene before the Sui reunited the Empire in 581. At the fall of the Han Dynasty in 220 China was divided into the Three Kingdoms of Wu, Wei, and Shu; in 280 it was once more reunited under a Wei king who named his dynasty Chin. Beyond the northern frontiers, the Hsiung-nu and the Hsien-pi were watching with interest the incessant civil wars to which the now-shrunken Empire was victim. When, soon after 300, two rival princes rashly appealed to them for aid, they promptly advanced into China. In 311 the Hsiung-nu captured Loyang, massacred twenty thousand of its inhabitants and took the Emperor prisoner; they then moved on to Ch'ang-an, which they put to the sack, while the Chin court fled in panic to Nanking. The Hsiung-nu and Hsien-pi were not the only tribes to take advantage of China's weakness to invade the north; sixteen petty barbarian kingdoms were to rise and fall before the Toba Wei, a Turkish tribe, brought the whole of North China under their rule in 439. They established their capital near Ta-t'ung in northern Shensi, abandoned their nomadic way of life and adopted Chinese dress, eventually becoming so sinicized that the use of the Toba language was forbidden altogether. At the same time, they energetically defended their northern borders against other and more barbarous tribes, and pushed their cavalry as far as Kucha in the Tarim Basin, thus reopening the great trade-route into Central Asia.

The invasions had split China into two countries, with two cultures. While the north sank into barbarism, tens of thousands of Chinese refugees migrated to the south. Nanking now became the cultural and political centre of 'free China', to which merchants and Buddhist missionaries came from South-east Asia and India. Yet this region too was in a perpetual state of turmoil and unrest, in which enormous quantities of art treasures were destroyed. Four more dynasties – the Liu Sung, Ch'i, Liang and Ch'en – ruled from Nanking before the split between north and south was healed. The Confucian order was undermined, and the southern Buddhist temples and monasteries now grew to such vast proportions – particularly under Liang Wu Ti (502–50) – that they constituted a serious threat to the political and economic stability of the realm. With the eclipse of the Confucian bureaucracy it was often the great landed families who exerted the most influence on politics and the arts, outliving the dynasties themselves.

TAOISM

Many intellectuals in the south sought escape from the chaos of the times in Taoism, music, calligraphy, and the delights of pure talk (*ch'ing-t'an*). Taoism came into its own in the third and fourth centuries, for it seemed to answer the yearnings of men of feeling and imagination for a vision of the eternal in which they could forget the chaos of the present. This conglomeration of folklore, nature-worship and metaphysics was rooted in the native soil of China. It had first become a cult in the Late Han, when Chang Tao-ling, a mystic and magician from Szechwan who called himself the *T'ien-shih*, 'Heavenly Master,' gathered round him a group of followers with whom he roamed the countryside in search of the elixir of life. Sometimes he would take them to the top of the Cloud Terrace Mountain (Yün-t'ai-shan) and there invent ordeals to test their magic powers. By the Chin Dynasty the movement that had originated as a private revolt against the established order had grown into a fully fledged 'church', with a canon of scriptures, a hierarchy, temples and all the trappings of a formal religion copied from the Buddhists.

On a higher level, however, the Taoists were the intellectual *avant-garde*. The reaction against Confucianism had produced a 'thaw' in the rigidly traditional view of art and literature, and now the imagination took flight once more in poetry more inspired than any since the elegies of Ch'u. Typical of the age is the poet T'ao Yüan-ming (365–427), who, though forced several times to take office to support his family, retired whenever he could to his country cottage where he grew his own vegetables, drank excessively and read books, though he said he did not mind if he failed to understand them completely. This was not merely escape from political and social chaos; it was escape also into the world of the imagination.

AESTHETICS

For it was in these turbulent years that the Chinese painter and poet first discovered himself. Lu Chi's *Wen-fu* ('Rhyme-prose on Literature'), written in 300, is a penetrating, even passionate, rhapsody on that ordeal which T. S. Eliot called the 'intolerable wrestle with words and meanings', and on the mysterious sources of poetic inspiration. In the traditional Confucian view, art had served a primarily moral and didactic purpose in society. Now that position was abandoned, and new critical standards were evolved, culminating in Hsiao T'ung's preface of 530 to his anthology *Wen-hsüan*, in which he wrote that his selection had been guided not by moral considerations, but by aesthetic merit alone. This sophisticated position was not reached at once, however. Literary criticism in the third and fourth centuries had taken

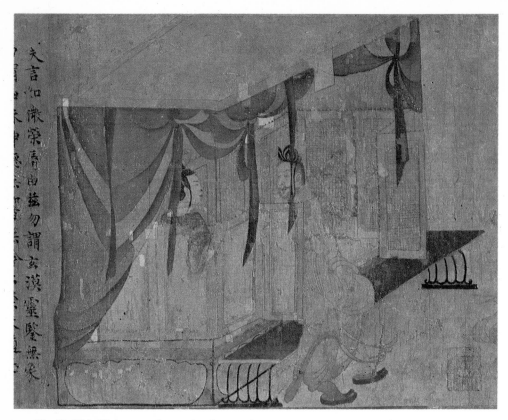

天言如微榮青由益勿謂玄漠靈鑒無象

71 After Ku K'ai-chih (*c.* 344–406). The Emperor with one of his concubines. Illustration to *The Admonitions of the Instructress*. Detail of a handscroll, ink and slight colour on silk. Ninth or tenth century.

the form of *p'in-tsao* – a mere classification according to merits and faults, first applied to statesmen and other public figures, then to poets. The great painter Ku K'ai-chih used it in discussing artists of Wei and Chin (if indeed the surviving text is from his hand). It was employed more methodically by Hsieh Ho in his famous *Ku hua p'in lu* (Ancient Painters' Classified Record), written in the second quarter of the sixth century, in which the author grades forty-three painters of former times into six classes, a useful but undistinguished contribution to art history. What has made this brief work so significant for the whole history of Chinese painting is its preface, which sets out the Six Principles (*liu fa*) by which paintings, and painters, are to be judged.

Much – perhaps too much – has been written about the Six Principles. But they cannot be passed over, for they have, with some variation or rearrangement, remained the pivot round which all subsequent art criticism in China has revolved. They are:

1 *Ch'i yün sheng tung:* Spirit Harmony – Life's Motion (Arthur Waley); Animation through spirit consonance (A. C. Soper).
2 *Ku fa yung pi:* bone-means use brush (Waley); structural method in the use of the brush (Soper).
3 *Ying wu hsiang hsing:* fidelity to the object in portraying forms (Soper).

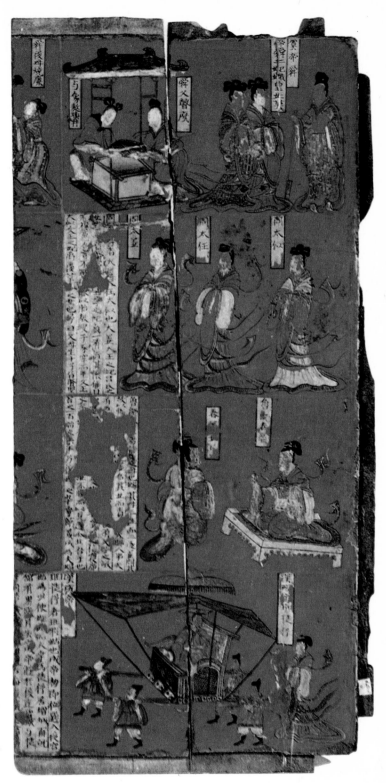

72 Filial piety scenes; the bottom panel, illustrating the story of the Emperor Ch'eng and Lady Pan, perhaps reproduces a design of Ku K'ai-chih. Panel from a wooden screen painted in lacquer. From a tomb dated 484 at Ta-t'ung, Shansi. Northern Wei Dynasty.

4 *Sui lei fu ts'ai:* conformity to kind in applying colours (Soper).

5 *Ching ying wei chih:* proper planning in placing (of elements) (Soper).

6 *Ch'uan i mu hsieh:* that by copying, the ancient models should be perpetuated (Sakanishi).

The third, fourth and fifth Laws are self-explanatory. The sixth involves on the one hand the need to train one's hand and acquire an extensive formal repertoire, and on the other a reverence for the tradition itself, of which every painter felt himself to be in a sense a custodian. Making exact copies of ancient, worn masterpieces was a way of preserving them; while, at a later date, working 'in the manner of great painters of the past, while adding something of oneself, was a way of putting new life into the tradition.

The experience of the painter – what Cézanne called, in a celebrated phrase, 'une sensation forte devant la nature' – is enshrined in the phrase *ch'i yün*, Soper's 'spirit consonance'. *Ch'i* is that cosmic spirit (literally breath or vapour) that vitalizes all things, that gives life and growth to the trees, movement to the water, energy to man, and is exhaled by the mountains as clouds and mist. It is the task of the artist to attune himself to this cosmic spirit and let it infuse him with energy so that in a moment of inspiration – and no word could be more appropriate – he may become the vehicle for its expression. William Acker once asked a famous calligrapher why he dug his ink-stained fingers so deep into the hairs of his huge brush when he was writing; the calligrapher replied that only thus could he feel the *ch'i* flow down his arm, through the brush and on to the paper. The *ch'i* is a cosmic energy that, as Acker puts it, 'flows about in ever-changing streams and eddies, here deep, there shallow, here concentrated, there dispersed'. It infuses all things, for there is no distinction between the animate and the inanimate. Seen in this light the third, fourth and fifth principles involve more than mere visual accuracy; for, as the living forms of nature are the visible manifestations of the workings of the *ch'i*, only by representing them faithfully can the artist express his awareness of this cosmic principle in action.

The quality in a painting through which awareness of the inner vital spirit is expressed is the second of Hsieh Ho's principles, *ku*, the 'bone', the structural strength of the brushstroke itself, whether in painting or calligraphy. The sudden flowering of calligraphy at the end of the Han Dynasty as an art form in its own right was partly due to the development of the *ts'ao-shu* 'draft script', the cursive style which freed the scholar from the formal angularity of the typical Han *li-shu*, official or clerical script, and enabled him to express himself in a style more personal, more charged with energy and grace, than any other writing that man has devised. (These and other styles are discussed on page 183.) It is no accident that many of the greatest calligraphers of this period, including Wang Hsi-chih and his son Hsien-chih, were ardent Taoists. Both the techniques and the aesthetic of this subtle art had a considerable influence upon the development of Chinese painting during the three centuries following the fall of the Han.

The Taoist ideal in action is illustrated in the life and work of Tsung Ping, a distinguished Buddhist scholar and painter of the early fifth century, who spent his life wandering amid the beautiful hills of the south with his equally romantic wife and who, when he was too old to wander any more, re-created the landscapes that he loved on the walls of his studio. A short *Preface on Landscape Painting* (*Hua shan-shui hsü*), one of the earliest surviving writings on this new art form, is attributed to him. In it he maintains that landscape-painting is a high art because landscapes 'both have material existence, and reach out into the realm of the spirit'. He declares that he would like to be a Taoist mystic, meditating upon the void. He has tried it and is ashamed to confess that he failed; but, he asks, is not the art of the landscape-painter, who can reproduce the very forms and colours that inspire the Taoist adept, even more wonderful? He is innocently amazed at the power of the artist to bring a vast panorama of mountains within the compass of a few inches of silk. Visual accuracy he holds to be essential, for if the landscape is well and convincingly executed, if the forms and colours in the picture correspond to those in nature, then 'that correspondence will stir the spirit, and when the spirit soars, truth will be attained. . . . What more,' he asks, 'could be added to this?'

Another brief essay, attributed to Wang Wei, a scholar, musician and man of letters who died in 443 at the age of twenty-eight, starts by pointing out that paintings must correspond to the *pa kua*, the 'eight trigrams', meaning that just as the *pa kua* is a symbolic diagram of the workings of the universe, so must landscape-painting be a symbolic language through which the painter may express not a relative, particularized aspect of nature seen at a given moment from a given viewpoint, but a general truth, beyond time and place. Though he, too, is full of wonder at the artist's mysterious power of pictorial compression, he insists that painting is more than the exercise of skill: 'the spirit must also exercise control over it; for this is the essence of painting'. The landscapes of Wang Wei, Tsung Ping and their contemporaries have all been lost centuries ago, but the ideals that are enshrined in these and other writings of this critical formative period have been the inspiration of Chinese painters up to the present day.

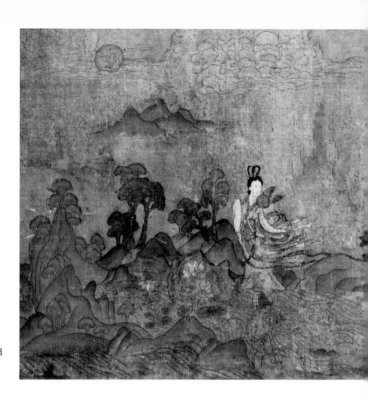

73 After Ku K'ai-chih (c. 344–406). Illustration to *The Fairy of the Lo River*. Detail of a handscroll, ink and slight colour on silk. Southern Sung period, about the twelfth century.

KU K'AI-CHIH AND THE BIRTH OF LANDSCAPE-PAINTING

The life and work of Ku K'ai-chih (c. 344–406), more perhaps than that of any other creative personality of this time, seem to embody the forces that inspired men in these turbulent years. Himself wildly unconventional and yet a friend of the great at court, a calligrapher and painter of Taoist landscapes who yet was seldom far from the hurly-burly of intrigue in the capital, he moved unharmed among the rival politicians and war-lords, protecting himself by the aura of idiocy which the Taoists held to be the only true wisdom. His biography tells us that he was famous for his portraits, in which he captured not merely the appearance but the very spirit of his subject.[1] A fascinating essay attributed to him describes how he would go about painting the Cloud Terrace Mountain and the ordeal to which Chang Tao-ling subjected one of his disciples on the top of a precipice. The text shows that he conceived of the mountain in strictly Taoist terms, bracketed east and west by the green dragon and the white tiger, its central peak ringed with clouds and surmounted by the strutting phoenix, symbol of the south. We do not know whether he ever painted this picture or not, though he probably did.

Only three paintings associated with Ku K'ai-chih's name have survived. One, of which there are Sung versions in the Freer Gallery, Washington, D.C., and in the Palace Museum, Peking, illustrates the closing moments in the *fu* of 'The Fairy of the Lo River' by Ts'ao Chih. Both these copies preserve the archaic style of Ku's time, particularly in

98

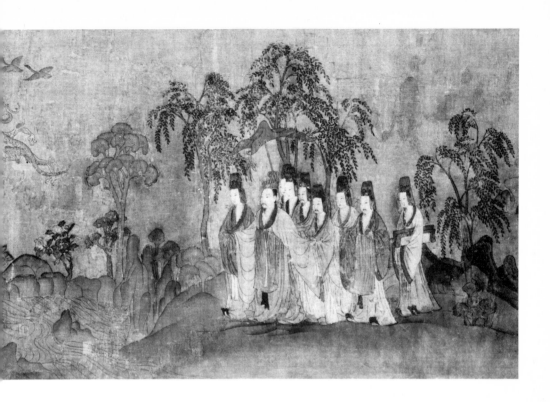

the primitive treatment of the landscape, which provides the
setting for the scene where the fairy bids farewell to the
young scholar who had fallen in love with her, and sails
away in her magic boat. In this painting (known as the 'Lo-
shen scroll') Ku makes use of the technique of continuous
narration, in which the same characters appear several times,
whenever the story requires it. This device seems to have
come from India with the introduction of Buddhism, for
there is no evidence of it in Han art. Probably the artists of
the Han scrolls most often used the convention which is
employed in the two other surviving works connected with
Ku K'ai-chih, the *Lieh-nü t'u*, illustrating four groups of
famous women of antiquity, with their parents,[2] and the
Admonitions of the Instructress to the Court Ladies, in which the
text alternates with the illustrations.

The *Admonitions* scroll, illustrating a poem by Chang Hua,
is not included among recorded works of Ku in T'ang texts,
and is first attributed to him in the catalogue of the collection
of the Sung Emperor Hui-tsung; there are, indeed, details in
the landscape treatment which indicate that it is unlikely to
be earlier than the tenth century. Yet it clearly derives from a
painting by a Six Dynasties master, whether or not it is from
the hand of Ku K'ai-chih himself. The scene which I have
illustrated depicts the Emperor gazing thoughtfully at one of
his concubines, wondering, perhaps, if she has deceived him.
Another scene illustrates Lady Pan refusing to distract the
Han Emperor Ch'eng from the affairs of state by going out

with him in his litter. To show the interior of the litter, the artist has used the technique that the Han artists employed, pulling the front round till it is almost parallel with the nearest side, in such a way that instead of diminishing in width and distance it seems to become wider. The same scene, and almost the same composition, painted on a wooden screen, was discovered in 1965 in the tomb of a Chinese official who died at Ta-t'ung in 484. While it is tempting to think that it was inspired by a version of a painting by Ku K'ai-chih that had already reached North China, both may be based on an older, traditional rendering of the theme.

When Liang Yüan Ti abdicated in 555, he deliberately consigned to the flames over two hundred thousand books and pictures from his private collection, so it is not surprising that nothing has survived of the works of the other leading masters of the Southern Dynasties who were active in Nanking. The ninth-century *Li-tai ming-hua chi*, however, records the titles of some paintings of this period, from which we know what subjects were popular. There were the stock Confucian and Buddhist themes, great panoramas illustrating the descriptive *fu* and other shorter poems, landscapes depicting famous mountains and gardens; there were scenes of city, village and tribal life, fantastic Taoist landscapes and pictures of the figures symbolizing the constellations, illustrations of historical events, legends such as the story of Hsi Wang Mu. Most must have had landscape settings, while several were pure landscapes, and at least three paintings of bamboo are recorded. The great majority were presumably either standing screens or long handscrolls.

We can obtain some notion of the style of the time from the paintings that line the walls of tombs in North Korea, notably the Tomb of the Dancing Figures and the Tomb of the Wrestling Scene at T'ung-kou on the Yalu River. Although painted as late as the sixth century, these lively scenes of feasting and hunting amid mountains are in the tradition of the Han tomb-paintings at Liao-yang. But to see the most advanced treatment of landscape in this indigenous style we must look not at the provincial tomb decorations, but at the engraved slabs from North China, of which the most beautiful examples are the sides of a stone coffin now in the Nelson Gallery, Kansas City, adorned with incidents in the lives of six famous filial sons of antiquity. The figures seem hardly more than the excuse for magnificent landscape panoramas, so richly conceived and so beautifully drawn that they must surely have been copied from a handscroll or, as Sickman suggests, a wall-painting by an accomplished artist. Each incident is set off from its neighbours by hills with overlapping tops called *ch'üeh*, which have powerful Taoist associations; half a dozen kinds of tree are distinguishable, tossed by a great wind that sweeps through their branches, while above the distant hills the clouds streak across the sky. The scene in which the filial Shun escapes from the well into which his jealous stepfather Yao had

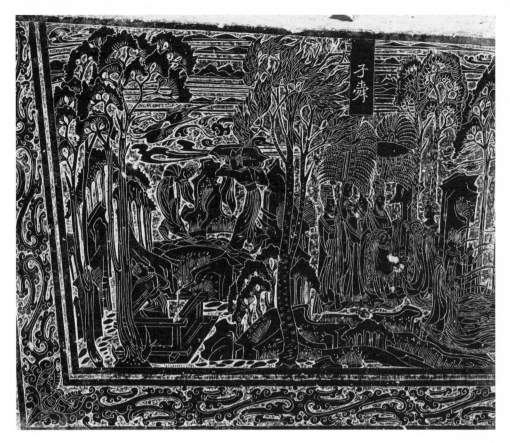

74 The story of the Filial Shun. Detail of an engraved stone slab from a sarcophagus. Late Northern Wei Dynasty, *c.* 520–30.

cast him is astonishing in its animation, and only in his failure to lead the eye back through a convincing middle distance to the horizon does the artist reveal the limitations of his time. Though its subject is respectably Confucian, its treatment exudes a wild and exultant joy in the face of living nature that is purely Taoist. It serves also to remind us that, in spite of the ever-growing demands of Buddhism for art of an entirely different kind, there already existed at this time a purely native landscape tradition allied to calligraphy and based on the language of the brush.

Buddhist communities were already established in North China before the end of the Han Dynasty. Now, however, political and social chaos, loss of faith in the traditional Confucian order and the desire to escape from the troubles of the times all contributed to a wave of remarkable religious enthusiasm, and the new doctrine spread to every corner of the Empire. Its acceptance, except among the lowest strata of society, was not due to blind and innocent faith – for that is not a sentiment to which the educated Chinese are prone –

BUDDHISM

but perhaps to the fact that it was new, that it filled a big gap in men's spiritual lives, and that its speculative philosophy and moral justification of the renunciation of worldly ties appealed to intellectuals who were now often reluctant to take on the perilous responsibilities of office. The new faith must have proved an effective consolation, if we are to judge by the vast sums spent on the building of monasteries and temples and their adornment during these troubled years.

We must pause in our narrative for a moment to consider the life and teachings of the Buddha, which form the subject-matter of Buddhist art. Gautama Śākyamuni, called the Buddha, or the Enlightened One, was born in about 567 B C, the son of a prince of the Śākya clan ruling on the border of Nepal. He grew up surrounded by the luxuries of the palace, married, and had a son, Rāhula. His father deliberately shielded him from all contact with the miseries of life beyond the palace gates, but in spite of the care with which his excursions were planned for him, Śākyamuni was finally confronted with the reality of old age, sickness and death, and he saw a vision of an ascetic, pointing to his future path. Deeply disturbed by his experience, he resolved to renounce the world and search for the cause of so much suffering. One night he stole out from the palace, cut off his hair, bade farewell to his horse and groom, and embarked upon his quest. For many years he wandered, seeking, first with one teacher and then with another, the answer to the mystery of existence, and a way of release from the intolerable cycle of endless rebirths to which all living things are subject according to *karma*, the inexorable law of cause and effect. Then one day at Bōdhgayā he entered into a trance seated under a pippala tree. For three days and nights he remained motionless. The demon Māra sent his host to assault him and his three lovely daughters to dance seductively before him, but, without moving from where he sat, the Lord rendered the former powerless while the latter he transformed into withered hags. Finally, in the moment of enlightenment, the answer came to him. In his first great sermon in the Deer Park at Benares, he gave his message to the world in the form of the Four Noble Truths:

> All existence is suffering (*dukkha*).
> The cause of suffering is craving, lust, desire – even desire for existence itself.
> There is an end to suffering, for this craving can be suppressed.
> There is a way of suppression, through the Noble Eightfold Path.

The Buddha also taught that there is no such thing as a soul, but that all life is transitory, all in a perpetual state of becoming. By following the Eightfold Path, which involves right conduct, right belief and right meditation, the devotee can break the cycle of rebirths which binds us eternally to the wheel of existence, and so secure his release and his final merging in eternity, as a cup of water poured into the sea.

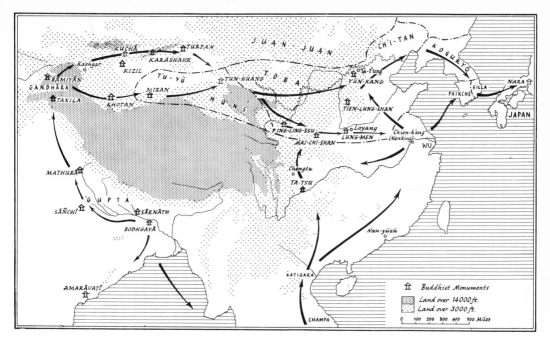

The spread of Buddhism into central and east Asia.

Śākyamuni achieved enlightenment in his lifetime, although he continued to walk the earth, gathering disciples, performing miracles and spreading his teaching, until his final departure, the *Mahāparinirvāna*, at the age of eighty. His teaching was austere, and, moreover, only for the chosen few who were prepared to renounce the world and face the rigours of life as a mendicant or, later, the regimen of the monastery. Its appeal lay partly in its simplicity – a welcome relief from the complexities of Hindu theology and metaphysics – and partly in the hope it offered of release from a destiny from which Hindu doctrine saw no escape.

The new faith grew slowly, and it was not until it was embraced by King Aśoka (272?–232) that it became a truly national religion. That monarch devoted himself with such tremendous energy to its propagation that legend has it that he erected eighty-four thousand *stūpas* (relic-mounds) in a single day, while his monastic and temple foundations were on a scale which many a pious Buddhist ruler has since tried to emulate. His missionary activities brought the faith to Ceylon and to Gandhāra in North-west India, where it came in contact with the religious ideas and artistic forms of the provincial Graeco-Roman world. It was probably in Gandhāra that, under these influences and encouraged by the great conference organized during the second century A D by King Kanishka of the Kushans, the first great development in Buddhist doctrine took place. The core of the dogma remained unaltered, but the new schools – who called themselves Mahāyāna (Greater Vehicle), referring derogatively to the more conservative sects as the Hīnayāna (Lesser Vehicle) – taught that salvation was open to all men, through

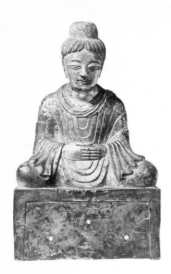

75 Śākyamuni Buddha. Gilt-bronze. Dated equivalent to 338.

faith and works. Now the Buddha ceased to be an earthly teacher, but was conceived of as pure abstraction, as the universal principle, the Godhead, from whom Truth, in the form of the Buddhist *dharma* (law), radiates with a blinding light across the universe. By this elevation to a status parallel to that of the Hindu Brahmā, the Buddha receded far beyond the reach of mortal man. *Bhakti*, the adoration of a personal god, expressed in Hinduism in the love of Krishna, demanded a more approachable deity. So there came into existence the *bodhisattva*, 'one destined for enlightenment', who has postponed his own end that he may bring help and comfort to suffering mankind. Of the *bodhisattvas* the most popular was Avalokiteśvara, 'the Lord who looks down [in mercy]', who on his translation to China as Kuan-yin became identified both with his female reflex Tārā and with the ancient Chinese mother-goddess, and thus imperceptibly acquired a sex – a process that was complete by the end of the tenth century. Almost as important were Mañjuśrī (Chinese Wen-shu), the god of wisdom, and Maitreya, the deity who, though now still a *bodhisattva*, will in the next cycle descend to earth as the Buddha; to the Chinese he has become Mi-lo-fu, the pot-bellied 'god of wealth' who sits grinning at the entrance of every temple. In time the pantheon grew to extraordinary proportions, the vast array of Buddhas and *bodhisattvas* being attempts to express the infinite aspects and powers of God. These developments were, however, for the theologians and metaphysicians. The common man needed only the comfort of Avalokiteśvara, or the secure knowledge that, merely by speaking once the name of the Buddha Amitābha, he would on quitting this world be reborn in his Western Paradise beyond the sunset.

It was probably in Gandhāra, and under Western influence, that the Buddha was first represented in sculpture. The style of Gandhāra is a curious mixture of the classical realism of Graeco-Roman provincial art with the Indian genius, fostered at the southern Kushan capital of Mathura, for giving concrete, plastic expression to an abstract, metaphysical concept. From Gandhāra Buddhism, and with it this new synthetic art, spread northwards across the Hindu Kush to Central Asia, there to run like a powder-trail along the string of oases to north and south of the Tarim Basin.

BUDDHIST ART REACHES CHINA Buddhist sculpture preceded Buddhist architecture into China, for it was the images – brought in the luggage of missionaries, travellers and pilgrims, who were no doubt prepared to swear that what they carried was an exact replica of some famous icon in India or Central Asia – which were most deeply venerated. The earliest known dated Chinese Buddhist image, cast in 338, is clearly an imitation of a Gandhāran prototype. Such icons were set up in shrines built in the traditional Chinese style, which grew until the monastery or temple became a kind of palace, with court-yards, pavilions, galleries and gardens. No attempt was made

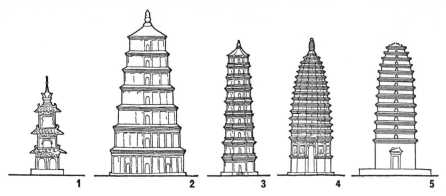

Types of pagodas. 1–3 derived from the Han timber *lou*: 1. Yünkang (Northern Wei); 2. Sian (T'ang); 3. Canton (Ming). 4 and 5 derived from the Indian *stūpa*: 4. Sung-shan (*c.* 520; see Ill. 76). 5. Sian (T'ang).

in these timber buildings to imitate the Indian temple. But the *stūpa* presented a different kind of challenge. The monk Sung Yün, returning from Gandhāra early in the sixth century, had described (as doubtless had many before him) the gigantic *stūpa* erected by King Kanishka, one of the wonders of the Western world. Built in timber, it was no less than seven hundred feet high, in thirteen storeys, capped by a mast with thirteen golden discs. The Chinese already possessed, in the towers called *lou* and *ch'üeh*, multi-storeyed timber buildings which could be adapted to this new purpose (see figure). The Chinese examples of this period have all perished, but the pagodas at Hōryūji and Yakushiji near Nara in Japan still stand as monuments to this simple, graceful style. The earliest surviving datable pagoda on Chinese soil, however, is the twelve-sided stone tower on Mount Sung in Honan, erected in about 520. It has no Chinese antecedents. Its profile echoes the curve of the Indian *śikhara* tower; the arched recesses on the main faces recall the niches on the great *stūpa* at Bōdhgayā, and, as A. C. Soper has observed, many of the details are Indian, or based on Southeast Asian modifications of the Indian style found in the kingdom of Champa, with which China was now in contact. But gradually the Indian elements were absorbed, and the architects of the later stone and brick pagodas were to imitate, in surface treatment, the posts, brackets and projecting roofs of the Chinese timber prototypes of these buildings.

At Bāmiyan in Afghanistan a high cliff more than a mile in length had been hollowed out into cave-shrines decorated with frescoes, and bracketed at either end by colossal standing Buddha figures carved out of the rock, plastered and painted. This fashion for decorated cave-shrines, which had originated in India, spread to Khotan, Kucha and other Central Asian city-states, where the already syncretic Graeco-Indian tradition of painting and sculpture became mixed with the flat, heraldic, decorative style of Parthia and Sasanian Persia. The routes that skirted the Taklamakan Desert joined at

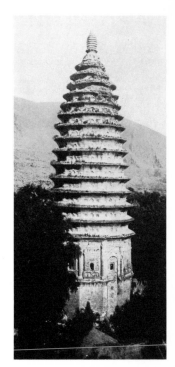

76 Twelve-sided pagoda of Sung-yüeh-ssu on Mount Sung, Honan. Late Northern Wei Dynasty, *c.* 520.

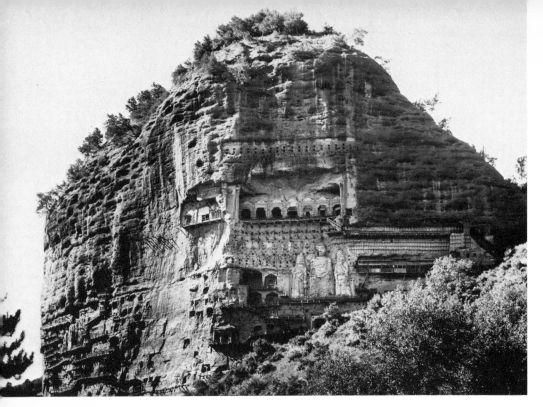

77 Mai-chi-shan, general view from the south-east.

Tun-huang, the gateway to China. There in AD 366 pilgrims had hewn from the soft rock the first of what were to develop during the next thousand years into a range of nearly five hundred chambers and niches, set about with plaster sculpture and adorned with frescoes. Further stages of the pilgrim-route into China were marked by cave-shrines at Ping-ling-ssu, about fifty miles south-west of Lanchow, and Mai-chi-shan, twenty-eight miles south-east of T'ien-shui. The former was only rediscovered in 1951, while restoration of the latter, which had always been known to the people of the T'ien-shui district, did not begin till 1953. In their spectacular sites and the quality and richness of their sculpture these shrines surpass Tunhuang, whose glory lies chiefly in its paintings.

BUDDHIST SCULPTURE UNDER
THE NORTHERN WEI:
THE FIRST PHASE

In 386 the Toba Turks established their ascendancy over North China as the Wei Dynasty, with their capital at Ta-t'ung. Their rulers had embraced Buddhism with enthusiasm for, like the Kushans in India, they were excluded from the traditional social and religious system of those they had conquered.[3] At the urging of the overseer of monks, T'an-yao, they began in 460 to hew out of the cliffs at Yünkang a series of shrines and colossal figures, possibly in emulation of the 'thousand foot' Maitreya at Darel, which were to be a monument not only to Buddhism but also to the splendour of the royal house itself. By the time the capital was moved south to Loyang in 494, twenty large caves and some minor ones had been excavated, while work was resumed between 500 and 535, and again between 916 and

1125, when Ta-t'ung became the western capital of the
Liao Dynasty. The earliest caves – those numbered XVI to
XX – were dedicated by the conqueror to himself and to the
spirits of four of his predecessors. They are cut into the living
rock, to expose colossal seated Buddhas carved almost in the
round, and originally protected by a timber roof which in
some of the cave-shrines was to develop into an elaborate
façade in several storeys. The colossus in Cave XX, forty-
five feet high, sits in an attitude of meditation; his shoulders
and chest are massive and yet finely proportioned, his face is
clear-cut with something of the mask-like quality often
found in Gandhāran art, while the drapery is suggested by
flat strap-like bands which disappear into points as they pass
round the contour of arm or shoulder. Perhaps, as Sickman
has suggested, this curious convention is the result of the
sculptor's following, and not properly understanding, a
line-drawing of some Western prototype, for great pains
were taken to copy the style of the more venerated images as
closely as possible.

By the end of the fifth century the native predilection for
abstract expression in terms of rhythmic line had begun to
modify this all-too-solid and somewhat ungainly imported
style. The carvings in Cave VII, one of the most richly
decorated of all, bear witness to this transformation. This is
one of the 'paired' caves dedicated by members of the
imperial family in about 480–90. Every inch of the walls

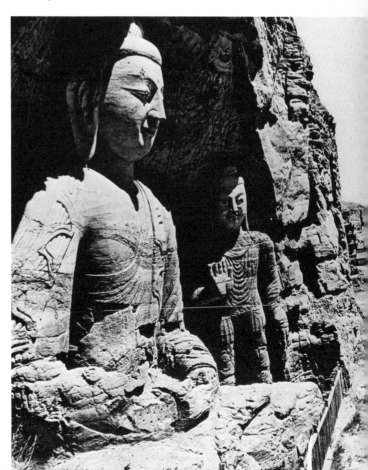

78 Śākyamuni Buddha with
attendant Buddha, perhaps Maitreya,
Yünkang. Northern Wei Dynasty,
c. 470–80.

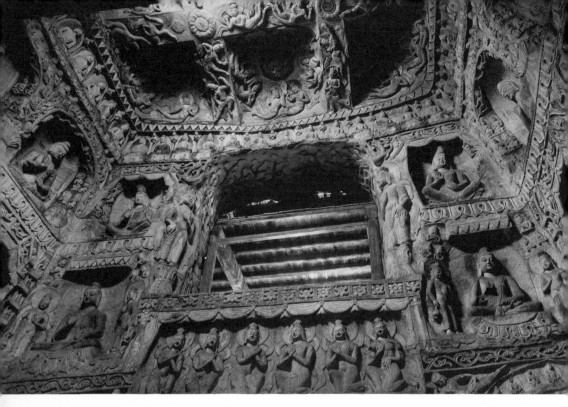

79 Interior of Cave VII, Yünkang. Northern Wei Dynasty, late fifth century.

and great central core is decorated with vigorous reliefs which were once painted in bright colours, and testify to the gratitude, to the generosity, and perhaps also to the anxiety about their future destiny, of the imperial donors. In long panels the life of the Buddha is told in a series of vivid reliefs, while above is the heavenly host – Buddhas, seated or standing, *bodhisattvas*, flying *apsarases*, musicians and other celestial beings. The decoration of this cave reminds us, in its wealth of detail, its contrast between the realism of the earthly figures and the serenity of the heavenly ones, of the beatific visions of the Italian primitives.

BUDDHIST SCULPTURE: THE SECOND PHASE

The Loyang region was closer to the centre of the purely Chinese tradition of pictorial expression in linear, as opposed to plastic, terms; and so it was inevitable that this tendency, already becoming apparent in the later caves at Yünkang, should have found its fulfilment after the move to the south in 494. At Lungmen, only ten miles from the new capital, sculptors found a fine grey limestone which permitted of greater refinement of expression and finish than the coarse sandstone of Yünkang. The new style reached its culmination in the cave known as Pin-yang-tung, commissioned by the Emperor Hsüan-wu and probably completed in 523. Against each of the interior walls is a large figure of the Buddha, attended by standing *bodhisattvas* or the favourite disciples Ananda and Kāśyapa. On either side of the entrance the walls were decorated with godlings in relief, *Jātaka* tales, scenes of the celebrated debate between Vimalakīrti and Mañjuśrī and two magnificent panels showing the Emperor

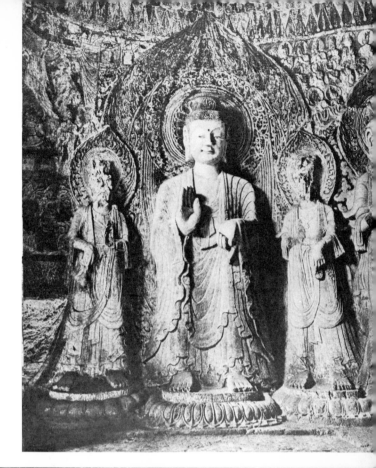

80 Buddha group, south wall of
Pin-yang-tung Cave, Lungmen.
Late Northern Wei Dynasty,
probably completed in 523.

81 The Wei Empress in procession
with court ladies. Restored relief
panel from Pin-yang-tung Cave,
Lungmen. Late Northern Wei
Dynasty.

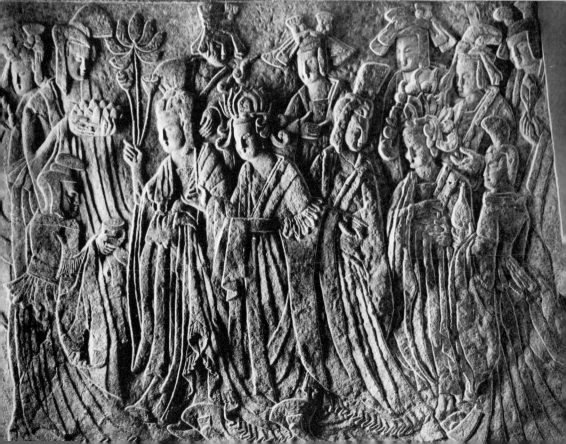

and Empress coming in procession to the shrine, attended by their retinue. The Empress panel, hacked out of the wall by robbers, has been restored and now forms part of the important Chinese collection in the Nelson Gallery, Kansas City. Executed in flat relief, its sweeping linear rhythms and wonderful sense of forward movement suggest the translation into stone of the style of wall-painting which must have been current at the Wei court, and is further proof that besides the imported, hieratic forms reserved for the deities themselves there existed another and more purely Chinese style, to which painters and sculptors instinctively turned when representing secular themes.

Because of the great scarcity of Buddhist sculpture from the southern kingdoms, we are apt to think that the stylistic revolution which reached its culmination at Lungmen must have originated in the north and gradually spread southwards. But recent discoveries and research suggest that the opposite was the case, and that it was the art of the southern courts centred in Nanking which was the dominating factor in the development of Buddhist sculpture during the Six Dynasties. One of the earliest innovators had been Tai K'uei, a contemporary of Ku K'ai-chih at the Chin court in Nanking. His work, in which he is said to have raised the art of sculpture to a new level, very probably reflected the style of contemporary painting – the flat, slender body, sweeping robes and trailing scarves that we see in copies of the Ku K'ai-chih scrolls. This concept of figure and drapery does not appear in the sculpture of the north until a century later, when we first encounter it in the later stages at Yünkang and the earliest caves at Lungmen, and there is much evidence to show that it was introduced by artists and sculptors from the south.

The arrangement of the Pin-yang-tung cave at Lungmen was probably intended to suggest the interior of the temple, whose equipment would also have included free-standing images in stone, stone votive stelae and gilded-bronze images. The stelae were carved and set up in or near the temple as an act of piety or gratitude by one or more subscribers, whose names they often bear. They consisted either of a flat slab, shaped like a pippala leaf, against which one figure, or more often a group of three figures, stands out almost in the round; or of a rectangular slab decorated, often on all four sides, with Buddhas, bodhisattvas and lesser deities, illustrations to favourite texts such as the Lotus Sūtra (Saddharmapundarīka Sūtra), and scenes from the life of the Buddha carved in relief. Their peculiar interest and value lie in the fact that they concentrate in little space the essentials of the style and iconography of the period, and that they are frequently dated.

In Cave 133 at Mai-chi-shan a group of eighteen of these stelae still stand in their original positions against the walls where they were set up by pious devotees. Three of these are splendid examples of the mid-sixth-century style; one is a veritable 'poor man's bible'. The upper central panel is

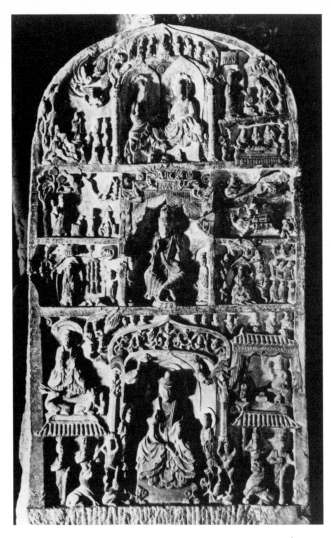

82 Stele illustrating scenes from the life of the Buddha and the Teachings of the *Lotus Sūtra*. Stone. In Cave 133, Mai-chi-shan, Kansu. First half of the sixth century.

devoted to the incident in the *Lotus Sūtra* in which Śākya-muni, by the power of his preaching, causes Prabhūtaratna, a Buddha of the distant past, to appear beside him. In the centre and below are Buddhas flanked by *bodhisattvas* – a simple presentation of the Paradise theme. The side panels show (on the left, going downwards): Śākyamuni descending from the Tuṣita Heaven, where he had preached to his deceased mother; Śākyamuni as a young prince; the Renunciation, and the First Preaching in the Deer Park. On the right, the panels show: a *bodhisattva* meditating under a tree; the *Mahāparinirvāna*; Samantabhadra on his elephant; the Temptations of Māra; and the theological disputation between Manjuśrī and Vimalakīrti (holding the fan).

Very few of the great bronze images of this period have survived. They were nearly all destroyed or melted down in the persecutions which intermittently scarred the history of Buddhism in China. To see the largest, if not the finest,

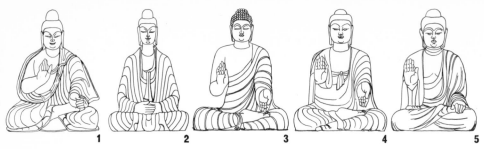

The development of the Buddha image. 1. Yünkang (*c.* 460–90); 2. Lungmen (*c.* 490–550); 3. Ch'i-chou (*c.* 550–580); 4. Sui (*c.* 580–620); 5. T'ang (*c.* 620–750).

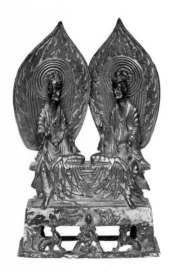

83 Prabhūtaratna and Śākyamuni. Gilt-bronze, dated equivalent to 518. Northern Wei Dynasty.

example of an altarpiece in the Wei linear style we must journey to Japan where, in the Kondō (Golden Hall) of the Monastery of Hōryūji at Nara, is a Buddha triad which, though executed by the grandson of an immigrant from Korea in 623, is a late survival of the style of mid-sixth-century China. Some of the smaller gilded-bronze images, made most probably for domestic chapels, escaped destruction. Because of the precision of their modelling and the beauty of their material, these bronzes – ranging from simple seated Buddhas to elaborate altar groups, complete with stand, flame mandorla and attendant deities – are among the supreme examples of Chinese Buddhist art. The earliest surviving dated specimen, cast in 338, has all the squat clumsy charm of an archaic piece. One of the most perfect examples of the mature Wei style is the exquisite group of Śākyamuni and Prabhūtaratna, Buddha of the remote past, dated 518, in the Musée Guimet, Paris. The form is expressively attenuated; the eyes slant, the mouth wears a sweet, withdrawn smile, while the body seems about to disappear altogether under a cascade of drapery that no longer defines the figure beneath, but, like the drapery of the Romanesque sculpture of Moissac or Vézelay, in its expression of a state of spiritual ecstasy seems to deny the body's very existence. Here, the influence on sculpture of the sweeping rhythms of the painter's brush is very apparent.

BUDDHIST SCULPTURE: THE THIRD PHASE

After the middle of the sixth century a further, equally momentous change came over the style of Chinese Buddhist sculpture. Now the body began to expand once more, filling the robes which, instead of fluttering free with a life of their own, began to mould themselves to the cylindrical form, subtly accentuating its mass. Against these now smooth surfaces the jewellery of the *bodhisattvas* provides a contrasting ornament. The head becomes rounded and massive, the expression austere rather than spiritual. In the stone sculpture of Northern Ch'i Chinese craftsmen developed a style in which precision of carving and richness of detail are subordinated to a total effect of grave and majestic dignity. While the change was stimulated by a renewal of Indian influence on Chinese Buddhist art, this time the influence came not across Central Asia, where contact with the West was now broken by fresh barbarian incursions into the Tarim Basin, but up from the Indianized kingdoms of South-east Asia, with which the court at Nanking had close diplomatic and cultural relations. There are abundant records of Buddhist images being sent to Nanking from Indochina in the sixth century, though none of these have yet been identified. However, in 1953 there was found in the ruins of a temple at Chengtu in Szechwan a buried hoard of about two hundred pieces of Buddhist sculpture, much of it in exotic style. Some of these pieces show the indirect influence of Gupta art, others have stylistic affinities with the sculpture of the Dvāravatī kingdom of Thailand, and with figures and reliefs excavated at Dong-duong and other sites in the ancient kingdom of Champa (present-day South Vietnam). Nothing comparable to the Chengtu find has yet been unearthed at Nanking itself, where the destruction of early Buddhist monuments was almost complete; but there is no doubt that Chengtu was strongly influenced by artistic developments at the southern capital.

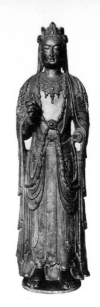

84 *Bodhisattva*. Stone. Northern Ch'i Dynasty.

BUDDHIST PAINTING

As with sculpture, so did the introduction of Buddhism give birth to a new school of painting of which both the content and the forms were largely foreign. A Sung writer tells of a certain K'ang Seng-hui, a Sogdian, who in AD 247 came to the Wu Kingdom (Nanking) by way of Indochina, 'to instal icons and practise ritual circumambulation. It so happened that Ts'ao Pu-hsing saw his iconographic cartoons for Buddhas [in the style of] the Western Regions, and copied them; whence it came about that the Ts'ao [style] has been popular through the generations all over the world.' (By the end of the sixth century, however, nothing survived of Ts'ao's work 'except the head of one dragon in the Privy Pavilion'.) The new style culminated in the work of Chang Seng-yu, the greatest of the painters working for the Liang emperors at Nanking. His work was remarkable – according

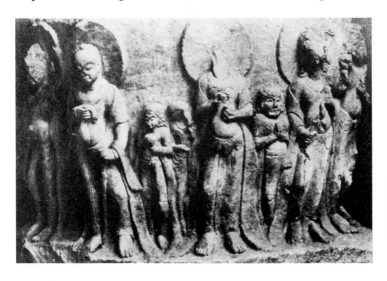

85 Worshippers. Fragment of a Buddhist stone relief from Wan-lo-ssu, Ch'iung-lai, Szechwan. Sixth to seventh century.

to contemporary accounts – for its realism; he painted dragons on the wall of An-lo-ssu, and when, in spite of his warning, he was persuaded to paint in their eyes, they flew away amid thunder and lightning. He decorated many Buddhist and Taoist temples in Nanking with frescoes; he was a portraitist, and also executed long scrolls illustrating such homelier themes as Han Wu Ti Shooting the Dragon, the Drunken Monk, and Children Dancing at a Farmhouse. But all these works were lost centuries ago, and none of the later pictures claiming to be copies of his work, such as the *Five Planets and Twenty-four Constellations* in the Abe Collection in Osaka, give more than a hint of his style. Nevertheless, we may be sure that one feature of this imported manner was the Indian technique of arbitrary shading, found in the wall-paintings at Ajantā, which was used to give an effect of roundness and solidity unlike anything that China had seen before.

WALL-PAINTINGS AT TUNHUANG Fortunately the wall-paintings at Tunhuang, Mai-chi-shan and Ping-ling-ssu have survived – though for the most part they are but a faint echo of the grand manner of metropolitan China. The first chapel at Tunhuang had been dedicated in 366. Today paintings of the Northern and Western Wei can be seen in thirty-two of the caves, and there were probably many more before dilapidation and later repainting took their toll. Of these the finest are in Caves 257 (P. 110) and 249 (P. 101).[4] The vigorous rendering of the preaching Buddha in Cave 249 is a good example of the mixture of styles that we find everywhere at Tunhuang. The stiff heraldic pose of the Buddha shows how the 'painterly' Chinese manner which we have already seen influencing the sculpture of the period has been frozen into a flat decorative pattern, indicating perhaps the hand of some itinerant painter from Central Asia, who has also attempted, not very successfully, to suggest an Indian fullness in the modelling of his attendant *bodhisattvas* and *apsarases*. The subjects of these early frescoes are generally Buddhist trinities, scenes from the Life, and endless *Jātaka* tales which, under the guise of recounting incidents in the Buddha's previous incarnations, draw upon a rich storehouse of Indian legend and folklore. It is these delightful scenes, and not the hieratic Buddhas and *bodhisattvas* in which the painter crudely copied some Western model, that reveal the Chinese journeyman artist at his most spontaneous: indeed, it is not unlikely that while some of the main figures were executed by artists from Central Asia and beyond, donors were content to leave the rendering of these accessory scenes to local talent.

A famous panel in Cave 257 tells the story of the Buddha's incarnation as a golden gazelle. The simple humped hills slant back diagonally in rows, like the seated figures in the Han banqueting scenes. Between them the participants are painted almost in silhouette on a flower-strewn ground. The sense of open space is Chinese, as is the emphasis on linear

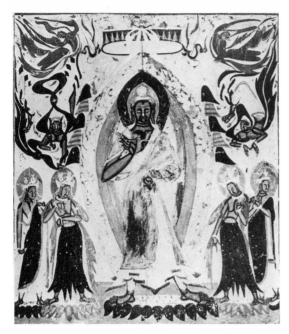

86 Buddha preaching the law; wall-painting in Cave 249 (Pelliot 101), Tunhuang. Northern Wei Dynasty.

87 The Buddha incarnate in a golden gazelle (the *Rūrū Jātaka*). Wall-painting in Cave 257 (Pelliot 110), Tunhuang. Northern Wei Dynasty.

88 Hunting scene on the lower part of the ceiling of Cave 249 (Pelliot 101), Tunhuang. Northern Wei Dynasty.

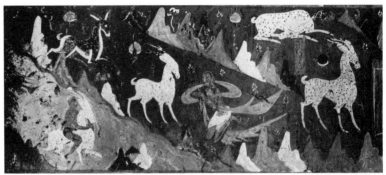

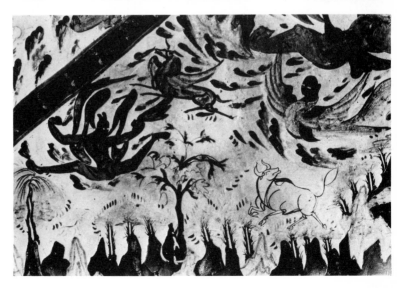

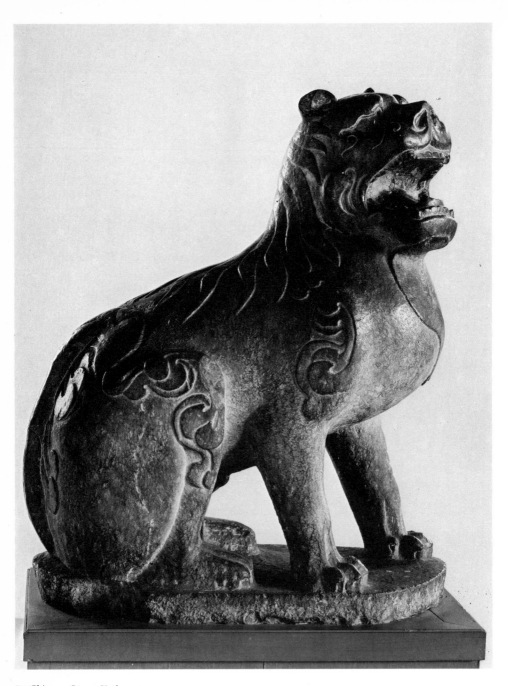

89 Chimera. Stone. Sixth century.

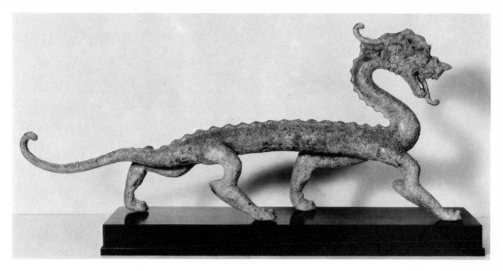

movement; but the decorative flatness of the figures, the dappled deer and flower-sprinkled ground have a Near Eastern origin. Most striking are the decorations on the sloping tent-like ceiling of Cave 249 (P. 101), painted early in the sixth century. While Buddhas dominate the main walls, the ceiling is a riot of celestial beings – Buddhist, Hindu and Taoist, the latter including Hsi Wang Mu and Tung Wang Kung, with lesser deities. Beneath them runs a frieze of gaily coloured mountains over which mounted huntsmen pursue their quarry after the fashion of Han decorative art. These paintings are a vivid illustration of the way in which Chinese Buddhism, at least at the popular level, came to terms with Taoism and native folklore.

90 Dragon. Gilt-bronze. Sixth century.

Although this was the heyday of Buddhism in China, the Confucian rites and ceremonies were not altogether neglected, and the imperial burials – particularly in the south – were as spectacular as ever. Liang Wu Ti, although a pious Buddhist, was buried outside Nanking in the most splendid fashion in a tomb whose 'spirit way' was lined on either side with heraldic lions carved in the native tradition, like the magnificent winged beast which I have illustrated. These creatures have about them a dynamic linear movement which also found expression in miniature in the beautiful gilt-bronze lions, tigers and dragons of which there are many examples in Western museums. But, on the whole, there seem to have been fewer elaborate tombs than before, and, indeed, until the last few years so few had been reliably excavated that experts were very reluctant to ascribe any grave goods to this period at all.

FUNERARY SCULPTURE

The ceramics industry in North China only gradually recovered from the disasters of the fourth century. The quality and variety of the *ming-ch'i* deteriorated. Much rarer now are the farms and pig-sties that give so delightful a

CERAMICS

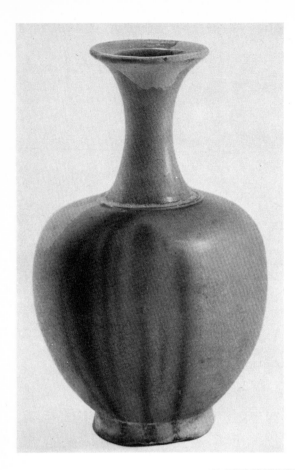

91 Vase. Stoneware, slipped and splashed with green under a crackled white glaze. From a tomb dated 575 at Anyang, Honan. Northern Ch'i Dynasty.

92 Flask. Stoneware, decorated with dancer and musicians in relief under a golden-brown glaze. From a tomb dated 575 at Anyang, Honan. Northern Ch'i Dynasty.

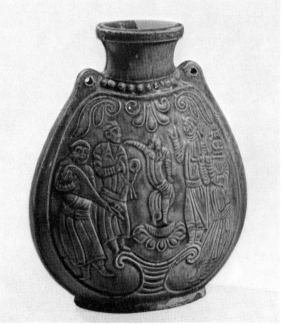

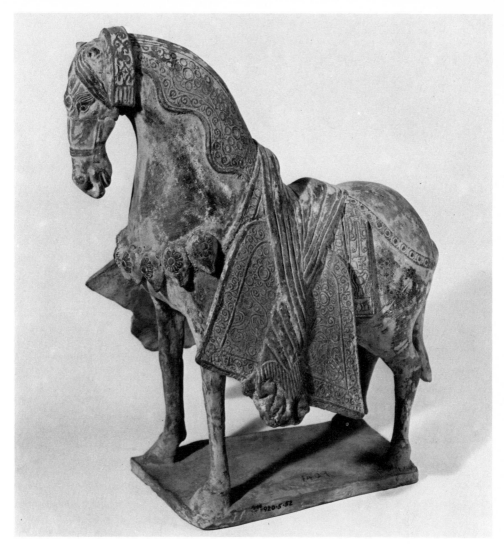

93 Horse. Painted pottery. Said to be from a tomb dated 525 near Loyang, Honan. Northern Wei Dynasty.

picture of Han rural economy. But to compensate, the best of the grave figurines have an almost fairy-like elegance which reminds us of the ladies in the Ku K'ai-chih scrolls, while the horses are no longer the tough, stocky, deep-chested creatures of Han art; they seem rather in their heraldic grace of form and the richness of their trappings to evoke a bygone age of chivalry. The Wei figurines are usually.dark-bodied and unglazed, but some are painted with colours that have mellowed to soft reds and blues through long burial.

It was not until the sixth century that really fine-quality wares were being made in the north. One of the most beautiful of recent discoveries is the porcellanous flask from the tomb of a Northern Ch'i official buried at Anyang in 575. It is covered with an ivory-white crackled glaze splashed with green – a technique hitherto thought to have been unknown

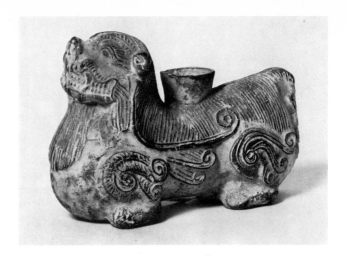

94 Water-container in the form of a lion (or dog?). Stoneware covered with olive-brown glaze, Yüeh ware. Chin Dynasty, 265–316.

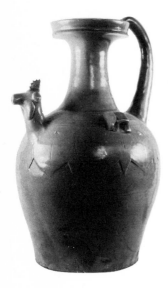

95 'Chicken ewer'. Stoneware covered with olive-brown glaze, Yüeh ware. Sixth century.

in China before the T'ang Dynasty. The tomb also contained pottery flasks with Sasanian figure subjects in relief under a brown glaze. A similar mixture of Chinese and western Asiatic motifs can be seen in other crafts in China at this time, notably metal-work and relief sculpture, showing that the cosmopolitanism that we think of as typical of the first half of the T'ang Dynasty was already well established in the sixth century.

So far, very few Six Dynasties kiln-sites have been discovered in the north. The position in the Lower Yangtse Valley is quite different. Kilns have been located in ten counties in Chekiang alone, while many of their products have been unearthed from dated tombs of the third and fourth centuries in the Nanking region. Of these pottery centres the most important were those in Shang-yü-hsien and round the shores of Shang-lin-hu in Yü-yao-hsien, active into the T'ang and Five Dynasties. In addition to celadon, the kilns at Te-ch'ing, north of Hangchow, also produced a ware with a rich black glaze. But in general the early Chekiang celadons show, in the growing strength and purity of their shapes, the final emancipation of the Chinese potter from his earlier bondage to the aesthetic of the metal-worker.

Indeed, freedom in the arts seems to be the keynote of this period – not only in technique and design, but also in the attitude of the privileged classes to the arts. For this was the age of the first critics and aestheticians, the age of the first gentlemen painters and calligraphers, the age of the first great private art collections and of the birth of such cultivated pursuits as garden-designing and conversation as a fine art. Just as the sixth-century anthologist Hsiao T'ung selected the poems for his *Wen-hsüan* on grounds of literary merit alone, so it seems did patrons during the Six Dynasties come for the first time to value their possessions – whether paintings or calligraphy, bronzes, jade or pottery – simply because they were beautiful.

7 The Sui and T'ang Dynasties

The Six Dynasties had been a period when new forms, new ideas and values were first, and often tentatively, tried out – ideas which could not find their fullest expression in those restless centuries, but needed an era of stability and prosperity to bring them to fruition. The founder of the Sui Dynasty was an able general and administrator, who not only united China after four hundred years of fragmentation, but also carried the prestige of her arms out into Central Asia. But his son Yang Ti squandered the resources of the Empire on palaces and gardens built on the scale of Versailles, and on vast public works. These included a long section of the Grand Canal, constructed to link his northern and southern capitals, for the building of which over five million men, women and children were recruited into forced labour. These huge projects, as a Ming historian put it, 'shortened the life of his dynasty by a number of years, but benefited posterity unto ten thousand generations'. Combined with four disastrous wars against Korea, they were too much for his long-suffering subjects, who rose in revolt. Soon a ducal family of the name of Li joined the insurrection, and the Sui Dynasty collapsed. In 617 Li Yüan captured Ch'ang-an, and in the following year was placed on the throne as first Emperor of the T'ang Dynasty by his able and energetic son Li Shih-min. In 626 Li Yüan abdicated in favour of Shih-min, who then at the age of twenty-five ascended the throne as T'ang T'ai-tsung, thereby inaugurating an era of peace and prosperity which lasted for well over a century.

T'ang culture was to the culture of the Six Dynasties as was Han to the Warring States, or, to stretch the parallel a little, Rome to ancient Greece. It was a time of consolidation, of practical achievement, of immense assurance. We will not find in T'ang art the wild and fanciful taste of the fifth century, which saw fairies and immortals on every peak. Nor does it carry us, as does Sung art, into those silent realms where man and nature are one. There is metaphysical speculation, certainly, but it is that of the difficult schools of Mahāyāna idealism which interested a small minority, and is expressed, moreover, in forms and symbols which touch neither the imagination nor the heart. For the rest, T'ang art has incomparable vigour, realism, dignity; it is the art of a people thoroughly at home in a world which they knew to be secure. There is an optimism, an energy, a frank acceptance of tangible reality which gives the same character to all T'ang art, whether it be the most splendid fresco from the hand of a master or the humblest tomb figurine made by the village potter.

By the time of his death in 649, T'ai-tsung had established Chinese control over the flourishing Central Asian kingdoms of Kucha and Khotan, the conquest of Korea had been begun, Tibet had been linked to the royal house by marriage, and relations had been established with Japan and the Southeast Asian kingdoms of Funan and Champa. Ch'ang-an, laid out by the Sui, now became a city of a size and splendour rivalling, if it did not surpass, Byzantium. It was planned on a grid seven miles by six. In the northern sector lay the government buildings and, outside the wall, the royal palace, Ta-ming Kung, which has been located and partially excavated. In its streets one might have encountered priests from India and South-east Asia, merchants from Central Asia and Arabia, Turks, Mongols and Japanese, many of whom are humorously caricatured in the pottery figurines from T'ang graves. Moreover, they brought with them their own faiths, which flourished in an atmosphere of rare religious tolerance and curiosity. T'ai-tsung himself, though personally inclined towards Taoism, at the same time for reasons of state supported the Confucians and strengthened the administrative system. This astonishing man also treated the Buddhists with respect – notably that great traveller and theologian Hsüan-tsang, who had left China in defiance of an imperial order in 629 and after incredible hardships and delays reached India, where he acquired a reputation as a scholar and metaphysician. In 645 he returned to Ch'ang-an, bringing with him the texts of the idealistic Vijñānavādin School of the Mahāyāna. The Emperor came out to meet him, and his entry into the capital was a public triumph. Never before had Buddhism stood so high in Chinese history; but it was not the only foreign religion on Chinese soil. There were also Zoroastrian temples, and Manichaean and Nestorian Christian churches in the capital, and, from the mid eighth century onwards, Muslim mosques; and the art of this period is as full of imported motifs as were the streets of Ch'ang-an with foreigners.

That China enjoyed a hundred years of peace and prosperity at home and enormous prestige abroad was due not only to the achievement of T'ai-tsung but also to two outstanding personalities who succeeded him. His former concubine Wu Tse-t'ien was to be Empress only from 683 to 705, but throughout the reign of her predecessor Kao-tsung (649–83) she was the able and unscrupulous *éminence grise* behind the throne. A woman capable of the most bestial cruelty and the profoundest Buddhist piety, she ruled China with a rod of iron until she was forced to abdicate at the age of eighty-two. Seven years later the throne passed to the man who, as Hsüan-tsung (Ming Huang, 713–56), was to preside over the most brilliant court in Chinese history, a period comparable to the Gupta in the reign of King Harsha or Florence under Lorenzo dei Medici. Like T'ai-tsung, he cherished and upheld the Confucian order, and in 754 founded the Imperial Academy of Letters (Han-lin Yüan), · which, as Joseph Needham has observed, is older than any existing European academy by nearly a millennium. All the talent and wealth of the country which was not given to the construction and adornment of Buddhist temples seemed to be concentrated on his court, his palaces, his favourite scholars, poets and painters, his schools of drama and music, his orchestras (two of which came from Central Asia) – and his mistress, the lovely Yang Kuei-fei. Through her influence, An Lu-shan, a general of non-Chinese origin, had become a favourite with Ming Huang. Suddenly in 755 he revolted, and the Emperor and his court fled in panic from Ch'ang-an. To appease his escort, Ming Huang, now over seventy, was forced to hand his favourite over to the soldiers, who promptly strangled her. A few years later the Empire was restored by the efforts of his son Su-tsung; but its power was broken, its glory past.

In 751 Chinese armies in Central Asia had been heavily defeated by Muslims advancing from the west, and eventually Chinese Turkestan came permanently under Muslim influence. The Arab conquest of Central Asia began the destruction of that chain of prosperous, civilized kingdoms which had provided the overland link between China and the West in the seventh century, a process which was in due course to be completed by the ferocity of the Mongols. However, contact with the Western world was maintained by way of the southern ports. The bustling quays of Canton were thronged with Chinese and foreigners who lived in peaceful prosperity with each other until Huang Ch'ao massacred the latter in 879, while at Ch'üan-chou in Fukien (Marco Polo's Zayton) recent excavations have revealed that as late as the thirteenth century Hindus, Arabs, Manichaeans and Jews were settled in that great trading-port, whose cosmopolitanism is symbolized by the 'twin pagodas' of the K'ai-yüan Temple, built in the twelfth century by Chinese and Indians working side by side.

As so often happens in history, China became less tolerant as her power declined, and the foreign religions suffered accordingly. The Taoists were jealous of the political power of the Buddhists and succeeded in poisoning the mind of the Emperor against them, while the Confucians had come to look upon Buddhist practices (particularly celibacy) as 'un-Chinese'. The government also viewed with increasing alarm the vast sums spent on the monasteries and their unproductive inmates, who now numbered several hundred thousand. In 845 all foreign religions were proscribed, and all Buddhist temples confiscated by imperial edict. The ban on Buddhism was later relaxed, but in the meantime so thorough had been the destruction and looting that today very little survives of the great Buddhist architecture, sculpture and painting of the seventh and eighth centuries.

ARCHITECTURE

123

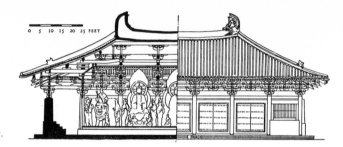

Main hall of Fo-kuang-ssu, Wu-t'ai-shan, ninth century.

Again, we must look to Japan, and it is the monasteries at Nara, itself a replica of Ch'ang-an, that preserve some of the finest of T'ang art. Tōdaiji was not an exact copy of the T'ang monastery, but in its grandeur of scale and conception it was designed to rival the great Chinese foundations. It was built on a north–south axis with pagodas flanking the main approach. A huge gateway leads into a courtyard dominated by the great Buddha Hall (Daibutsuden), 290 feet long by 170 feet deep by 156 feet high, housing a gigantic seated Buddha in bronze, consecrated in 752. Much restored and altered, this is today the largest wooden building in the world, though in its time the Chien-yüan-tien at Loyang, since destroyed, was even larger.

The earliest known T'ang wooden temple building is the small main hall of Nan-ch'an-ssu in Wu-t'ai-hsien, Shansi, built in 782; the largest is the main hall of Fu-kuang-ssu on Wu-t'ai-shan, built in the mid ninth century. Its roof-line is still practically straight in silhouette, though the eaves and corners are beginning to show that graceful lift which from the tenth century onwards was to impart such lightness and grace to Chinese architecture. Much has been written about this curve; it has even been seriously suggested that it was an attempt to imitate the sagging lines of the tents used by the Chinese in some long-forgotten nomadic stage. It is more likely that it was influenced by the architecture of China's

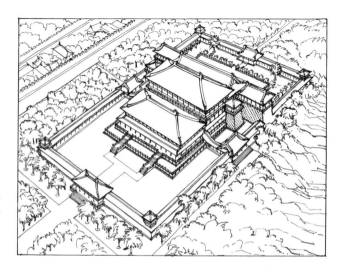

Conjectural reconstruction of the Lin-te-tien of the Ta-ming Kung, Ch'ang-an. T'ang Dynasty.

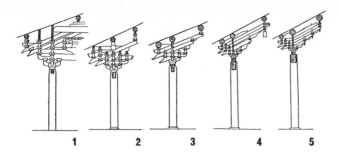

The development and decline of the bracket order. 1. T'ang (857); 2. Sung (1100); 3. Yüan (1357); 4. Ming; 5. Ch'ing (1734).

neighbours in South-east Asia, with whom she was now coming into close contact for the first time.

The sketch which I have reproduced shows a conjectural restoration of one of the buildings of the imperial palace at Ch'ang-an, the Ta-ming Kung. It is interesting to compare this with the three great halls of the Forbidden City in Peking (see pages 180–81). While the latter is far larger in scale, the grouping of the buildings is much less interesting. The interlocking of masses on ascending levels, buttressed at the sides by wings and towers, which gives such strength to the T'ang complex, was not attempted in Peking. T'ang (and indeed Sung) palaces seem to have been not only more enterprising architecturally but also more livable in than the vast, isolated and coldly ceremonial structures of the Ch'ing Dynasty, and suggest a more human concept of the role of the Emperor. By the T'ang Dynasty the heavy bracketing system (which, with the column it is poised upon, constitutes the nearest that Chinese architecture comes to an 'order' in the Western sense), is becoming a little more complex; the brackets extend outwards and upwards to support two slanting cantilever arms called *ang*, the inner ends of which are anchored to a cross-beam (1). In Sung and Yüan construction, the *ang* ride freely balanced on the bracketing systems (2 and 3), creating a dynamic and meaningful play of forces that reminds us of Gothic vaulting. During the Ming and Ch'ing, however, as the details become increasingly fussy and elaborate, the true function of *ang* and bracket is lost, and the whole degenerates into an intricate but structurally meaningless assemblage of carpentry, a mere decorative frieze running along under the eaves (4 and 5).

A few T'ang stone and brick pagodas have survived. Some – the pagoda built for Hsüan-tsang's ashes at Sian, for example – are straightforward translations of a form of construction derived from the Han timber tower (*lou*). The Chien-fu-ssu at Sian (see page 105), on the other hand, derives ultimately from the Indian *śikhara* tower of stone, which we have already encountered in its purest form in the pagoda on Mount Sung (see page 105). Imitation of Indian forms is carried still further in the Treasure Pagoda of the Fu-kuang Temple of Wu-t'ai-shan, which originally had a dome, copied perhaps from a sketch or souvenir brought back by a returning pilgrim. Under the influence of the

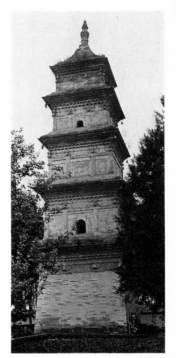

96 Brick pagoda of Hsing-chiao-ssu, Sian, Shensi. Built *c.* 699 to receive remains of Hsüan-tsang. Rebuilt 882. T'ang Dynasty.

mystical Mahāyāna sects, an attempt was even made to incorporate the dome of the *stūpa* into a timber pagoda; none survive in China, but the twelfth-century Tahōtō of Ishiyamadera is a Japanese example of this odd misalliance.

BUDDHIST SCULPTURE:
THE FOURTH PHASE

Until the dissolution of the monasteries in 845, their insatiable demands for icons, banners and wall-paintings absorbed the energies of the great majority of painters and sculptors. Some of the sculptors' names are recorded: we read in Chang Yen-yüan's history, for example, of Yang Hui-chih, a painter in the time of Wu Tao-tzu, who, 'finding that he made no progress, took to sculpture, which he thought was an easier craft'. Chang also mentions other pupils and colleagues of Wu's who became noted for their work in clay and stone; indeed, as we shall see, T'ang sculpture in its extraordinary linear fluidity seems often to have been formed by the brush rather than the chisel. Very little secular sculpture was carried out, if we except the guardian figures and winged horses and lions which lined the 'spirit way' leading to the tombs. The earliest and most famous example of T'ang funerary sculpture is the set of panels depicting in relief the six favourite chargers of T'ang T'ai-tsung, executed, according to tradition, after designs by the great court painter Yen Li-pen; the style is plain and vigorous, the modelling so flat that the origin of these monumental silhouettes in line-drawings seems not at all improbable.

The great Buddhist bronzes of the seventh and eighth centuries have all disappeared, melted down in the persecution of 845 or lost through subsequent neglect, and the style can best be seen in the temples at Nara in Japan. Only in the cave-shrines has stone and clay sculpture survived in any quantity. At Lungmen, in 672, the Emperor Kao-tsung ordered the carving of a colossal figure of the Buddha Vairoćana, flanked by the disciples Ananda and Kāśyapa,

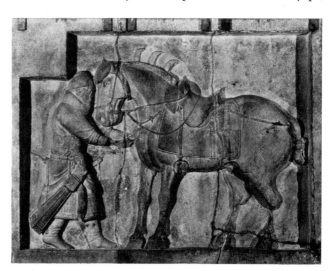

97 Charger and his groom. Stone relief from the tomb of the Emperor T'ai-tsung (died 749). T'ang Dynasty.

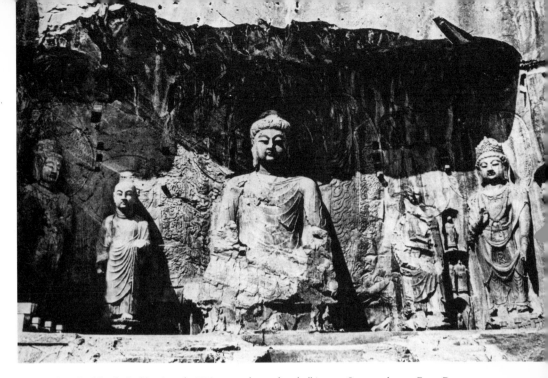

98 Vairoćana Buddha flanked by Ananda, Kāśyapa, and attendant *bodhisattvas*. Stone sculpture. From Feng-hsien-ssu, Lungmen, Honan. T'ang Dynasty, 672–75.

with attendant *bodhisattvas*. Obviously intended to rival in size and magnificence the great Buddha of Yünkang, this figure of the Buddha of Boundless Light far surpasses it in power of modelling, refinement of proportion and subtlety of feeling. Even though badly damaged, the Vairoćana well expresses the ideal of the Mahāyāna, which saw the Buddha not as a great teacher but as a universal principle radiating out in all directions for all time. More directly modelled on an Indian prototype – perhaps on a version of the celebrated sandalwood image reputedly made by King Udayāna in the Buddha's lifetime, a copy of which was brought back by Hsüan-tsang in 645 – is the thoroughly Gupta torso in marble from Ch'ü-yang-hsien, Hopei, in the Victoria and Albert Museum, London. This tendency to treat stone as though it were clay reached its climax in the cave-shrines carved out at T'ien-lung-shan during the reigns of Wu Tse-t'ien and Ming Huang. Here the figures are carved fully in the round with the exquisite grace and richly sensuous appeal that we find in Greek sculpture of the fourth century BC. The modelling has an all-too-Indian suavity and voluptuousness; the drapery seems as though poured over the fleshy body, the face is over-full, the mouth small and pouting. But, to compensate, there is a new mobility of movement. In these figures the Indian feeling for solid, swelling form and the Chinese genius for expression in terms of linear rhythm are at last successfully fused and reconciled, to produce a style which was to become the basis of all later Buddhist sculpture in China.

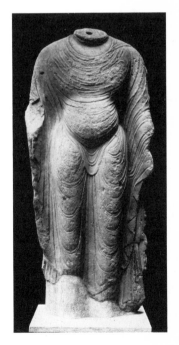

99 Torso of standing Buddha, Udyāna type. White marble. From Hsiu-te Pagoda near Ch'ü-yang, Ting-chou, Hopei. T'ang Dynasty, seventh century.

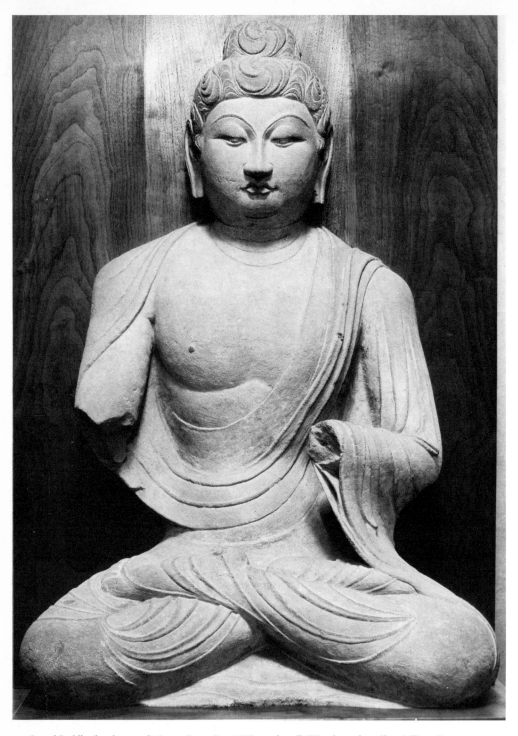

100 Seated Buddha (head restored). Stone. From Cave XXI, north wall, T'ien-lung-shan, Shansi. T'ang Dynasty

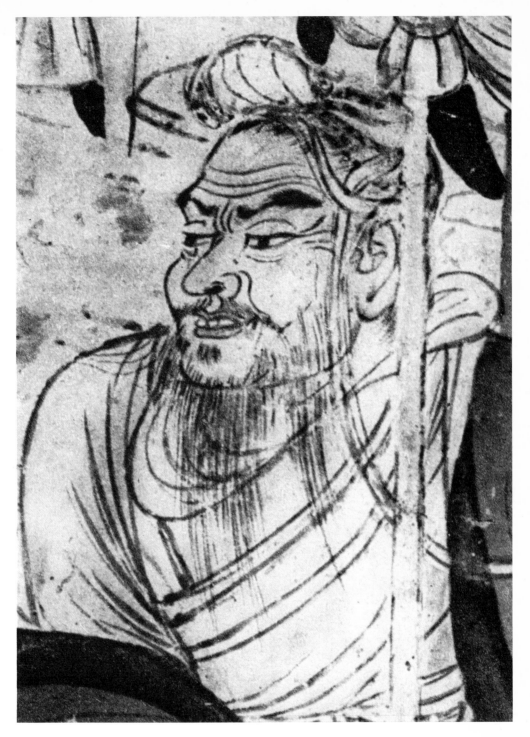

101 The sage Vimalakīrti. Detail of a wall-painting in Cave 103 (Pelliot 137M), Tunhuang. T'ang Dynasty, eighth century.

The Buddhist painting of this period must have contained as rich a mixture of native and foreign elements as did the sculpture. During the seventh century the most popular subjects were those that illustrated the teachings of the T'ien-t'ai sect based on the *Lotus Sūtra*, an encyclopaedic text which, in its combination of theology and metaphysics, ethics, magic and simple human appeal, seemed to satisfy all human needs; we have already encountered some of its themes on the sculptured stelae of the Northern Wei. Even more popular were the teachings of the Ching-t'u (Pure Land) school, which had cut its way through the growing forest of metaphysical abstractions of the later Mahāyāna with the doctrine that through simple faith one might be reborn in one of the Buddhist Paradises and so find release and eternal bliss. By the mid-seventh century, however, new concepts were coming into Buddhism which were eventually to bring about its decline. The later Mahāyāna in India had become deeply coloured by a highly abstract and idealistic metaphysics on the one hand, and by the practices of the Tantric sects of revived Hinduism on the other. Tantrism held that by sheer concentration of will-power, aided by magic spells (*mantra*) and diagrams (*mandala*), a deity could be invoked and desirable changes in the order of things thus brought about. This school also believed in the Hindu concept of the *Śakti*, a female emanation, or reflex, of a deity who would be doubly efficacious if represented clasping her in ecstatic union. At its finest this new art has a formidable power that is overwhelming, but it too easily degenerated into the soulless repetition of magical formulae.[1] It found its true home in the bleak wastes of Tibet, whence it reached out to paralyse the art of Tunhuang during the Tibetan occupation from about 750 to 848. In course of time, the revolt of the Chinese spirit against the sentimental, the over-intellectual and the diabolical aspects of these sects found expression in the Ch'an (Zen) school of contemplative mysticism, but as this doctrine did not greatly affect painting until the Sung Dynasty I will defer discussion of it to the next chapter.

Chang Yen-yüan's catalogue in the *Ming-hua chi* of frescoes in the temples of Loyang and Ch'ang-an is as full of the names of great painters and their works as Baedeker's guide to Florence; but the persecution of 845, coupled with wars and rebellions, fire and sheer neglect, have destroyed them all. According to contemporary accounts the work of the foreign painters aroused much interest and had considerable influence on local artists. During the Northern Ch'i there had been Ts'ao Chung-ta, whose figures 'were clad in garments which clung to the body; they looked as if they had been drenched in water' – an apt description also of the sculpture at T'ien-lung-shan. The Khotanese painter Yü-ch'ih (or Wei-ch'ih) Po-chih-na had come to Ch'ang-an during the Sui Dynasty; he specialized not only in Buddhist subjects but also in strange objects from foreign lands, and flowers which he painted with great realism. His son (?) I-seng was honoured by T'ai-tsung with a ducal title. 'His [I-seng's] paintings,' says the *T'ang-ch'ao ming-hua lu*, 'whether votive images, human figures, or flowers and birds, were always foreign-looking and not like Chinese things', while Chang Yen-yüan said of his brushwork that it was 'tight and strong like bending iron or coiling wire'. A Yüan critic wrote of him that 'he used deep colours which he piled up in raised layers on the silk'. His work has of course long since been lost, but a painting of Śākyamuni standing under a flowering tree, which bears the inscription 'Ch'en Yung-chih [an eleventh-century painter] respectfully copied', now in the Boston Museum of Fine Arts, has all the characteristics of the Yü-ch'ih style – flowers painted in relief, fine wire-like brush-lines and strong colour – and may possibly be based on one of his paintings, although recent cleaning has revealed it as a Ming work. It seems that his 'relief style' of flower-painting was not a subtle use of shading to give an effect of solid volume, but a much cruder technique wherein the pigment was piled up in a heavy impasto till the flowers actually *did* stand out from the wall.

While some T'ang painters were no doubt seduced by such devices into thoroughly un-Chinese experiments, Wu Tao-tzu, the greatest of them all, seems from contemporary accounts to have subordinated them into a truly Chinese style, which in its grandeur of conception and fiery energy of execution makes him one with Michelangelo. Born about 700, he is said before he died to have painted three hundred frescoes (using the term in the general sense) in the temples of Loyang and Ch'ang-an. None of his pictures have survived; indeed, by the eleventh century the poet Su Tung-p'o could say that he had seen but two genuine ones, his friend Mi Fei three or four. But we can obtain a vivid idea of the vigour, solidity and realism of his work from descriptions written by those who had seen it – certainly a more vivid idea than is provided by the third-hand copies, odd rubbings and sketches on which our estimates are generally based. The twelfth-century writer Tung Yu said of him, 'Wu Tao-tzu's figures remind me of sculpture. One can see them sideways and all round. His linework consists of minute curves like rolled copper wire [another writer says this was more characteristic of his early work: it suggests the influence of Yü-ch'ih I-seng]; however thickly his red or white paint is laid on, the structure of the forms and modelling of the flesh are never obscured.' Earlier Tung Yu had remarked that 'when he paints a face, the cheek-bones project, the nose is fleshy, the eyes hollow, the cheeks dimpled. But these effects are not got by heavy ink shading. The shape of the features seems to have come spontaneously, yet inevitably.' All spoke of the whirlwind energy of his brush, so remarkable that crowds would gather to watch him as he worked. Perhaps his technique is reflected in the head of the Indian sage

WU TAO-TZU

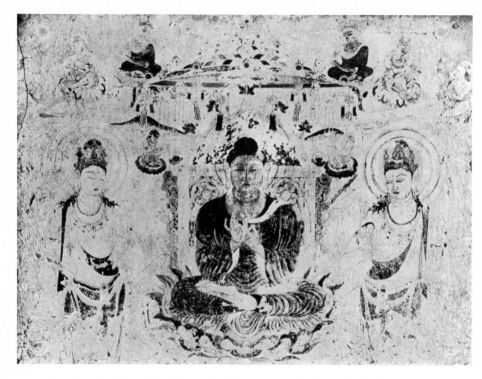

102 The Paradise of Amitābha. Detail of a wall-painting in the Kondō (Golden Hall) of Hōryūji, Nara, Japan.

Vimalakīrti, painted by an unknown eighth-century artist on the wall of Cave 103 (Pelliot 137M) at Tunhuang.

THE HŌRYŪJI KONDŌ CYCLE No major works survive in China itself to demonstrate that fusion of Indian formal ideals with the traditional Chinese language of the brush, which took place during the T'ang Dynasty and which I have already referred to, in writing of sculpture, as the Fourth Phase. But such a fusion did take place, and was in turn passed on to Korea and Japan. Early in the eighth century, the walls of the Kondō (Golden Hall) of the Monastery of Hōryūji at Nara were decorated by an unknown master with four large square panels depicting the Paradises of the Buddhas of the four directions, and eight vertical panels with bodhisattvas. These paintings, after miraculously surviving for twelve hundred years, were almost totally destroyed by fire in 1949, a disaster to the art of the world as great as if the frescoes in the Sistine Chapel or those in the cave-temples of Ajānta had perished. I have illustrated a part of the most popular Paradise, that of Amitābha. The composition is a simple and serene arrangement of deities, the bodhisattvas Mahāsthāmaprāpta and Avalokiteśvara standing on either side of Amitābha, who sits turning the wheel of the law on his lotus throne beneath a bejewelled canopy. The figures are drawn with a sweeping brush-line of extraordinary delicacy and precision which evokes a feeling of the solid form, from which the Indian tactile sensuality has been abstracted. Indeed, except for the iconography and the contours themselves there is little that is Indian here. Arbitrary shading is used with great restraint to amplify the roundness of an arm or chin, but much more is accomplished by the almost imperceptible modulations of the brush-line itself, while the folds of the drapery are emphasized by a kind of shading which – if the *Admonitions* scroll is a faithful copy of the style of Ku K'ai-chih – goes back to the fifth century. Only in the jewellery is there a hint of that rich impasto with which the Yü-ch'ih had astonished Ch'ang-an. Apart from these details, the forms, as Tung Yu said of Wu Tao-tzu, 'seem to have come spontaneously, yet inevitably'.

Long after Buddhism began to lose its hold on the intelli‐ gentsia it lived on in the hearts and minds of ordinary folk, who must have gazed with awe and wonder at the huge visions of Amida's Paradise which filled the walls of the temples and cave-shrines. In the walled-up storeroom at Tunhuang Sir Aurel Stein found a great hoard of manu‐ scripts and silk banners. Many were craftsmen's work, but, taken as a whole, they represent the only considerable group of undoubtedly genuine Chinese silk-paintings from the T'ang Dynasty that have survived. The most remarkable is a banner on which are very carefully drawn a series of Buddha figures almost certainly copied from sketches of well-known Indian images made on the spot. One represents the Buddha of the Enlightenment at Bōdhgāya, two are faithful reproductions of Gandhāran models, another shows the Buddha preaching on the Vulture Peak, while Stein identified yet another as identical in style with two great stucco reliefs which he discovered in the ruins of a monastery in Khotan. The banners also include a number of Paradises, and single deities (especially the increasingly popular Kuanyin), painted in warm colours, with a wealth of detail and floral ornament. The most appealing and lively parts of these banners are the little panels at the sides which, like the predella of a quattrocento altarpiece, tell in miniature the story of the Buddha's life on earth, generally in a landscape setting. It seems that until Tibetan esoteric Buddhism laid its cold hand on Tunhuang, the Chinese painters there used a landscape setting wherever they could. Sometimes, indeed, it dominates the theme in a thoroughly un-Indian fashion. In Caves 103 (P. 154) and 217 (P. 70), for example, the old subdivision into superimposed horizontal scrolls has been replaced by a panoramic landscape of towering peaks which fills the whole wall. There is still a tendency to break it up into smaller connected 'space cells', and the transition through the middle distance to the horizon is hardly better managed than on the stone sarcophagus in the Nelson Gallery, Kansas City. But other paintings at Tunhuang, notably the land‐ scape vignettes in Cave 323, show that this problem was successfully solved in the eighth century.

TUNHUANG

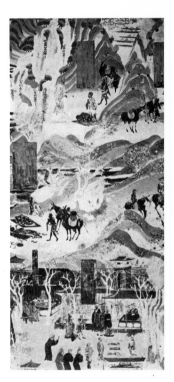

103 Pilgrims and travellers in a landscape. Wall-painting in Cave 217 (Pelliot 70), Tunhuang. T'ang Dynasty, eighth century.

We must return from the rustic pleasures of Tunhuang naturalism to the splendour of the T'ang court. A famous scroll in the Boston Museum of Fine Arts, bearing portraits of thirteen emperors from Han to Sui, has traditionally been attributed to Yen Li-pen, the son and brother of two famous artists, who had been a court painter in attendance (*tai-chao*) to T'ai-tsung and rose to the high office of Minister of the Right under his successor. This handscroll – or part of it, for more than half is a copy dating from the Sung Dynasty – is the very epitome of the Confucian ideal, now restored to its proper place as the pivot of Chinese society. While each group makes a monumental composition by itself, together they form a royal pageant of incomparable dignity. The figures are full, the robes ample, the brush-line fluent and of even thickness. Arbitrary shading is used with restraint to give volume to the faces, more generously in the folds of the robes, as on the *Amitābha* in the Kondō of the Monastery of Hōryūji.

Is it perhaps the hand of a pupil of Yen Li-pen that we see in the lovely paintings that line the tomb of Princess Yung-t'ai near Sian? The unfortunate girl was murdered at the age of seventeen by the 'Empress' Wu Tse-t'ien. When that monstrous woman died, the restored Emperor built, in 706, a huge subterranean tomb for his daughter, of which the walls were adorned with the figures of serving-girls. The drawing is free and vivacious, sketchy yet perfectly controlled. These paintings, executed solely for the pleasure of the dead Princess, bring us probably as close as we shall ever get to T'ang courtly wall-painting as it approached its climax in the eighth century.

The quality of T'ang court life is further revealed in the paintings attributed to Chou Fang and to Chang Hsüan, a court painter under Ming Huang who was chiefly celebrated for his paintings of 'young nobles, saddle horses and women of rank'. So far as is known none of his works survive in the original, but there exists what is probably a careful copy of his *Court Ladies preparing Silk*, attributed to the Sung Emperor Hui-tsung, but more likely a product of his palace studio: it is hard to imagine the Emperor having the time for making replicas of this sort, although he often put his name to them. We see a lady, about to pound the silk strands, rolling up her sleeves; another draws out the thread, a third is sewing, on the left a servant fans the charcoal brazier. The colour is rich and glowing, the detail of jewel-like precision. There is neither ground nor background, but the picture has depth, and there is a subtle and uniquely Chinese sense of almost tangible space between the figures.

Court painters such as Chou Fang and Chang Hsüan were kept busy by the Emperor, as were the poets, in celebrating the more memorable social and cultural events of court life, and in portrait-painting. This included portraits not only of the Emperor's favourite concubines and virtuous Ministers, but also of strangers from the West whose exaggerated

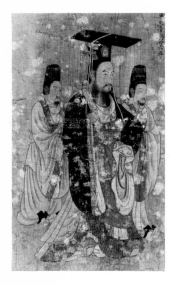

104 Yen Li-pen (died 673). Detail of the handscroll of the Thirteen Emperors from Han to Sui. Ink and colours on silk. T'ang Dynasty.

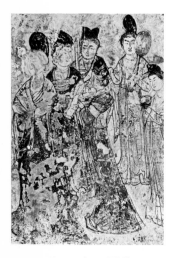

105 Female attendants. Wall-painting from the tomb of Princess Yung-t'ai near Sian, Shensi. T'ang Dynasty, about 706.

134

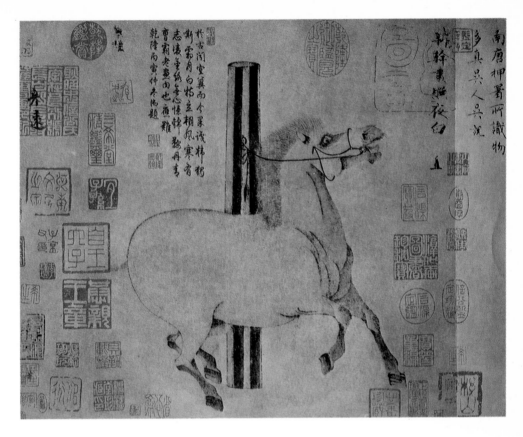

features have been a never-failing source of delight to the Chinese. In more serious vein were portraits of Buddhist priests, such as the series of the patriarchs of the Chen-yen (Shingon) sect, painted by Li Chen, a contemporary of Chou Fang. Long forgotten in China, the work of this artist has been cherished in Japan for its austere and noble evocation of the spirit of mystical Buddhism.

Court artists were not always treated with the respect they felt was due to them. Chang Yen-yüan noted the indignity to which the great Yen Li-pen was once subjected, when he was peremptorily summoned, sweating and panting, to sketch an unusual bird that had alighted on the lake in front of T'ai-tsung, after which he advised his son never to become a court painter. Ming Huang was passionately fond of horses, particularly the tough, stocky ponies from the western regions, and is said to have had over forty thousand in his stables. The striking painting of one of his favourites, Light of the Night, has long been attributed to the noted horse-specialist Han Kan. Tethered to a post, he rears up with eyes dilated as though suddenly startled. All but the head, neck and forequarters are the work of a later restorer (who also forgot the tail), but enough remains to suggest a dynamic energy of movement and solidity of modelling such as we find also in the best of the T'ang pottery figurines.

106 Han Kan (active 740–60). Painting of Light of the Night, a favourite horse of T'ang Ming-huang. Detail of a handscroll. Ink on paper.

During these prosperous years, when painters were busily occupied with Buddhist frescoes, portrait-painting and other socially useful activities, their hearts, if not their feet, were roaming the hills and valleys far from the glitter of the capital. The tradition of landscape-painting which was later to rise to such supreme heights had been born during the Six Dynasties, but it had advanced little – partly because of the ever-increasing demands for Buddhist icons, partly because artists were then still struggling with the most elementary problems of space and depth. But during the T'ang Dynasty these difficulties were mastered.

According to later Chinese critics and historians, two schools of landscape-painting came into being during the T'ang Dynasty. One, created by the court painter Li Ssu-hsün and his son Li Chao-tao, painted in the precise line technique, adding decorative mineral colours; the other, founded by the poet-painter Wang Wei, developed mono-chrome landscape-painting in the p'o-mo (broken ink) manner. The first, later called the 'northern school', became in course of time the special province of court painters and professionals, while the second, the so-called 'southern school', was the natural mode of expression for scholars and amateurs. As we shall see when we come to a discussion of Ming painting, this doctrine of the northern and southern schools, and of the founding role of Wang Wei, was invented by a group of Late Ming scholar-critics to bolster up their belief in the superiority of their own kind of painting over that of the professionals and court painters of the day. In fact, the line between the two kinds of painting was not so sharply drawn during the T'ang Dynasty. Wang Wei's elevation to this pinnacle in the history of Chinese painting was an expression of the belief, shared by all scholar-painters from the Sung Dynasty onwards, that a man's painting, like his handwriting, should be the expression not of his skill, but of his quality as a man. Because Wang Wei was the ideal type of man, it was argued, he must also have been the ideal type of painter.

A gifted musician, scholar and poet, Wang Wei (699–759) joined the brilliant group of painters and intellectuals round Ming Huang's brother, Prince Ch'i. He got into political difficulties at the time of the An Lu-shan Rebellion, but was extricated by his brother and restored to imperial favour. When his wife died in 730 he became a devout Buddhist, though whether this influenced his painting is not known. He was famous in his lifetime for his snow landscapes, but the work for which he is best remembered by later painters was the long panoramic handscroll depicting his country estate, Wang-ch'uan, outside Ch'ang-an. This picture dis-appeared long ago, and although the general composition has been preserved in many later copies, one of which was engraved on stone during the Ming Dynasty, these give little idea of the style, still less of the technique of the original. Perhaps the nearest we shall ever get to him is the beautiful little *Riverside under Snow*, formerly in the Manchu House-hold Collection and now believed to be lost. To judge from reproductions, it might be a Late T'ang or tenth-century painting. The landscape conventions are archaic, the technique is simple, yet no early Chinese landscape painting evokes more movingly the atmosphere of a river-bank in the depths of winter, when the snow covers the ground, the roofs and the bare branches, and men hurry home to their cottages at dusk.

Wang Wei was not regarded by early critics as a pioneer. Far more daring with the brush was Chang Tsao (late eighth century), a southerner, who in his landscapes is said by contemporary accounts to have achieved dramatic effects by the rich texture of his ink alone. In the last century of the T'ang, the general breakdown of orthodoxy produced techniques of ink flinging and splashing quite as wild as those of the New York School of the 1950s. The work of these 'expressionists', all of whom lived not in Loyang or Ch'ang-an but in the Lower Yangtse Valley, is lost, but their styles were taken up by some of the Zen painters of the tenth century and again during the Late Southern Sung.

A brilliant example of the so-called 'northern' tradition of Li Ssu-hsün (651–716) and Li Chao-tao (died about 735) is the small hanging scroll called *Ming Huang's Journey to Shu*, in the Palace Museum Collection in Taiwan. This jewel of a picture is believed to illustrate the flight of the Emperor from An Lu-shan in 756, though the tragic event is here

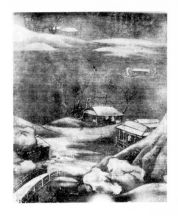

107 Style of Wang Wei (?). *Riverside under Snow*. Part of a handscroll (?). Ink and colour on silk. About the tenth century.

108 Anonymous. *Ming Huang's Journey to Shu*, or *An Imperial Excursion in the Hills*. Hanging scroll Ink and colour on silk. T'ang style, but painted during the Sung Dynasty or later.

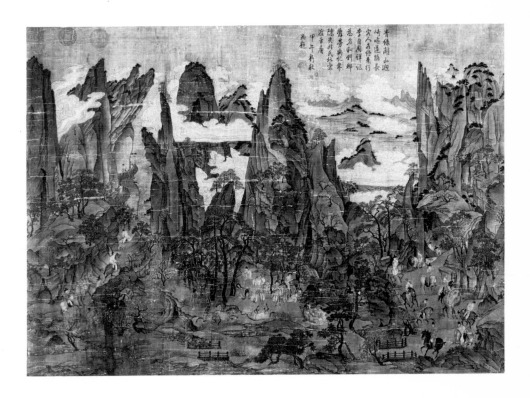

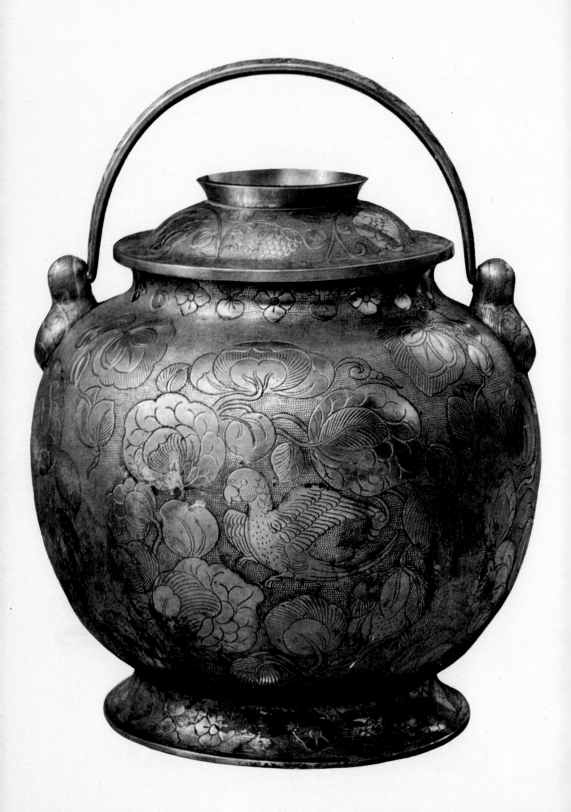

represented as a happy excursion through the mountains on a summer day. The tripartite division of the composition, the exaggerated peaks and slab-like *ch'üeh*, and the carefully drawn trees lining the edges of the contours, are all archaic features; the brush drawing is fine and precise, and a richly decorative effect is achieved by the use of malachite-green and azurite-blue – the so-called *ch'ing-lü* (blue and green) style. It is not known precisely when this picture was painted. Although it may be a copy of much later date, it seems to preserve many of the features of the T'ang courtly style of landscape-painting. This tradition was further developed during the Sung Dynasty by such painters as Chao Po-chü, and in later centuries by a host of academicians and professionals, of whom the most accomplished were T'ang Yin and Ch'iu Ying.

The objects, apart from paintings and sculpture, with which Western collections illustrate the achievements of T'ang culture are, for the most part, grave goods. These, though they have an appealing vigour and simplicity, bear little relation to the finest of T'ang decorative arts. But masterpieces of T'ang art were placed in the tomb as well, and sometimes buried for other reasons. In 1970 two large pottery jars were unearthed at Sian, crammed with gold and silver vessels believed to have been buried when the owner fled from the rebel An Lu-shan in 755 or 756. Among the finest pieces was the covered jar, decorated with parrots and peonies in gilt repoussé, which I have illustrated. But if all of it were put together it would not give the overwhelming impression of the splendour and refinement of T'ang decorative art that we get from one single collection in

DECORATIVE ARTS

109 Covered jar with swing handle, decorated with parrots amid peonies. Beaten silver with traced decoration in gilt. Excavated at Ho-chia-ts'un, Sian. T'ang Dynasty, mid eighth century.

110 Octagonal wine-cup. Beaten silver with traced and relief decoration in gilt. Excavated at Ho-chia-ts'un, Sian. T'ang Dynasty, mid eighth century.

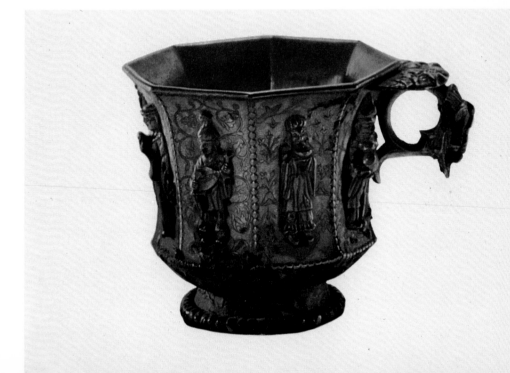

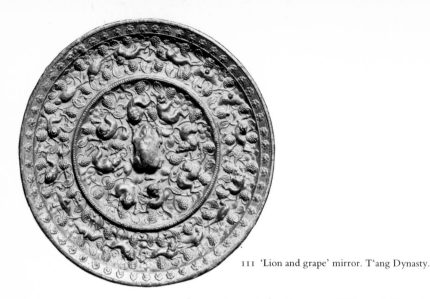

111 'Lion and grape' mirror. T'ang Dynasty.

Japan. In 756 the Empress Kōken dedicated to the great Buddha of Tōdaiji at Nara the treasures which her deceased husband Shōmu had collected in his lifetime. These and other objects were put in a treasury, called the Shōsōin, in which they have survived virtually intact until this day. This remarkable collection contains furniture, musical instruments and gaming-boards painted, lacquered or inlaid with floral and animal designs in mother-of-pearl, tortoise-shell, gold and silver; there are glass vessels from the Arab world, silver platters, jugs and ewers, mirrors, silk brocades, weapons, pottery, maps, paintings and calligraphy. What is astonishing about this collection is the triumphant confidence with which the Chinese craftsman – assuming most of these pieces to be of Chinese origin – has mastered foreign forms and techniques. This is particularly true of the arts of the goldsmith and silversmith, which came into their own during the T'ang Dynasty. Hitherto silverwork had been largely dominated by bronze design, but under Near Eastern influence it was emancipated. Some silver vessels, such as the two huge bowls in the Shōsōin, were cast, but precious metals were scarce, and a massive appearance was often achieved with little material by soldering thin sheets together to form the outer and inner surface, which also made it possible to trace designs in the metal inside and outside. Many of the shapes, such as the stem-cup, foliated bowl and flat platter with animal designs in repoussé, were of Persian origin; the decoration, applied with a typically T'ang combination of lavishness and delicacy, includes animals and figures, hunting scenes, flowers, birds and floral scrolls, generally chased or engraved, and set off against a background of rows of tiny punched circles, a technique borrowed from Sasanian metal-work.

The extravagant taste of the T'ang Dynasty also demanded that mirror-backs be gilded or silvered. The old abstract and magical designs were now replaced by a profusion of ornament whose significance is auspicious in a more general way. Symbols of conjugal felicity, entwined dragons, phoenixes, birds and flowers in relief or inlaid in silver or mother-of-pearl account for most of the designs. Two beautiful mirrors in the Shōsōin retain something of the ancient symbolism of the TLV design by bearing landscapes of foam-washed peaks ringed with clouds and set about with fairies, immortals and other fabulous creatures; while the influence of Manichaean symbolism may be seen, as Schuyler Cammann believes, in the 'lion and grape' design which was extremely popular for a short time; its sudden disappearance may have coincided with the suppression of foreign religions in 843–45.

T'ang ceramics, too, showed much use of foreign shapes and motifs. The metal ewer was copied in stoneware, often with appliqué designs in relief under a mottled green and brown glaze; the rhyton was reproduced from an old Persian shape; the circular pilgrim bottle, which appears in the blue-glazed pottery of Sasanian Persia, reappears in China, decorated rather roughly in relief with vintaging boys, dancers, musicians and hunting scenes. The Hellenistic amphora in Chinese stoneware loses its static symmetry; the playful dragon-handles, the lift and buoyancy of its silhouette, the almost casual way in which the glaze is splashed on, all bespeak the touch of the Chinese craftsman, who brings the clay to life under his hands. The T'ang Dynasty is notable in the history of Chinese ceramics for the dynamic beauty of its shapes, for the development of polychrome glazes, and for the perfecting of porcelain. Now no longer are potters limited to the simple green and brown-tinted glazes of the Han. A white ware with blue splashes was already being made in North China under the Northern Ch'i Dynasty (550–77). The fine white earthenware of the T'ang Dynasty is often clothed in a polychrome glaze, made by mixing copper, iron or cobalt with a colourless lead silicate to produce a rich range of colours from blue and green to yellow and brown; this glaze is applied more thinly than before, often over a white slip, is generally very finely crackled and stops short of the base in an uneven line. Dishes are stamped with foliate or lotus patterns and decorated with coloured glazes, which are confined by the incised lines of the central design, whereas elsewhere the colours tend to run together. The T'ang love of rich effects is seen also in the marbled wares, made by mixing a white and a brown clay together and covering the vessel with a transparent glaze. The more robust T'ang wares were exported to the Near East, where they were imitated in the poor-quality clays of Persia and Mesopotamia.

These coloured earthenwares were produced in a number of kilns in Honan and other parts of North China, though they were imitated elsewhere. But as T'ang China went into its long twilight after 756, the coloured wares also declined in quantity and quality, although they persisted in grave

CERAMICS

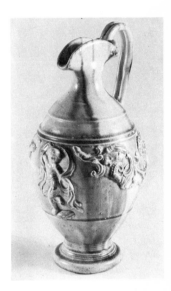

112 Phoenix-head ewer with relief decoration under a polychrome glaze. Stoneware. T'ang Dynasty, eighth century.

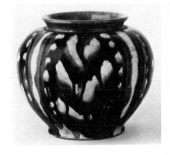

113 Jar, decorated with polychrome glazes. Stoneware. T'ang Dynasty.

figurines in Szechwan and in the ceramic sculpture of North China well into the Sung Dynasty. In the meantime, however, Yüeh ware had reached a high pitch of perfection at the Shang-lin-hu kilns near Hangchow. The body is porcellanous; bowls and vases (the most common shapes) bear moulded or incised decoration under an olive-green glaze. The soft-bodied North China wares have a flat or slightly concave base, but the Yüeh wares have a fairly high and often slightly splayed foot.

It was probably in the seventh century that the Chinese potters perfected true porcelain, by which is meant a hard, translucent ware fused at high temperature with the aid of a high proportion of felspar, causing it to ring when struck. In 851 a work entitled *The Story of China and India*, by an unknown author, appeared at Basra; it contained information about the Cantonese supplied by a certain merchant named Sulaiman, who writes of them, 'they have pottery of excellent quality, of which bowls are made as fine as glass drinking cups; the sparkle of water can be seen through it, although it is pottery'.[2] Indeed, this white ware was already in demand far beyond China's shores, for fragments both of green Yüeh ware and white porcelain were found in the ruins of the Abbasid city of Samarra, which was the summer residence of the Caliphs from 836 to 883. Although the site was occupied after that date, the greater part of the huge quantity of shards belongs to the years of its heyday and bears witness to a flourishing export trade in Chinese ceramics. What was this white ware? An *Essay on Tea*, the *Ch'a-ching*, written it is believed by the poet Lu Yü in the latter half of the ninth century, says that for drinking tea one should use Yüeh bowls (which give it the colouring of ice or jade) or the ware of Hsing-chou (which was as white as snow or silver). A number of pieces have been identified as possibly Hsing ware on account of their hardness, their creamy whiteness and their typically T'ang shapes, but the kilns have not yet been discovered and the identification of this ware remains uncertain.[3] In these white wares the most characteristic shapes are bowls, often with a slightly everted and foliated lip, globular jars and ewers of generous contour, and stem-cups imitating silver vessels.

The white porcelain soon became popular and was widely imitated, notably in the white-slipped stonewares of Hunan and Szechwan. At the same time the number of kilns making the finer wares begins to multiply. During the latter half of the dynasty white porcellanous wares were made – if a single reference in a poem of Tu Fu is acceptable evidence – at Ta-yi in Szechwan; while pale bluish-white ware, the predecessor of the lovely Sung *ch'ing-pai* (*ying-ch'ing*), was already being produced in the Shih-hu-wan kilns near Ching-te-chen, and at Chi-chou, both in Kiangsi. Yüeh-type celadons were being manufactured near Changsha in Hunan, and in Hsiang-yin-hsien, north of the city, where some of the earliest experiments in under-glaze and enamel-

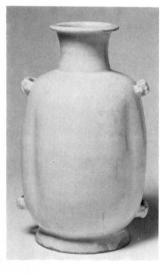

114 Vase, Hsing ware (?). White porcelain covered with a creamy-white glaze. T'ang Dynasty.

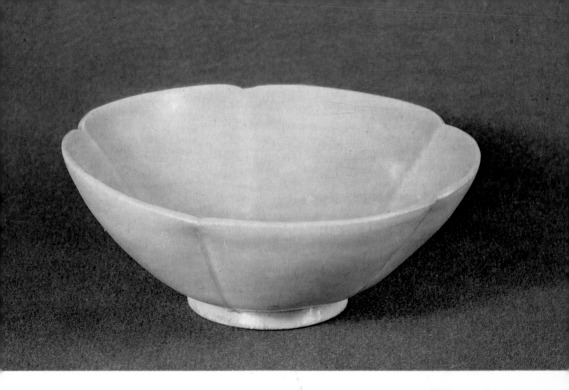

115 Lobed bowl, Yüeh ware. Stoneware covered with greyish-olive glaze. T'ang Dynasty.

painting in China were undertaken. A hard grey stoneware, ancestor of the famous splashed Chün wares of the Sung Dynasty, was made in kilns in Chia-hsien, not far from Chün-chou. The full massive shapes covered with a rich brown or black felspathic glaze are often made even more striking by bluish-white phosphatic splashes.

The fact that most of the T'ang wares that we enjoy today were made not for the collector's pleasure, not even for domestic use, but simply as cheap grave goods probably accounts for their unsophisticated charm and vigour. These qualities are most apparent in the great numbers of figurines placed in the tombs, which give a vivid picture of daily life in T'ang times. They vary in size from animals and toys a few inches high to gigantic horses, Bactrian camels, armed men and fantastic squatting guardian creatures popularly called *ch'i-t'ou* or *pi-hsieh*. They include a fascinating array of officials, servants, dancing-girls and musicians; indeed, among them women predominate. Women rode horseback with the men, and even played polo. A passage in the 'Treatise on Carriages and Dress' in the *Chiu T'ang-shu* (*Old T'ang History*) records that 'At the beginning of the K'ai-yüan period (713–42) the palace ladies who rode behind the carriages all wore Central Asian hats, exposing the face, without a veil. Suddenly their hair also was exposed when they broke into a gallop. Some were wearing men's dress and boots.'[4]

Something of the gaiety of this courtly life is recaptured in these pottery figurines. The fairy-like slenderness of the Six Dynasties women gives way in the fashion of the eighth century to an almost Victorian rotundity – Yang Kuei-fei

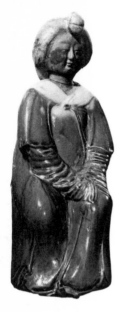

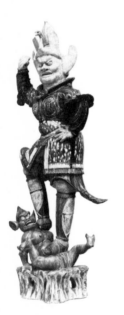

herself was said to have been plump. But these women make up in character for what they lack in elegance, while Chinese potters derived much amusement from caricaturing the extraordinary clothes, the beards and great jutting noses of the foreigners from Central and western Asia. The human figurines were almost always made in moulds, the front and back being cast separately, while the larger figures and animals were made in several pieces, generally with the base, or underside of the belly, left open. Though sometimes left in the slip and painted, they are most often lavishly decorated with three-colour glazes, which in time acquired a minute crackle very difficult for the forger to imitate.

The most spectacular of the T'ang figurines are the fierce armed men who are often represented standing on demons. These may represent actual historical figures. Once, when the Emperor T'ai-tsung was ill, ghosts started screeching outside his room and throwing bricks and tiles about. A General Chin Shu-pao, who claimed that he had 'chopped up men like melons, and piled up corpses like ant-hills', offered, with a fellow general, to stand guard outside the imperial sick-room, with the result that the screeching and brick-throwing abruptly ceased. The Emperor was so pleased that he had the generals' portraits painted to hang on either side of his palace gate. 'This tradition', the T'ang book tells us, 'was carried down to later years, and so these men became door-gods.'[5]

116 Seated woman. Earthenware, glazed and painted. From a tomb at Loyang, Honan. T'ang Dynasty.

118 Camel carrying a band of musicians. Earthenware, painted and polychrome glazed. From a tomb at Sian, Shensi. T'ang Dynasty.

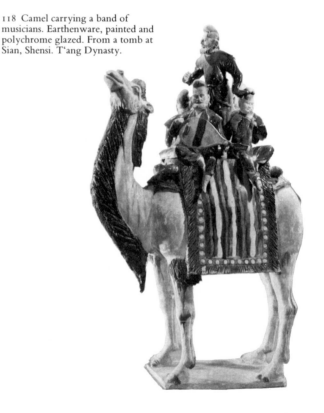

117 Tomb guardian trampling on a demon. Earthenware, painted and polychrome glazed. T'ang Dynasty.

8 The Five Dynasties and the Sung Dynasty

T'ang China never fully recovered from the An Lu-shan Rebellion, and gradually what had been a great empire shrank, both in body and spirit. The loss of Central Asia to the Uighurs, the Tibetan invasion, rebellions by local war-lords and the consequent breakdown in the irrigation and water transport system on which prosperity and good order depended, all made the downfall of the dynasty inevitable. In 907 China finally disintegrated into a state of political chaos, a period dignified with the name of the Five Dynasties. The title is an arbitrary one, chosen to cover those royal houses which had their capitals in the north-east; set up mostly by military adventurers, they had such grandiloquent names as Later T'ang, Later Han and Later Chou. Between 907 and 923 Later Liang had four rulers belonging to three different families. Although the south and west were divided among the Ten (lesser) kingdoms, in fact those regions were far more peaceful and prosperous. Szechwan, as before when the country was disunited, was, until the destruction of 'Former Shu' by Later T'ang in 925, a flourishing kingdom, distinguished for its scholars, poets and artists who had come as refugees from the T'ang court, bringing with them something of the imperial splendours of Ch'ang-an and Loyang. The style of late T'ang decorative art is reflected in the jades, wall-painting, silverwork and relief sculpture in the tomb of the Former Shu ruler Wang Chien, who died at Chengtu in 918.

Meanwhile, as before, the northern barbarians watched with patient interest the disintegration of their old enemy. In 936 the first ruler of Later Chin made the fatal gesture of ceding to the Khitans the area between Peking and the sea south of the Great Wall, with the result that once again the northern nomads had a footing on the edge of the North China plain. Ten years later they established the kingdom of Liao over a wide area of North China, which was not to be finally restored to Chinese hands for over four hundred years.

In 959 the last Emperor of the Later Chou died and in the following year the Regent, General Chao K'uang-yin, was persuaded to ascend the throne as the first Emperor of a new dynasty. At first it seemed that the Sung would be just one more in a succession of short-lived houses. But Chao was an able man; in sixteen years of vigorous campaigning he had practically united China, though, as L. Carrington Goodrich observed, his armies never succeeded in breaking the iron ring that had been forged round the imperial

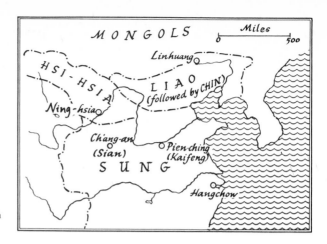

North China during the eleventh century.

boundaries by the Khitan (until 1125), the Jurchen Tungus (until 1234) and the Mongols in the north; by the Tangut, a Tibetan people (c. 990–1227), and the Mongols in the north-west; and by Annam and Nan Chao in the south-west. In 1125 the dynasty suffered a disaster from which it barely recovered, when the Jurchen raided the capital at Kaifeng and captured the whole court, including the Emperor Hui-tsung, famous throughout history as a painter, collector and connoisseur. In 1127 a young prince and the remaining officials fled south beyond the barrier of the Yangtse, where the court wandered from place to place for several years before they set up what they hoped was to be their temporary capital at Hangchow. The Jurchen, who named their dynasty Chin, were now in control of all China north of the Yangtse-Yellow River watershed. Like the Liao, they were only prevented from making further incursions into Sung territory by the enormous tribute which China paid every year, chiefly in coin and rolls of silk, until Genghis Khan with his savage hordes descended from the north, obliterating friend and foe alike.

Hemmed about by hostile powers, Sung China looked inward upon herself. Han China had lived in a fabulous world whose boundaries were the mythical K'un-lun and P'eng-lai, far beyond the horizon; T'ang China had flung out her arms to embrace Central Asia and welcome all that the West had to offer. Sung China, at peace with herself and buying peace with her neighbours, proceeded to examine the world with a new curiosity, a deeper reverence. She rediscovered the world of feeling and imagination which had been revealed to her during the Six Dynasties, but had been lost again under the strong light of T'ang positivism. It was this depth of philosophical insight, combined with a perfect balance of creative energy and technical refinement, that made the tenth and eleventh centuries one of the great epochs in the history of Chinese art.

During this time, China was ruled by a succession of emperors more truly cultivated than any before or since.

Under them the intellectuals who ran the government were an honoured élite, permitted to remain seated in the imperial presence, and to debate rival policies with complete freedom. Their prestige was perhaps partly due to the rapid spread of printing, for which Chengtu, the capital of Shu, was already the chief centre in the ninth century. There the first paper money had been printed and the first edition of the Classics was issued in 130 volumes between 932 and 953; likewise the Buddhist *Tripitaka* in over five thousand volumes and the Taoist canon before the end of the tenth century. With the aid of this new craft it became possible to synthesize knowledge as never before, and there began the unending compilation of dictionaries, encyclopaedias and anthologies which was to become ever more characteristic of Chinese intellectual activity until the Revolution. It was this desire for intellectual synthesis which led to the founding by Chou Tun-i and Chu Hsi of the doctrine of Neo-Confucianism, in which Confucian morality (*li*) became identified with the Taoist first cause (*t'ai-chi*) seen as a moral force, and at the same time was enriched by a theory of knowledge and a way of self-cultivation derived partly from Buddhism. To the Neo-Confucianist *li* became the governing principle which gives to each form its inherent nature. By 'investigating things' – that is, by a process of study, part scientific, part intuitive, and leading outwards from the near and familiar – the cultivated man could deepen his knowledge of the world and of the workings of *li*. The trend in Sung painting (particularly in bird-and-flower and bamboo painting) towards the intimate 'close-up' bears witness to the profound and subtle examination of the visible world which found philosophical expression in Neo-Confucianism.

An important by-product of the Confucian revival, or parallel manifestation of the same backward-looking impulses perhaps, was the new interest taken in ancient arts and crafts, creating a demand for reproductions of archaic ritual vessels and implements, in bronze and jade, which was to grow with the centuries. Some Sung copies of ancient bronzes are hard to distinguish from Shang and Chou pieces with any certainty. They are of superb craftsmanship (even the patina was imitated), less vigorous in form than their ancient models, but much closer to them than the fanciful archaisms of the Ch'ien-lung period. Illustrated catalogues of the Sung imperial collections were compiled, but they only survive in late, unreliable editions, and are of little help in separating Sung reproductions from the genuine archaic bronzes and jades which enthusiastic antiquarians were beginning to unearth.

ARCHITECTURE

It is also in character with the 'intellectualizing' trend of the period that the first great manual of architectural practice, the *Ying-tsao fa-shih* (presented to the Emperor in 1100), should have been written during the Sung Dynasty. The author, Li Chiai, a practising architect in the service of the state, combines historical scholarship with a considerable amount of straightforward technical information on materials and construction, which in this time was becoming increasingly complex and refined – if not so grand in scale as during the T'ang Dynasty. The *ang*, for example, was now no longer a simple cantilevered arm jutting out to hold up the eaves; it was cut loose from supports at either end and poised on the top of an intricate bracketing system, held in balance by a complex play of stresses and strains. In time this intricacy for its own sake was to lead to degeneration, but in Sung timber construction it combined structural boldness with refinement of detail. Sung taste also preferred the delicate to the robust, the tall and slender to the gigantic and solid, and Kaifeng was a city of spires. Temples had roofs of yellow tiles and were floored with yellow and green. Timber and stone pagodas now acquired little projecting roofs at each storey, curving up at the point where two faces met.

On the subject of curved roofs, A. C. Soper quotes a remark made by the master-builder Yü Hao, who had come up to the capital from the south early in the dynasty: 'They certainly were capable enough in those days,' he is reported to have said, on looking at a T'ang gate tower. 'The only thing is, they didn't understand how to curve up their eaves.' We have seen that the curving eaves and sweeping roof-line began in the south, possibly under the influence of China's South-east Asian and island neighbours; they were used on some Five Dynasties pagodas in the Yangtse region and, perhaps, were brought to Kaifeng by Yü Hao himself. Whatever the origin of the curve, it could not have been adopted by the Chinese if they had employed the rigid triangular roof-truss of Western architecture. The Chinese system, whereby the rafters rest on purlins supported by a framework of cross-beams and queen-posts, made it possible for the roof to take any profile desired; the architect had to vary merely the height of the queen-posts. It may be, after all, that the curve was adopted simply because it was beautiful.

Sung temples were further embellished with elaborate timber cupolas over the images, while libraries had model pavilions surmounting each bay, and huge revolving book-cases for the *sūtras*, such as that which still survives in the eleventh-century Lung-hsing-ssu at Cheng-ting-hsien in Hopei. Slightly later but more splendid in total effect is the Buddha Hall of Upper Hua-yen Monastery at Ta-t'ung in Shansi, dedicated in 1140. Here, architect, sculptor and fresco-painter have combined their arts in the service of theology to create a fabulous Buddha-world by which the worshipper, on entering the hall, is surrounded and enveloped. Buddhas, *bodhisattvas*, guardians and *arhats* take their apportioned place in a gigantic three-dimensional *mandala*, the total effect of which is to saturate the eye, and the mind, of the believer with the manifold and all-embracing powers of God.

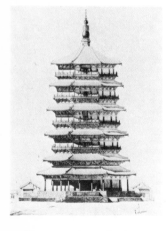

119 Twelve-sided pagoda of Fu-kuang-ssu, Ying-hsien, Shensi. Sung Dynasty, 1058.

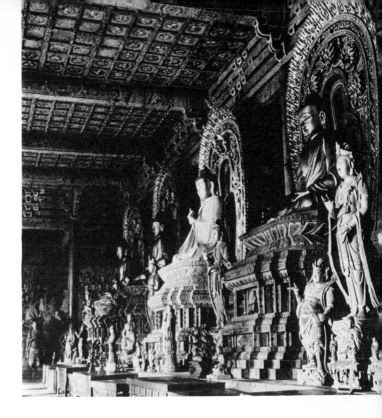

120 Interior of the Buddha Hall of
Upper Hua-yen Monastery,
Ta-t'ung, Shansi. Dedicated 1140.
Chin Dynasty.

As the Toba Wei had fostered Buddhism because they themselves were aliens on Chinese soil, so did the Liao and Chin,
and under their patronage the old faith was vigorously
revived. The largest surviving bronze image in China, a
many- armed Kuanyin consecrated in 971, can still be seen in
its temple at Cheng-ting-hsien in Liao territory, but it is a
wretched effort. Rather more successful and interesting are
the colossal Buddhas and *bodhisattvas* carved at Yünkang, in
so close an imitation of the Sui work near by that their Liao
date has only recently been established by Japanese scholars.
Perhaps the most impressive – and deceptive – achievement
of Liao-Chin sculpture is the set of pottery figures of *lohan*
(*arhats*) which were found some years ago in a cave at I-chou
near Peking. One figure is in the British Museum, London,
five others are in other Western collections. The vigorous
modelling, the dignity and realism, and above all the three-
colour glaze, all suggested a T'ang date at a time when the
possibility of art of any quality being produced under the
Liao and Chin was not seriously considered. But it is now
known that North China at this time was the centre of a
flourishing culture in which the traditions of T'ang art were
preserved, with subtle differences, not only in sculpture but
also in ceramics, and there is no disgrace in assigning them to
the Liao or Chin. These figures, and others executed in dry-
lacquer, are not so much portraits of individual monks, as
expressions of a variety of spiritual states. In the face of the
young *arhat* in the Nelson Gallery, Kansas City, is portrayed
all the inward struggle, the will to triumph, the intensity of

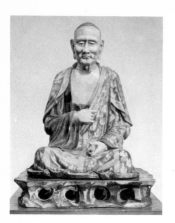

121 Lohan. Earthenware, decorated with polychrome glazes. From I-chou, Hopei. Liao-Chin Dynasties.

concentration of the meditative sects of which Zen was the chief. When we turn to the figure in the Metropolitan Museum, New York, we see in the bony skull, lined features and deep-set eyes of an old man, the outcome of that struggle; it has taken its toll of the flesh, but the spirit has emerged serene and triumphant.

But not all sculpture of this period was an archaistic revival, or a prolongation of the T'ang tradition. The figures in wood and plaster, of which a number still stand in the temples of North China, represent an evolution beyond the T'ang style. The Buddhas and *bodhisattvas* are still fully modelled – even to the extent of a fleshiness that can be displeasing – but what they have lost in dynamic energy they gain in a new splendour of effect. They stand against walls covered with huge frescoes painted in the same ample and spectacular manner – such as can still be seen today in the Buddha Hall of Upper Hua-yen Monastery at Ta-t'ung. In fact, so closely does the style of the one echo that of the other that Laurence Sickman's vivid description of the sculpture could apply equally to the painting:

> An almost uncanny impression of movement, as though the gods were stepping forward with an easy, stately pace, or had just taken their seats on the lotus thrones, is produced by the great agitation and restless movement of the garments and encircling scarves. These latter accessories are especially important in creating an almost spiral movement in three dimensions as the long, broad ribbons trail over the arms, loop across the body and curve around the back. In the actual carving the folds are deep, with sharp edges, so that the maximum contrast is obtained between highlight and shadow. Frequently the ends of garments and scarves are caught up in whorls and spirals obviously derived from the calligraphic flourishes of paintings.[1]

This suave and restless splendour was clearly designed, like that of the Baroque art with which it has so much in common, to capture the attention of the worshipper through its emotional appeal. It is no accident that it finds its most splendid expression in the figures of Kuanyin, the comforter, the giver of children, the preserver from peril of all those who call upon her name. She looks down upon suffering humanity with calm detachment; yet she is not indifferent, and her regard is full of sweetness without being sentimental. In this beautiful figure a potential extravagance of effect is held delicately in check by the refinement of Sung taste.

At another level, Sung sculpture could be anything but refined. Although after the Middle T'ang period institutional Buddhism appealed less and less to the intelligentsia, its doctrines of rewards and punishments continued to exert their hold on the common people. Some of the most vigorous examples of Sung religious art were produced for the edification of the masses. Perhaps the most astonishing

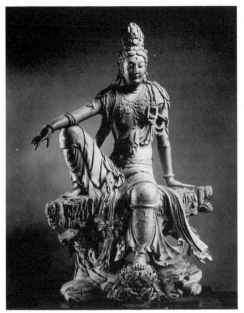
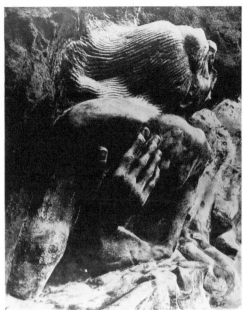

122 Kuanyin. Sculpture in wood and gesso, painted and gilded. Sung Dynasty, late twelfth century.

123 Soul suffering the torments of Hell. Stone relief sculpture on a cliff at Ta-tsu, Szechwan. Sung Dynasty.

example of Sung sculptural realism is the figure of a soul suffering the torments of Hell, one of hundreds of reliefs carved by unknown craftsmen on the cliff at Ta-tsu in Szechwan.

Buddhism as a popular religion never recovered from the suppression of 845. During the Later T'ang the speculative and Tantric sects decayed, partly because they had no roots in Chinese soil. But for the Ch'an sect (known in Japan as Zen) the position was different. Like Taoism, it emphasized quietism, self-cultivation, the freeing of the mind from all intellectual and material dross, so as to leave it open and receptive to those flashes of blinding illumination when suddenly, for a moment, the Truth is revealed. To create the right atmosphere for meditation, the Ch'an monks built their temples in beautiful secluded places, where the only sound might be the wind in the trees and the rain falling on the stones of the temple courtyard. Their aims, and the very techniques by which they were to be realized, were almost identical with those of the Taoists. So it was that after Buddhism had been on Chinese soil for nearly a thousand years, it finally came to terms with Chinese ideals.

In seeking a technique with which to express the intensity and immediacy of his intuition, the Ch'an painter turned to the brush and monochrome ink, and with the fierce concentration of the calligrapher proceeded to record his own moments of truth in the outward forms of Buddhas and

CH'AN PAINTING DURING THE FIVE DYNASTIES

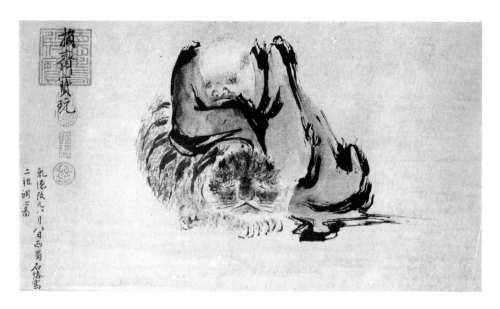

124 In the manner of Shih K'o (active mid tenth century). *Two Minds in Harmony*. Part of a handscroll. Ink on paper. Sung Dynasty (?).

arhats. Already in the last century of the T'ang Dynasty there were artists practising techniques as wildly eccentric as those of any modern Western 'action painter'. None of their work survives, but contemporary descriptions of it suggest that these individualists were either Zen adepts or were fired by the same impulse towards irrationality and spontaneity as that which inspired the Zen painters. Only slightly later was Kuan-hsiu, who, after a lifetime of painting Buddhist subjects in the Lower Yangtse region, came, full of years and honour, to the court of Wang Chien at Chengtu, where he died in 912. His *arhats* were drawn with that exaggeration bordering on perversity which is typically Zen; with their bony skulls, huge eyebrows and pronounced Indian features, they have the ugliness of caricatures, as if only by deliberate distortion could the sudden, electrifying experience of the Ch'an mystic be suggested. For the experience itself is incommunicable: all the artist can do is to give the viewer a shock which may jolt him into awareness. The few surviving copies of Kuan-hsiu's work are treasured in Japan, where Zen long outlasted its popularity in China. When Kuan-hsiu died his mantle fell upon Shih K'o, a wild and eccentric individual who, according to an eleventh-century historian, 'liked to shock and insult people and compose satirical rhymes about them'. By this time writers were fond of classifying painters into three grades: *neng* (capable), *miao* (wonderful) and *shen* (divine, superhuman); but for Shih K'o and his like even *shen* was not enough, for it still implied obedience to the rules. For them the critics coined the term *i*, meaning 'completely unrestrained by rules'. 'Painting in the *i* style,' said another author, 'is most difficult; those who follow it . . . despise refinement and rich colouring and draw the forms quite sketchily, but they grasp the natural [*tzu-jan*] spontaneously.'

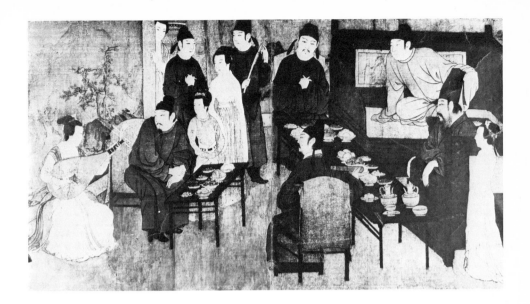

In the meantime quite another tradition was flourishing at Nanking, whose painters must have raised their hands in horror at the antics of the *fauves* up in Chengtu. There Li Hou-chu, the 'Emperor' of Southern T'ang, had re-created in miniature the luxury and refinement of the T'ang court under Ming Huang. One recent writer describes the art produced under his patronage as the twilight of the T'ang, another as 'premature Sung'; all we can say is that it provides an important link between the two great epochs. Under his patronage the spirit of Chou Fang and Chang Hsüan was reborn in Chou Wen-chü and Ku Hung-chung. The painting of which I have reproduced a detail is probably a very close copy, dating from about the twelfth century, of a scroll by Ku Hung-chung depicting the nocturnal revels of the Vice-President Han Hsi-tsai, rumours of whose thoroughly un-Confucian behaviour with singing- and dancing-girls, of whom he had at least a hundred, had reached the ears of the 'Emperor'. Li Hou-chu sent a Painter in Attendance (*tai-chao*) to observe and record what was going on, and then confronted Han Hsi-tsai with the evidence of his dissipation. The scene looks respectable enough, but the casual attitudes of Han, his friends and his singing-girls, the meaningful glances, the figures half hidden behind bed-curtains, are all highly suggestive; indeed, not the least intriguing thing about this picture is the way in which licentiousness is suggested in a formal language of such exquisite refinement and dignity. The painting, which the fourteenth-century writer T'ang Hou considered 'not a pure and fitting object for a high-class collection', is also extremely revealing as a document on tenth-century costume, furniture and porcelain, and shows also how lavishly paintings, including monochrome landscapes, were used in interior decoration, forming panels on the beds as well as tall free-standing screens. It

125 Attributed to Ku Hung-chung (tenth century). *A Night Entertainment of Han Hsi-tsai.* Detail of a handscroll. Ink and colour on silk. Probably a twelfth-century copy. Sung Dynasty.

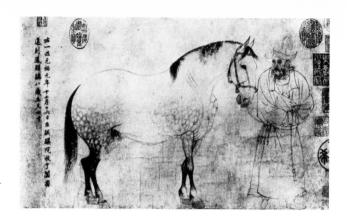

126 Attributed to Li Lung-mien
(c. 1040–1106). *A Horse*. One of five
tribute horses. Detail of a handscroll.
Ink and slight colour on paper.
Sung Dynasty.

would seem that the hanging scroll had not yet become
fashionable.

The last great exponent of the T'ang figure-painting tradition was Li Kung-lin (1040–1106), better known as Li
Lung-mien, from the name of his country estate, of which
he, in emulation of Wang Wei, painted a long panoramic
handscroll. Several versions of it exist. Li Lung-mien moved
in an intellectual circle at court that included the poet Su
Tung-p'o and the historian Ou-yang Hsiu, while it is recorded that even the great statesman Wang An-shih, who
was 'careful in choosing his friends', condescended to visit
him. In early life he was a famous painter of horses – until, so
the story goes, a Taoist told him that if he continued much
longer in this vein he would become like a horse himself,
whereupon he switched to other themes. He was thoroughly
eclectic, spending years in copying the old masters, and
though his own technique was restricted largely to ink-line
(*pai-miao*), his subject-matter included everything from
horses and *genre* scenes to Taoist fairy landscapes, Buddhist
figures and paintings of Kuanyin amid rocks, of which he
created an ideal conventional type.

CONNOISSEURSHIP The reverence for the past revealed in Li Lung-mien's
sedulous copying of the old masters is from now on to loom
large in Chinese connoisseurship, and to present the most
formidable problems to the expert. In the case of a master we
may assume that his motives were the honourable ones of
training his hand and of transmitting the ancient models in
the spirit of the sixth principle of Hsieh Ho. To paint in the
manner of Wu Tao-tzu, therefore, was no less 'original' than
for a pianist to play the works of Bach and Beethoven; for
what the artist sought was not originality but a sense of
identity, both with nature and with the tradition itself. The
Western artist particularizes; and each painting is the result
of a direct examination of what is before his eyes. The
Chinese painter generalizes, and his work, ideally, reveals
not the particular but the quintessential forms of nature,
animated by his *élan*, and by his mastery of the brush. To

achieve this he must, like the pianist, have the language of expression at his fingertips so that no technical impediment, no struggle with form or brushwork, should come between the vision and its realization. An important part of his training is the study of the old masters. He might perhaps make an exact reproduction by tracing (*mu*), he might copy the picture with the original before him (*lin*), or he could freely interpret the manner of the master (*fang*). Paintings in either of the first two categories which passed into the hands of unscrupulous collectors or dealers would often acquire false signatures, seals and colophons, and the new attribution would then be attested by further colophons. In many cases, such are the vicissitudes through which the painting has passed that the truth can never be known, and the most that can be said is that a given work is in the style of a certain master or period and *looks* old enough, and good enough, to be genuine. Sometimes a painting is exposed as a copy by the subsequent appearance of a still finer version. In this most difficult branch of connoisseurship there is not an expert who has not been deceived, and the recent tendency in the West has been towards a perhaps excessive caution not shared by the majority of Chinese and Japanese connoisseurs.

This uncertainty applies particularly to the few great landscape-paintings of the Five Dynasties and Early Sung which are generally attributed to such masters as Ching Hao, Li Ch'eng, Tung Yüan and Chü-jan, all of whom were working in the tenth century, and Fan K'uan, Hsü Tao-ning and Yen Wen-kuei, who were active into the eleventh. In the hundred years between 950 and 1050 a host of great names succeed each other in what must be looked upon as perhaps the supreme period in classical Chinese landscape-painting. Ching Hao, who was active from about 900 to 960, spent much of his life in retirement amid the mountains of eastern Shansi. An essay attributed to him, the *Pi-fa chi* (*Record of Brush Methods*) or *Hua shan-shui lu* (*Essay on Landscape Painting*), puts his thoughts on the art into the mouth of an old man whom he pretends he met when wandering in the mountains, and who gave him a lecture on principles and technique. The old man tells him of the six essentials in painting: the first is spirit, the second rhythm, the third thought, the fourth scenery, the fifth brush, the sixth ink – a more logical system than that of Hsieh Ho, for it proceeds from the concept to its expression, and thence to the composition, truth to nature (scenery), and finally technique. The sage further distinguishes between resemblance, which reproduces the outward, formal aspect of objects, and truth, which involves a perfect integration of form and content. He seeks a just correspondence of the type of brushstroke with the object depicted. He insists that flowers and trees should be those appropriate to the season, and that men be not larger than trees – not simply for the sake of objective realism, but because only by faithfully reproducing the

LANDSCAPE-PAINTING: THE CLASSICAL IDEAL IN NORTH CHINA

155

visible forms of nature can the artist hope to express, through them, their deeper significance. To default in this, therefore, is a sign that the artist has not fully attuned himself.

This doctrine of a realism raised to the level of idealism is elaborated in a well-known essay by the eleventh-century master Kuo Hsi, who combined in his spectacular landscapes the strong drawing and jagged silhouette which we associate with Li Ch'eng with a modelling of relief in ink wash which was probably derived from the late T'ang individualists. Kuo Hsi was to Sung landscape what Wu Tao-tzu had been to T'ang Buddhist art – a painter of enormous energy and output, who loved to cover large walls and standing screens with monumental compositions. In his *Advice on Landscape Painting* (*Shan-shui hsün*), he insists again and again on the necessity, amounting to an ethical obligation, for the artist to study nature in every aspect, to mark the procession of the seasons, the way the same scene may look at morning and evening; to note and express the particular, unique character of every changing moment; to select with care; to impart movement to water and cloud, for, as he says, 'watercourses are the arteries of a mountain; grass and trees its hair; mist and haze its complexion'. Indeed, as the painter knows the very mountains to be alive, so must he transmit that life (*ch'i*) into the mountains that he paints.

PERSPECTIVE How was it then, one might ask, that the Chinese painter, who insisted on truth to natural appearance, should have been so ignorant of even the elementary laws of perspective as the West understands it? The answer is that he deliberately avoided it, for the same reason that he avoided the use of shadows. Scientific perspective involves a view from a determined position, and includes only what can be seen from that single point. While this satisfies the logical Western mind, it is not enough for the Chinese painter: for why, he asks, should we so restrict ourselves? Why, if we have the means to depict what we know to be there, paint only what we can see from one viewpoint? In the Sung Dynasty Shen Kua criticized Li Ch'eng for 'painting the eaves from below' and thereby putting an arbitrary restriction on his power to 'view the part from the angle of totality'. 'When Li Ch'eng paints mountains, pavilions and buildings,' he writes in his *Meng-ch'i pi-t'an*,

> he paints the eaves from below. He believes that looking up one perceives the eaves of a pagoda as a person on the level ground and is able to see the beams and rafters of its structure. This is absurd. All landscapes have to be viewed from 'the angle of totality to behold the part', much in the manner in which we look at an artificial rockery in our gardens. If we apply Li's method to the painting of real mountains, we are unable to see more than one layer of the mountain at a time. Could that be called art? Li Ch'eng surely does not understand the principle of viewing the part from the angle of totality. His measurement of height and distance certainly is a fine thing. But should one attach paramount importance to the angles and corners of buildings?[2]

The composition of a Chinese painting is not defined by the four walls of its mount as is a European painting within its frame. Indeed, the Chinese artist hardly thinks of it as a 'composition' at all. Those formal considerations to which the Western painter devotes so much attention he takes very largely for granted. Rather is his picture, as Shen Kua suggests, a fragment – chosen as it were at random, yet profoundly significant – of eternity. What the Chinese artist records is not a single visual confrontation, but an accumulation of experience touched off perhaps by one moment's exaltation before the beauty of nature. The experience is transmitted in forms that are not merely generalized, but are also richly symbolic. This kind of generalization is quite different from that of Claude and Poussin, in whose idyllic landscapes the evocation of a Golden Age is deliberate. The Chinese artist may paint a view of Mount Lu, but the actual shape of Mount Lu is of little interest to him in itself; the mountain is significant only if, in contemplating it, wandering through it, painting it, he is made aware of those things that for him make Mount Lu, for the moment, the very embodiment of 'mountainness'. Likewise, the bird on a branch painted by some Sung academician is not a thing in itself, defined by its frame, but seems poised in limitless space, a symbol chosen by the artist to express what we might call the 'bird-on-bough' aspect of Reality. We are often told that the Chinese painter leaves large areas of the picture space empty so that we may 'complete it in our imagination'. But that is not so. The very concept of completion is utterly alien to the Chinese way of thinking. The Chinese painter deliberately avoids a complete statement because he knows that we can never know everything, that what we can describe, or 'complete', cannot be true, except in a very limited sense. All he can do is to liberate the imagination and set it wandering over the limitless spaces of the universe. His landscape is not a final statement, but a starting-point; not an end, but the opening of a door. For this reason, Rembrandt's drawings, and the work of the modern Abstract Expressionists, are much closer to the spirit of Chinese art than are the idealized, classical compositions of the great European landscape-painters of the seventeenth century.

In the passage I have quoted above, Shen Kua clearly explains the attitude behind the 'shifting perspective' of Chinese painting, which invites us to explore nature, to wander through the mountains and valleys, discovering fresh beauty at every step. We cannot take in so great a panorama at a glance; indeed, the artist intends that we should not. We would need perhaps days or weeks to walk the length of the stretch of countryside he presents in his scroll; but by revealing it to us little by little as we proceed, he combines the element of time with that of space, in a four-dimensional synthesis such as Western art has not achieved until modern times.

This power in a great Chinese landscape-painting to 'take

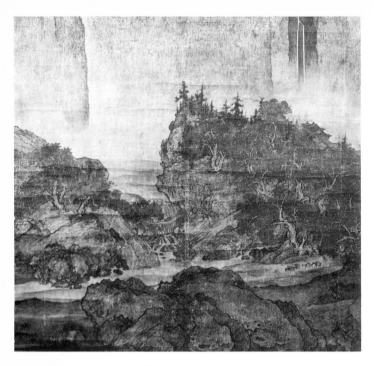

127 Fan K'uan (late tenth to early eleventh century). *Travelling amid Mountains and Gorges.* Detail of a hanging scroll. Ink and colour on silk. Sung Dynasty.

us out of ourselves' was widely recognized as a source of spiritual solace and refreshment. Kuo Hsi opens his essay by declaring that it is the virtuous man above all who delights in landscapes. Why the virtuous man particularly? Because, being virtuous (in other words, a good Confucian), he accepts his responsibilities to society and the state, which tie him down to the urban life of an official. He cannot 'seclude himself and shun the world', he cannot wander for years among the mountains, but he *can* nourish his spirit by taking imaginary journeys through a landscape-painting into which the artist has compressed the beauty, the grandeur and the silence of nature, and return to his desk refreshed.

FAN K'UAN The great masters of the tenth and eleventh centuries are sometimes called 'classical' because they established an ideal in monumental landscape-painting to which later painters returned again and again for inspiration. In nearly every case the attributions to such masters as Ching Hao, Li Ch'eng, Kuan T'ung and Kuo Chung-shu are merely traditional. But, by a miracle, there has survived one masterpiece bearing the hidden signature of the great Early Sung painter Fan K'uan which is almost certainly an original from his hand. Born in about the middle of the tenth century, and still living in 1026, Fan K'uan was a shy, austere man who shunned the world. At first, like his contemporary Hsü Tao-ning, he modelled himself on Li Ch'eng, but then it came to him that nature herself was the only true teacher, and he spent the rest of his life as a recluse in the rugged Ch'ien-t'ang Mountains of Shansi, often spending a whole day gaz-

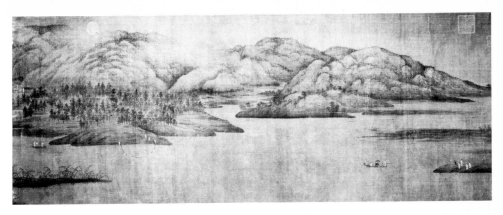

128 Attributed to Tung Yüan (tenth century). *Scenery along the Hsiao and Hsiang Rivers.* Detail of a handscroll. Ink and slight colour on silk. Early Sung Dynasty (?).

ing at a configuration of rocks, or going out on a winter's night to study with great concentration the effect of moonlight upon the snow. If we were to select one single painting to illustrate the achievement of the Northern Sung landscape-painters we could not do better than to choose his *Travelling amid Mountains and Gorges*, in which we see a train of pack-horses emerging from a wood at the base of a huge precipice. The composition is still in some respects archaic; the dominating central massif goes back to the T'ang Dynasty, the foliage retains several early conventions, while the texture-strokes (*ts'un*) are still almost mechanically repeated and narrow in range; their full expressive possibilities are not to be realized for another two hundred years. Yet this painting is overwhelming in its grandeur of conception, its dramatic contrasts of light and dark in the mist, rocks and trees, and above all in a concentrated energy in the brushwork so intense that the very mountains seem to be alive, and the roar of the waterfall fills the air around you as you gaze upon it. It perfectly fulfils the ideal of the Northern Sung that a landscape-painting should be of such compelling realism that the viewer will feel that he has been actually transported to the place depicted.

The painters I have been discussing were all men of North China, nurtured in a hard, bleak countryside whose mood is well conveyed in the austerity of their style. The painters of the south lived in a kinder environment. The hills of the Lower Yangtse Valley are softer in outline, the sunlight is diffused by mist, and winter's grip less hard. In the works of Tung Yüan and Chü-jan, both active in Nanking in the latter half of the tenth century, there is a roundness of contour and a looseness and freedom in the brushwork that is in marked contrast to the angular rocks and crabbed branches of Li Ch'eng and Fan K'uan. Shen Kua said that Tung Yüan 'was skilled in painting the mists of autumn and far open views', and that 'his pictures were meant to be seen at a distance, because their brushwork was very rough'. Tung also, rather surprisingly, worked in a coloured style like that of Li Ssu-hsün. The revolutionary impressionism which

TUNG YÜAN AND CHÜ-JAN

159

Tung Yüan and his pupil Chü-jan achieved by means of broken ink washes and the elimination of the outline is well illustrated by Tung Yüan's scroll depicting scenery along the Hsiao and Hsiang rivers in Hunan, sections of which are now in the museums in Peking and Shanghai. In this evocation of the atmosphere of a summer evening, the contours of the hills are soft and rounded, the mist is beginning to form among the trees, the diminutive figures of fishermen and travellers catch the last rays of the setting sun. Over the scene hangs a peace so profound that we can almost hear their voices as they call to each other across the water. Here an element of pure lyricism appears in Chinese landscape-painting for the first time.

THE PAINTING OF THE LITERATI

The high point of Northern Sung realism, shown in a remarkable documentary scroll depicting life in the capital on the eve of the Ch'ing-ming Festival, was reached shortly before the débâcle of 1125. The painter, Chang Tse-tuan, a member of the official class, shows not only acute powers of observation but also mastery of shading and foreshortening, techniques which were to be almost completely abandoned after the fall of the Northern Sung. For even while this climax was approaching, elsewhere the subtle change which first showed itself in the work of some of the T'ang scholar-painters was coming out into the open, and the tradition of the painting of the literati, the *wen-jen hua*, was being firmly established. By the eleventh century, and indeed long before, the scholars had come to look on the kind of painting they did as being different in kind from that produced by professional artists. To the literati, painting was, like poetry and calligraphy, primarily a means of self-expression. They painted not so much to evoke in the viewer the same kind of feelings that he would have before a real scene, as to convey to others of their class something of themselves. Of the panorama of the Hsiao and Hsiang rivers the scholar-painters might say, not 'From this you can see what the scenery of Hsiao and Hsiang is like,' but 'From this, you can tell what kind of a man Tung Yüan was.'

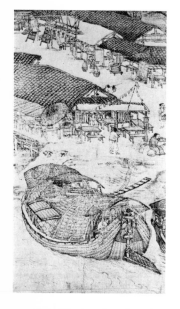

129 Chang Tse-tuan (late eleventh to early twelfth century). *Life along the River on the Eve of the Ch'ing-ming Festival*. Detail of a handscroll. Ink and slight colour on silk. Sung Dynasty.

In the landscapes of the scholar-painters, the passion of a Fan K'uan for the hills and streams gave way to a more urbane, detached attitude. They avoided becoming too deeply involved, either in nature or in material things. They spoke of merely 'borrowing' the forms of rocks, trees or bamboo as something in which, for the moment, to find 'lodging' for their feelings. Above all, they were amateurs. They affected to be merely playing with ink, even pretended to be clumsy, because mere skill was an attribute of professionals and court painters. By choice they painted, as the poets and calligraphers wrote, in ink on paper, deliberately avoiding the visual seductions of colour and silk. It is not surprising that of all the streams of Chinese painting, the *wen-jen hua* is the hardest to appreciate, even for the Chinese themselves. Like a rare, dry wine, it is often a little hard on

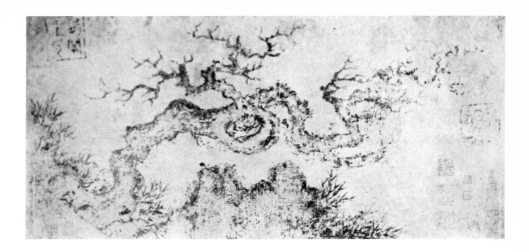

the palate at first, but deepening familiarity brings its rich rewards.

The Sung *wen-jen hua* crystallized round a group of remarkable personalities in the eleventh century that included the poet Su Tung-p'o (1036–1101) and his teacher in bamboo-painting Wen T'ung (died 1079), Mi Fu (or Mi Fei, 1051–1107), and the great calligrapher Huang T'ing-chien (1045–1105). No certain painting from the hand of Mi Fu or Su Tung-p'o has survived, and the short handscroll illustrated was first attributed to the latter in the thirteenth century. But it is typical of the taste and technique of the eleventh-century scholar-painters in its choice of medium, its dry, sensitive brushwork, its avoidance of obvious visual appeal, and in the sense that this is a spontaneous statement as revealing of the man himself as of what he depicts.

130 Attributed to Su Tung-p'o (1036–1101). *Bare Tree, Bamboo and Rocks*. Handscroll. Ink on paper. Sung Dynasty.

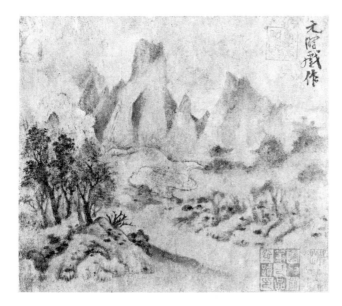

131 Mi Yu-jen (1086–1165). *Misty Landscape*. Hanging scroll. Ink on paper. Sung Dynasty.

The work of the early scholar-painters was always original, not because they strove for originality for its own sake, but because their art was the sincere and spontaneous expression of original personalities. One of the most remarkable of these men was Mi Fu, critic, connoisseur and eccentric, who would spend long evenings with his friend Su Tung-p'o, surrounded by piles of paper and jugs of wine, writing away at top speed till the paper and wine gave out, and the small boys grinding the ink were ready to drop with fatigue. In painting landscapes, Mi Fu, it is said, abandoned the drawn line altogether, forming his mountains of rows of blobs of ink laid on the paper with the flat of the brush. This striking 'Mi-dot' technique, as it came to be called, had its dangers, however; in the hands of the master or of his son Mi Yu-jen (1086–1165), who seems to have modified it somewhat, it achieved marvels of breadth and luminosity with the simplest of means, but it was fatally easy to imitate.

So radical was this technique of Mi Fu's that the Emperor Hui-tsung would have none of his work in the imperial collection, nor would he permit the style to be practised at court. It is not known whether an official painting academy ever existed before the Southern Sung. Painters at the T'ang court had been given a wide variety of civil and military ranks, most of which were sinecures. Wang Chien, ruler of Former Shu, seems to have been the first to give his painters appointments in his own Hanlin Academy of Letters, and this practice was followed by the Southern T'ang Emperor Li Hou-chu at Nanking, and by the first emperors of the Sung. Contemporary writers often speak of distinguished painters as being in attendance (tai-chao) in the Yü-hua-yüan (Imperial Academy of Painting); yet no such institution is ever mentioned in the Northern Sung history, and, if such a body did in fact exist, it was presumably a subdivision of the Hanlin Academy.

The tradition of direct imperial patronage culminated in Hui-tsung (1101–25), almost the last emperor of Northern Sung, whose passion for pictures and antiquities blinded him to the perils into which his country was drifting. In 1104 he set up an official School of Painting (Hua-hsüeh), in the palace, but in 1110 this was abolished and painting was once more placed under the supervision of the Hanlin Academy. Hui-tsung kept tight control over the painters at court. He handed out the subjects to be painted and set examinations as though the painters were candidates for administrative posts. The theme was generally a line from a poem, and distinction went to the most ingenious and allusive 'answer'. When, for example, he chose the theme A Tavern in a Bamboo Grove by a Bridge, the winner did not depict the tavern at all, but simply suggested it by a sign-board set among the bamboos. Thus what Hui-tsung required of these artists was not mere academic realism, so much as the kind of intellectual agility, the avoidance of the obvious, the play upon ideas that was

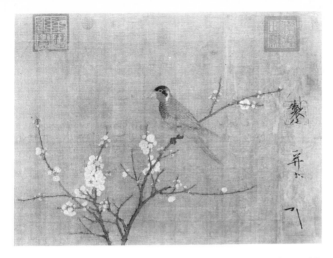

132 Sung Hui-tsung (reigned 1101–25). *The Five-colour Parakeet.* Hanging scroll. Ink and colour on silk. Sung Dynasty.

expected also of literary scholars. But the Emperor, himself a painter of great ability, tolerated no indiscipline in the ranks. He imposed a dictatorship of form and taste upon his academicians as rigid as that of Le Brun over the artists working for Louis XIV, who were in much the same position. The penalty for independence was dismissal. For all his talent and enthusiasm, his influence cannot have been beneficial. The imposition of a rigid orthodoxy laid the foundation for a decorative, painstaking 'palace style' which was to govern court taste until modern times, while his insatiable and somewhat unscrupulous demands as a collector – demands which no owner could refuse – helped to ensure the destruction, in the disastrous events of 1125–27, of most of the still-surviving masterpieces of ancient art.

Whenever Hui-tsung produced a masterpiece, the painters in the 'Academy' vied with each other in copying it and, if they were lucky, succeeded in having their versions stamped with the Emperor's own seal. So closely, indeed, did they model their work on his that it is now almost impossible to disentangle the one from the other, though some attempts have been made to do so. It would even be wrong to assume that the better the painting the more likely it is to be from the imperial hand. The pictures associated with his name are for the most part quiet, careful studies of birds on branches – *A Dove on a Peach Tree, Sparrows on Bamboo*, and so on – painted with exquisite precision, delicate colour and faultless placing. Often their beauty is enhanced by the Emperor's highly elegant calligraphy, which, we may be sure, was not infrequently applied also as a mark of approval to paintings executed by members of the Academy. A typical product of this sophisticated circle is the famous *The Five-colour Parakeet*, which bears a poem and signature penned by the imperial brush. This exquisitely balanced picture reveals a certain stiffness (much clearer in the original than in the photograph), an anxiety to be correct at all costs – just the qualities we might expect to find in Hui-tsung himself.

The art of flower-painting which Hui-tsung and his academicians practised was not, in origin, wholly Chinese. Buddhist banner-paintings brought from India and Central Asia were richly set about with flowers, painted in a technique which influenced the late sixth-century master Chang Seng-yu. Speaking of some of Chang's paintings in a temple at Nanking, a T'ang author had written, 'All over the gate of the temple "flowers-in-relief" are painted. . . . Such flowers are done in a technique brought here from India. They are painted in vermilion, malachite greens and azurite blues. Looking at them from a distance, one has the illusion that they are [carved] in relief, but close at hand they are seen to be flat.'[3] T'ang Buddhist art is rich in this decorative style of flower-painting, but by the tenth century it had become an art in its own right. Later painters loved to animate their flower studies with birds, and thus 'birds and flowers' (hua-niao) became recognized as an independent category in the repertoire.

The tenth-century master Huang Ch'üan is said to have invented a revolutionary technique of flower-painting at the court of Wang Chien in Chengtu. He would first sketch the outline very delicately in ink, then add colour in layered washes – a style that came to be known as kou-le tien-ts'ai, 'outline filled with colour'. The technique of his contemporary and great rival at Nanking, Hsü Hsi, was quite different. He drew his flowers and leaves swiftly in ink and wash with no outline, adding only a little colour. Later this manner developed into the mo-ku-hua, 'boneless painting'. Huang Ch'üan's style was considered the more skilful and decorative, and eventually became more popular with professionals and court painters, while Hsü Hsi's, because it was based on the free use of brush and ink, found favour among the literati. Huang's son Huang Chü-ts'ai, among others, successfully combined elements of both styles. No original from the hand of Huang Ch'üan or Hsü Hsi survives, but their techniques are still popular with flower-painters today.

A comment by the critic Shen Kua on the work of Huang and his son on the one hand and Hsü on the other throws an interesting light on the standards by which this kind of painting was judged in the Sung Dynasty. 'The two Huangs' flower paintings are marvellous [miao]', he writes, 'in their handling of colours. Their brushwork is extremely fresh and finely detailed. The ink lines are almost invisible, and are supplemented only by washes of light colours. Their sort of painting you might call sketching from life. Hsü Hsi would use his ink and brush to draw in a very broad way, add a summary colouring, and that would be all. With him the spiritual quality is pre-eminent, and one has a special sense of animation. Ch'üan disliked his technique, called his work coarse and ugly, and rejected it as being without style.'

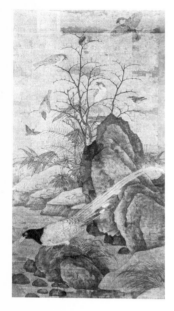

133 Attributed to Huang Chü-ts'ai (933–93). *Pheasant and Sparrows among Rocks and Shrubs.* Hanging scroll. Ink and colour on silk. Sung Dynasty.

LI T'ANG

When, after the disaster of 1125, the Sung shored up the ruins of their house amid the delights of their 'temporary' capital

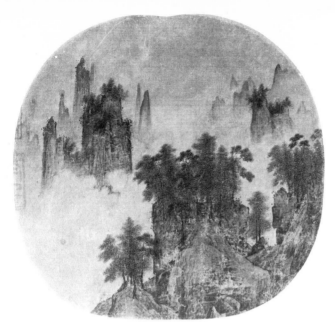

at Hangchow, they set out to recapture the dignity and
splendour of the old life at Kaifeng. At Wu-lin outside the
city a formal Academy of Painting (Hua-yüan) was set up,
for the first and only time in Chinese history. Venerable
masters from the north were assembled there to re-establish
the tradition of court painting, and no national catastrophe,
it seemed, provided that it was ignored, could disturb the
even tenor of their life and art. Or was it that, with the
northern barbarians in occupation of half of China, it was
impossible to tell when the final disaster might come?

Chao Po-chü, who excelled in panoramic landscapes with
figures in the archaistic green and blue style which originated
with Li Ssu-hsün, became a special favourite of Kao-tsung
(1127–62). The classic northern tradition was transformed
and transmitted to the Southern Sung by Li T'ang, doyen of
Hui-tsung's 'Academy'. History credits Li T'ang with a
monumental style based on the *fu-p'i ts'un*, 'axe-cut texture
stroke', a graphic description of his method of, as it were,
hacking out the angular facets of his rocks with the side of
the brush. A powerful landscape in this technique in the
Palace Museum, Taipei, signed and dated equivalent to 1124,
may be a later copy, and it is likely that no original from his
hand survives today. Perhaps the little fan-painting, *A
Myriad Trees on Strange Peaks*, brings us as close to his style as
we will ever get. He was an old man when Kaifeng fell, and
most of his work must have perished with the imperial
collection. But copies, attributed paintings and literary
sources suggest that his style and influence were dominant
in the twelfth century, making him the vital link between
the remote grandeur of Northern Sung and the brilliant
romanticism of Southern Sung painters such as Ma Yüan
and Hsia Kuei.

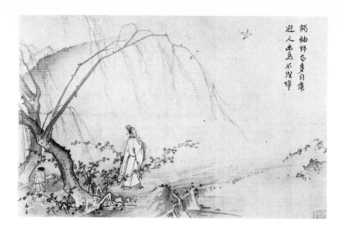

135 Ma Yüan (*fl.* 1190–1225). *On a Mountain Path in Spring*. With a poem written by the Empress Ning. Album-leaf. Ink and slight colour on silk. Sung Dynasty.

MA YÜAN AND HSIA KUEI Perhaps because of its obvious visual and emotional appeal, the work of the 'Ma-Hsia school', as it is called, has come in Western eyes to represent the very quintessence of Chinese landscape-painting, and not only in the West, for this style was to have a profound influence too on the development of landscape-painting in Japan. Its language of expression was not altogether new. We have found an anticipation of its spectacular tonal contrasts in Fan K'uan and Kuo Hsi, its claw-like trees and roots in Li Ch'eng, its axe-strokes in Li T'ang. But in the art of Ma Yüan and Hsia Kuei these elements all appear together, united by a consummate mastery of the brush which would border on mannerism if it were not so deeply infused with poetry. Without this depth of feeling, the style is in itself decorative and easily imitated in its outward aspects – qualities which were to be seized upon by the painters of the Kanō school in Japan. What is new is the sense of space, achieved by pushing the landscape to one side, opening up a vista of limitless distance. There are many night scenes, and the mood is often one of a poetic sadness that hints at the underlying mood of Hangchow in this age of deepening anxiety.

Ma Yüan became a *tai-chao* (Painter in Attendance) at the end of the twelfth century, Hsia Kuei early in the thirteenth. It is not always easy to disentangle the style of one from the other. If we say, looking at the *Four Old Recluses* in Cincinnati attributed to Ma Yüan, that his brushwork is bold and fiery, we will find the same quality even more brilliantly displayed in Hsia Kuei's *Pure and Remote View of Hills and Streams* in the Palace Museum Collection, Taipei. It is hard to believe that this almost violently 'expressionistic' work was painted by a senior member of the Imperial Academy. Both Hsia Kuei and Ma Yüan used Li T'ang's axe-stroke *ts'un* with telling effect; both exploited brilliantly the contrast of black ink against a luminous expanse of mist. All we can say is that, of the two, Ma Yüan generally seems the calmer, the more disciplined and precise; Hsia Kuei the 'expressionist', who may in a fit of excitement seem to stab and hack the silk with his brush. The brilliant virtuosity of his style appealed

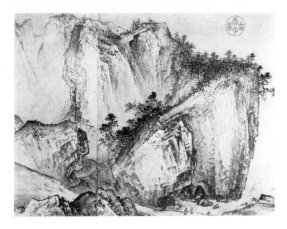

strongly to the Ming painters of the Che school, and there is little doubt that the great majority of the paintings generally attributed to Hsia Kuei are in fact pastiches by Tai Chin and his followers. For there is in the real Hsia Kuei a noble austerity of conception, a terseness of statement, a brilliant counterpoint of wet and dry brush, a sparing and telling use of *ts'un*, which his imitators failed altogether to capture.

The art of Hsia Kuei is not far removed, in the explosive energy of its brushwork, from that of the Ch'an Buddhist masters, who at this time were living not far from the capital in point of distance – their monasteries lay in the hills across the West Lake from Hangchow – but who were in their lives and art far removed from the court and all it stood for. Of these the chief were Liang K'ai, who, after rising to be *tai-chao* under Ning-tsung (1195–1224), retired to a temple, taking with him the brilliant brush style of Hsia Kuei, and Mu-ch'i, who from his monastery, the Liu-t'ung-ssu, dominated the painting of the Hangchow region throughout the first half of the thirteenth century. There was hardly a subject that Mu-ch'i did not touch. Landscapes, birds, tigers, monkeys, *bodhisattvas* – all were grist to his mill. In everything he painted he sought to express an essential nature that was not a matter of form – for his forms may break up or dissolve in mists – but of inner life, which he found because it was in the painter himself. His *Six*

CH'AN PAINTING OF THE
SOUTHERN SUNG DYNASTY

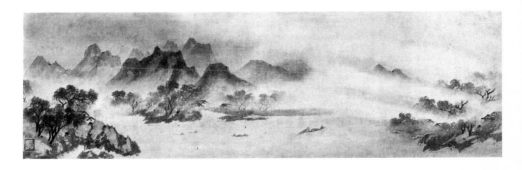

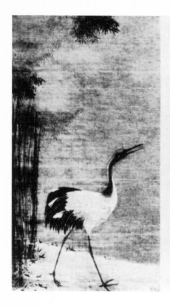
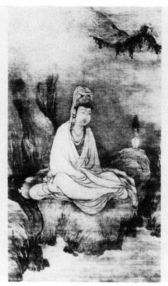
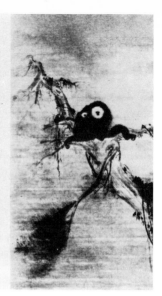

138 Mu-ch'i. *The White-robed Kuanyin.* Hanging scroll. Ink on silk. Sung Dynasty.

Persimmons is the supreme example of his genius for investing the simplest thing with profound significance. Less often recognized is his power of monumental design, shown above all in the central panel of his great triptych in Daitoku-ji, Kyōto, depicting the white-robed Kuanyin seated in meditation amid the rocks, flanked by paintings of a crane in a bamboo grove, and gibbons in the branches of a pine tree. Whether or not these pictures were painted to hang together is immaterial, for, in Ch'an Buddhism, all living things partake of the divine essence. What is most striking about these scrolls, and common to all the best Ch'an painting, is the way in which the artist rivets the viewer's attention by the careful painting of certain key details, while all that is not essential blurs into obscurity, as in the very act of meditation itself. Such an effect of concentration and control was only possible to artists schooled in the disciplined techniques of the Ma-Hsia tradition; the brush style of the literati, for all its spontaneity, was too relaxed and personal to meet such a demand.

DRAGONS   The influence of the academic attitude to art during the Sung Dynasty is revealed in a growing tendency to categorize. The catalogue of the Emperor Hui-tsung's collection, *Hsüan-ho hua-p'u,* for instance, was arranged under ten headings; Taoist and Buddhist themes (which, though less popular than before, still preserved a prestige conferred by tradition); figure-painting (including portraits and *genre*); palaces and buildings (particularly those in the ruled *chieh-hua* style); foreign tribes; dragons and fishes; landscapes; domestic animals and wild beasts (there was a whole school of painters specializing in water-buffaloes); flowers and birds; ink bamboo; and vegetables and fruit. The last category requires no special mention, and bamboo I will leave to the next chapter. But before leaving the subject of Sung painting we must say a word on the subject of dragons. To the 'man in the street' the dragon was a benevolent and generally auspicious creature, bringer of rain and emblem of the Emperor. To the Ch'an Buddhists he was far more than that. When Mu-ch'i painted a dragon suddenly appearing from the clouds, he was depicting a cosmic manifestation and at the same time symbolizing the momentary, elusive vision of Truth which comes to the Ch'an adept. To the Taoists, the dragon was the *Tao* itself, an all-pervading force which momentarily reveals itself to us, only to vanish again and leave us wondering if we had actually seen it at all. 'Hidden in the caverns of inaccessible mountains,' wrote Okakura Kakuzo, 'or coiled in the unfathomable depths of the sea, he awaits the time when he slowly rouses himself to activity. He unfolds himself in the storm clouds; he washes his mane in the blackness of the seething whirlpools. His claws are in the forks of the lightning, his scales begin to glisten in the bark of rain-swept pine trees. His voice is heard in the hurricane which, scattering the withered leaves of the forest, quickens the new spring. The dragon reveals himself only to vanish.'[4] Ts'ao Pu-hsing in the third century had been the first prominent painter to specialize in dragons, but the greatest of all was Ch'en Jung, who combined a successful career as an administrator during the first half of the thirteenth century with a somewhat unorthodox technique as a dragon-painter. His contemporary T'ang Hou tells us that when he was drunk he would give a great shout, seize his cap, soak it with ink and smear on the design with it, afterwards finishing the details with a brush. His celebrated *The Nine Dragons*, painted in 1244, could well have been executed thus, the dragons with his brush, the clouds with his cap; indeed, on the original the imprint of some textile in the clouds can be seen quite clearly. This, the finest dragon-painting in existence, and widely accepted as authentic, is now one of the treasures of the Boston Museum of Fine Arts.

139 Ch'en Jung (*fl.* 1235–*c.* 1260). *The Nine Dragons.* Detail of a handscroll. Ink on paper. Sung Dynasty.

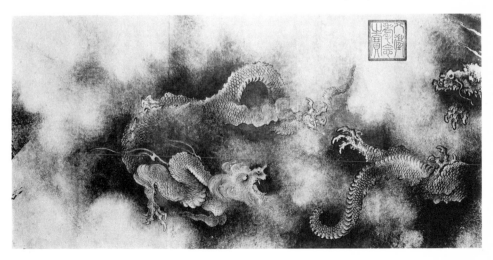

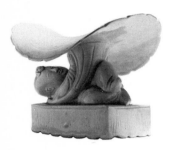

140 Funerary pillow. Ting ware. Porcelain. Sung Dynasty.

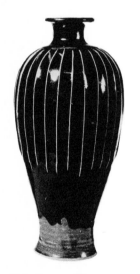

141 Mei-p'ing vase. Honan stoneware with black glaze. Sung Dynasty.

The art of the Sung Dynasty which we admire today was produced by, and for, a social and intellectual élite more cultivated than any other that has existed in Chinese history. The pottery and porcelain made for their use is a natural reflection of their taste. Some T'ang wares may be more robust, Ch'ing wares more refined, but the Sung have a classical purity of form and glaze which holds a perfect balance between the vigour of the earlier wares and the refinement of the later. Although some of the porcelain for the Northern Sung court came from kilns as far away as Chekiang and Kiangsi, the most famous of the Northern Sung *kuan* (official) wares was manufactured in the kilns at Ch'ien-tz'u-ts'un, near Ting-chou in Hopei, where a white porcelain with a greenish tint where it runs thick was already being made in the late T'ang Dynasty. The classical Ting ware is a finely potted, high-fired white porcelain, with a creamy-white glaze which has a brownish tinge where it runs into the 'tear-marks' described in early texts. The floral decoration of earlier pieces, such as the masterly tomb-pillow which I have illustrated, was freely carved in the 'leather-hard' paste before firing; later, more elaborate patterns were impressed in the paste from pottery moulds. As the vessels were fired upside down, the rims of bowls were left unglazed and often had to be bound with bronze or silver. Chinese connoisseurs recognize, in addition to the true *pai* (white) Ting, a fine-grained *fen* (flour) Ting, a *tzu* (purple – actually soya-sauce brown) Ting, and a coarse yellowish *t'u* (earth) Ting. Varieties of Ting and near-Ting, however, are not always easy to distinguish.

The extensive surveys and excavations of the past fifteen years have made it apparent that not only was one type of ware often made in a number of different kilns, with the inevitable local variations in character and quality, but also that one kiln centre might turn out a wide range of products. To take two examples, Fujio Koyama and more recent Chinese investigators discovered in the ruins of the Ting kilns white, black, and persimmon-red glazed porcelain, unglazed painted porcelain, pottery with white slip, with patterns in iron oxide, with carved designs, with black, and with buckwheat brown glaze. The Sung kilns at Hao-pi-chi, T'ang-yin-hsien, Honan, first investigated in 1955, while turning out chiefly plain white wares, also produced coloured wares, white wares with coloured decoration, cups glazed black outside and white inside, a high-quality Chün-type stoneware, and black-glazed vases with vertical yellowish ribs in relief, such as the lovely vessel in the collection of Mrs Alfred Clark. The value and beauty of the Ting wares lies not merely in their glaze and decoration but also in the exquisite purity of their shapes, many of which were copied not only in other Sung kilns but also in the Korean wares of the Koryŏ period. After the fall of Kaifeng in 1127, wares of Ting type were made at Chi-chou in central Kiangsi, very probably by refugee potters who had fled to the south. Before leaving the subject of the white wares, I must also mention the beautiful white stoneware jars and vases found in the ruins of the town of Chü-lu-hsien, between Ting-chou and Tz'u-chou, which was inundated and destroyed when the Yellow River changed its course in 1108. Long immersion in the river mud has given them a dull surface and large uneven crackle, and has stained them with subtle hues of pink and old ivory which by no means mar their beauty.

Since the Sung Dynasty, Chinese connoisseurs have classed Ting-yao as a 'classic' ware of Northern Sung, together with Ju-yao, Chün-yao, and the now legendary Ch'ia-yao, which had a glaze 'blue like the sky after rain'. When the too-fastidious Emperor Hui-tsung decided that, presumably because of its 'tear-drops' and metal rim, Ting-yao was no longer good enough for palace use, kilns were set up to make a new *kuan* ware, both at Ju-chou and within the confines of the capital itself. The latter kilns have long since been buried or swept away in the floods that periodically inundate the Yellow River Valley, and it is not known for certain what kind of porcelain they produced, although the Palace Museum authorities in Taiwan have recently documented a number of fine pieces, close both to Ju and to Hangchow *kuan*, as products of the Kaifeng imperial kilns. Ju-yao, one of the rarest of all Sung porcelains, has been more positively identified. It has a buff or pinkish-yellow body, covered with a bluish-grey glaze with a lavender tint, netted over with a fine crackle like mica. The shapes, chiefly bowls, brush-washers and bottles, are of an exquisite simplicity, matching the quality of the glaze. Ju-chou was also one of several centres in addition to the large factory in T'ung-ch'uan-hsien, north of Sian, which produced 'northern celadon' – an apt name for a stoneware often richly decorated with carved or moulded floral designs under a dull green glaze. A kind of celadon had been made at Yao-yao in T'ung-ch'uan-hsien as early as the Six Dynasties, but when the Sung expanded to absorb Chekiang, production and quality in the Yao-yao kilns seem to have been influenced by the Yüeh potters, some of whom may have been sent to North China.

Much more closely related to Ju, however, is the well-known Chün ware, made not only at Chün-chou and Ju-chou, but also at other centres in the neighbourhood of Hao-pi-chi, Anyang and Tz'u-chou. The finest Chün was of palace quality, and so is sometimes called '*kuan* Chün' by Chinese collectors. The potting is much heavier than that of Ju-yao, however, and myriads of tiny bubbles, which burst on the surface of the thick lavender-blue glaze, give it a seductive softness and warmth. It was the Chün potters who discovered that spots of copper oxidized in the glaze during firing produced crimson and purple splashes, a technique which they used with exquisite restraint. On later varieties of Chün ware, however, such as the numbered sets of

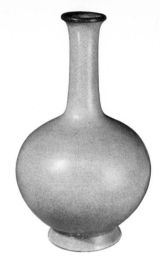

142 Bottle with copper-bound rim. Ju ware. Sung Dynasty.

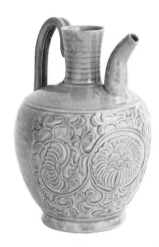

143 Vase. Northern celadon stoneware, with carved decoration under an olive-green glaze. Sung Dynasty.

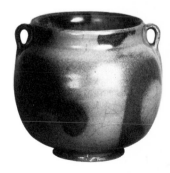

144 Jar. Chün stoneware, covered with a lavender-blue glaze splashed with purple. Sung Dynasty.

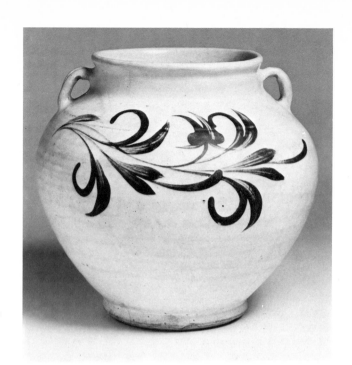

145 Jar. Tz'u-chou stoneware, painted in black under a transparent glaze. Sung Dynasty.

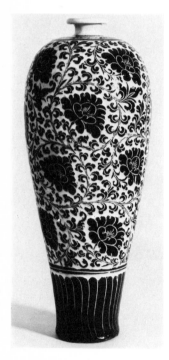

146 Mei-p'ing vase. Tz'u-chou stoneware, with design carved through black to white slip under a transparent glaze. Sung Dynasty.

flower-pots and bulb-bowls made during the Ming Dynasty at Te-hua and Canton, these 'flambé' effects are often used with tasteless extravagance.

The Tz'u-chou wares represent perhaps the most striking example of the extent to which the discoveries of the last twenty years have altered the ceramic picture. Tz'u-chou is a convenient name for a large family of North China stonewares decorated chiefly by painting under the glaze or by carving or incising through a coloured slip. The technique of underglaze painting may have been imported from the Near East, where it had long been known, but the magnificently buoyant shapes and the motifs used in the decoration are purely Chinese. The unaffected grace and confidence of the brush-drawing gives the Tz'u-chou wares an immediate appeal, although until very recently they have been considered too close to a peasant art to command the respect of educated people in China herself.

The kilns at Tz'u-chou are well known, and still active today, but recent Chinese excavation and research have revealed that the 'North China decorated stoneware', as perhaps it ought to be called, was made across the breadth of the country, from Shantung to Szechwan. Of the known kilns, the most important so far excavated, in addition to Tz'u-chou itself, are Hao-pi-chi, already mentioned, the stratified kiln-site at Kuan-t'ai on the Honan–Hopei border, among whose products were a white ware with designs incised or stamped through the glaze on to a darker body, and the kilns at Hsiu-wu (or Chiao-tso), on the Shansi–Honan border, which produced striking vases with floral

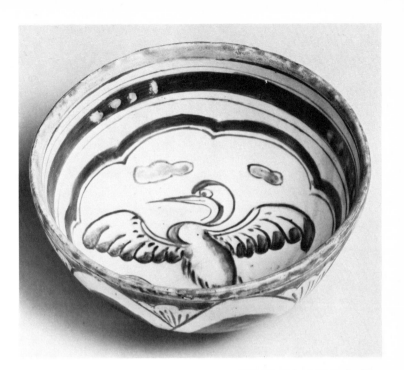

147 Bowl. Tz'u-chou stoneware, decorated with enamels over a creamy-white glaze. Sung Dynasty.

designs reserved on black or boldly carved through a black glaze.

Before the end of the Sung Dynasty, North China potters, at P'a-ts'un in Honan, at Pa-i in Shansi and at Te-chou in Shantung, had developed the revolutionary technique of overglaze painting. Their delightful bowls and dishes, decorated with birds and flowers swiftly sketched in tomato-red, green and yellow over a creamy glaze, are the earliest examples of the enamelling technique which was to become so popular during the Ming Dynasty.

At the fall of the T'ang, the north-east was lost to a Khitan tribe who called their dynasty 'Liao' (907–1124). I have already noted how a 'T'ang revival' school of Buddhist art was flourishing at Yünkang and elsewhere under their patronage, and have assigned the famous ceramic Lohans to this period. Liao sites in Manchuria have yielded fragments of Chün, Ting and Tz'u-chou-type wares, but Japanese scholars and collectors and, more recently, Chinese archaeologists have also recovered large quantities of a distinct local ware which combines something of the *sgraffito* floral decoration of Tz'u-chou with the three-colour glazes and the robust – though now provincial and often ungainly – shapes of the T'ang Dynasty, such as the chicken ewer, pilgrim flask and trumpet-mouthed vase. The finest Liao wares are the equal of Sung porcelains in elegance, and even the rough grave wares, such as the imitation of a leather water-flask carried at the saddle which I have illustrated, have the same spontaneous, unsophisticated charm that we admire in medieval European pottery.

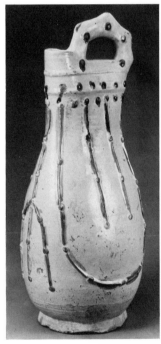

148 Traveller's flask. Stoneware, with cockscomb ornament in green enamel over white glaze. North China. Liao Dynasty.

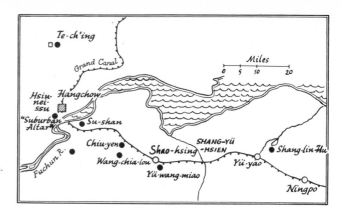

Te-ch'ing

Grand Canal

Miles
0 5 10   20

Hsiu-nei-ssu

Hangchow

"Suburban Altar"

Su-shan

Chiu-yen

Wang-chia-lou

Shao-hsing

Yü-wang-miao

SHANG-YÜ-HSIEN

Yü-yao

Shang-lin-Hu

Ningpo

Fuchun R.

Kiln sites in the Hangchow area.

CERAMICS: SOUTHERN WARES

Among the most striking of the northern wares are those with a black glaze, which used to be called 'Honan *temmoku*'. This name forms a link with South China, for it was in the south that tea-drinking had first become popular during the T'ang Dynasty and it was discovered that a black glaze effectively set off the pea-green colour of the tea. *Temmoku* is the Japanese equivalent of T'ien-mu, a mountain near Hangchow, whence certain of these southern wares were shipped to Japan. The true *temmoku*, made at Chien-an in Fukien as early as the tenth century, consisted almost exclusively of the type of tea-bowls which proved so popular in Japan. They have a dark stoneware body decorated with a thick, oily iron glaze running to big drops at the foot. The colour is basically a very dark brown verging on black, often streaked with blue or a steel-grey, producing marks known as 'hare's fur', or bluish 'oil spots', caused by the coagulation of grey crystals. These were imitated in a rather coarse lustre-less ware made at Chi-chou in Kiangsi, often confusingly called 'Kian ware' in older books, and at other kilns in Fukien such as Kuang-che, Fu-ch'ing and Ch'üan-chou.

When, after a few years at Hangchow, the Southern Sung court began to realize that this was to be more than a temporary halting-place, steps were taken to enlarge the palace and government offices, and to set up factories to manufacture utensils for court use which would duplicate as closely as possible those of the old northern capital. The Supervisor of Parks, Shao Ch'eng-chang, who was in charge of this work, established a kiln near his own office (Hsiu-nei Ssu) on Phoenix Hill just to the west of the palace, which lay at the southern end of the city. There, according to a Sung text, Shao's potters made 'a celadon which was called *Nei-yao* [palace ware]. Its pure body of exceptional fineness and delicacy, its clear and lustrous glaze, have been prized ever since.' The Phoenix Hill area has been repeatedly built over and the kilns have not been discovered, nor is it known how long they were in operation. But before long another imperial factory was set up to the south-west below the suburban Altar of Heaven (Chiao-t'an). This has become a

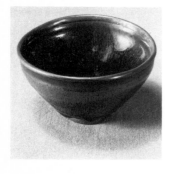

149 Tea-bowl. Fukien *temmoku* stoneware, with black 'hare's fur' glaze. Sung Dynasty.

place of pilgrimage to ceramics enthusiasts, who over the years have picked up quantities of shards of the beautiful 'southern *kuan*' which graces many Western collections. Its dark body is often thinner than the glaze, which is layered, opaque, vitrified and sometimes irregularly crackled, and ranges in colour from a pale bluish green through blue to dove-grey. The ware has an air of courtly elegance combined with quietness and restraint that made it a fitting adornment for the Southern Sung court.

We should not try to draw too sharp a line between Hangchow *kuan* ware and the best of the celadons made at Lung-ch'üan in southern Chekiang. The imperial kilns at Hangchow made a light-bodied ware in addition to the dark, while Lung-ch'üan produced a small quantity of dark-bodied ware as well as the characteristic light grey. It seems certain that the finest Lung-ch'üan celadons were supplied to the court, and could hence be classed as *kuan*.

Probably of all Sung porcelains the celadons are the most widely appreciated – outside China, at least. The name is believed to have been taken from that of Céladon, a shepherd dressed in green who appeared in a pastoral play, *L'Astrée*, first produced in Paris in 1610. These beautiful wares, known to the Chinese as *ch'ing tz'u* (blue-green porcelain), were made in a number of kilns, but those of Lung-ch'üan were the finest, as well as the most abundant, and were, indirectly, the heirs of the Yüeh wares. The light-grey body of Lung-ch'üan ware burns yellowish on exposure in the kiln, and wears an unctuous iron glaze ranging in colour from leaf-green to a cold bluish green, which is sometimes, though by no means always, crackled. Crackle, originally an accidental result of the glaze shrinking more than the body when the vessel cooled after firing, was often exploited for its decorative effect, as in the *ko*-type celadons, in which a closer secondary crackle was also developed. To the finest Lung-ch'üan celadons, which have a lovely cloudy blue-green colour, the Japanese gave the name *kinuta*

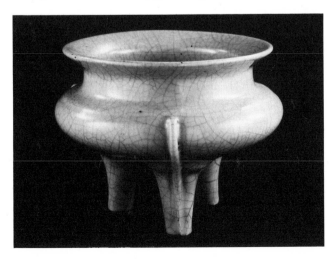

150 Tripod incense-burner. *Kuan* stoneware, carved with crackled bluish-green celadon glaze. Sung Dynasty.

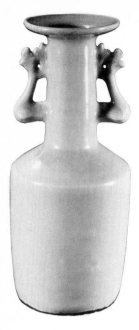

151 Vase. *Kinuta*, Lung-ch'üan stoneware, covered with a grey-green celadon glaze. Sung Dynasty.

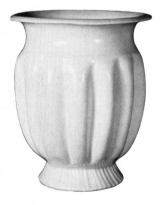

152 Vase. *Ch'ing-pai* ware, white porcelain. Sung Dynasty.

(mallet), perhaps after the shape of a particularly famous vase. Almost every shape appears in the Lung-ch'üan repertoire: many are purely ceramic, but we also encounter adaptations of archaic bronze forms, notably incense-burners in the form of the three- and four-legged *ting* – a mark of that antiquarianism which was now beginning to develop in Chinese court art and was to have an ever-increasing influence on cultivated taste. For the most part celadon relies for its beauty on the perfection of its form and glaze, but the bowls may be subtly decorated with lotus leaves on the outside, baluster vases and jars with flowers moulded in relief under the glaze; while in the fourteenth century spectacular effects were attained by leaving the decorative motifs in raised biscuit relief. We can trace the development of the Chekiang celadon wares through dated pieces well into the Ming Dynasty, when the potting became heavier, the glaze greener and more glassy and the scale more ambitious. From Southern Sung onwards they formed a large proportion of China's export trade. Thousands of shards of Lung-ch'üan ware, for instance, have been picked up on the beaches at Kamakura, near Tokyo. Until the Ming Dynasty, celadons, including much coarser imitations made in other kilns in Kiangsi and Fukien, formed the bulk of China's exports to Indo-China, Borneo, the Philippines, Malaya and Indonesia; while, as every amateur knows, the ware was much in demand among the potentates of the Arab world, because they believed that it would crack or change colour if it came into contact with poison.

Also exported in large quantities (although it was originally a purely domestic ware), was a beautiful translucent porcelain with a granular sugary body and pale bluish glaze. Some doubt as to its respectability in Chinese ceramic history was long caused by the fact that the name for it used in the West is *ying-ch'ing*, a recent term which was invented by Chinese dealers to describe its shadowy blue tint, and for which scholars had searched in vain in Chinese works. In fact its original name, *ch'ing-pai* (bluish white), occurs frequently in texts going back to the Sung Dynasty. Because of its high felspar content, the hard clay could be potted in shapes of wonderful thinness and delicacy. The tradition, which began humbly in the T'ang kilns at Shih-hu-wan some miles to the west of Ching-te-chen, achieved a perfect balance between living form and refinement of decoration in the Sung wares, whose shapes included teapots, vases, stem-cups and bowls, often with foliate rim and dragons, flowers and birds moulded or incised with incredible lightness of touch in the thin paste under the glaze. Already during the Sung Dynasty *ch'ing-pai* wares were being imitated in many kilns in South China, and a good proportion of their output was exported to South-east Asia and the Indonesian Archipelago, where the presence of *ch'ing-pai* or celadon in an archaeological site often provides the most reliable means of dating it.

9 The Yüan Dynasty

During the twelfth century China had come to uneasy terms with her northern neighbours and, after her custom, civilized them. But beyond them, across the deserts of Central Asia, there roamed a horde which C. P. Fitzgerald called 'the most savage and pitiless race known to history' – the Mongols. In 1210 their leader, the great Genghis Khan, attacked the buffer state of Chin, and in 1215 destroyed its capital, Peking. In 1224 he destroyed the Hsi-Hsia, leaving only one-hundredth of the population alive, a disaster by which the north-west was permanently laid waste. Three years later Genghis died, but still the Mongol hordes advanced, and in 1235 they turned southwards into China. For forty years the Chinese armies resisted them, almost un-supported by their own government. But the outcome was inevitable, and when in 1279 the last Sung pretender was destroyed, the Mongols proclaimed their rule over China, calling themselves the 'Yüan'. China was spared the worst of the atrocities which had been visited upon all their other victims, for, as a Khitan adviser had pointed out, the Chinese were more useful alive, and taxable, than dead. But the wars and break-up of the administration left Kubilai master of a weak and impoverished Empire, whose taxpayers had been reduced from a hundred million under the Sung to less than sixty million. Although Kubilai was an able ruler and a deep admirer of Chinese culture, the Mongol administration was not only utterly out of touch with the people but ruthless and corrupt as well. Seven emperors succeeded one another in the forty years following the death of Kubilai in 1294. Chinese discontent with the harsh rule of the last Khan broke into open rebellion in 1348. For twenty years rival bandits and war-lords fought over the prostrate country, which the Mongols had long since ceased to control effectively. Finally, in 1368, the last Khan fled northwards from Peking, the power of the Mongols was broken for ever, and the short, inglorious rule of the Yüan Dynasty was at an end. In conquering China, they had realized the age-long dream of all the nomad tribes, but in less than a century the Chinese drained them of the savage vitality which had made that conquest possible, and threw them back into the desert, an empty husk.

Politically, the Yüan Dynasty may have been brief and inglorious, but it was a period of special interest and importance in the history of Chinese art – a period when men, uncertain of the present, looked both backwards and

153 Aerial view of the heart of Peking. Down the centre runs the lake of the New Summer Palace, Wan-shou-shan; to the right is the moated rectangle of the 'Purple Forbidden City', with the three halls of state, San Ta Tien, clearly visible on the north–south axis. Prospect Hill lies in the rectangle to the north, while to the south is the main gate of the Forbidden City, T'ien-an-men. Since this photograph was taken, in about 1945, the area to the south of T'ien-an-men has been cleared to make a huge square, with the Great Hall of the People on the west side.

forwards. Their backward looking is shown in the tendency, in painting as much as in the decorative arts, to revive ancient styles – particularly those of the T'ang Dynasty, which had been preserved in a semi-fossilized state in North China under the alien Liao and Chin Dynasties. At the same time, the Yüan Dynasty was in several respects revolutionary, for not only were those revived traditions given a new interpretation, but the divorce between the court and the intellectuals, brought about by the Mongol occupation, instilled in the scholar class the conviction that they belonged to a self-contained élite that was not undermined until the mid-twentieth century, and was to have an enormous influence on painting. On the technological level, the brief Yüan period saw several major innovations, such as the introduction of ceramic decoration in under-glaze red and blue, and the carving of lacquer, that were to be fully exploited in succeeding centuries.

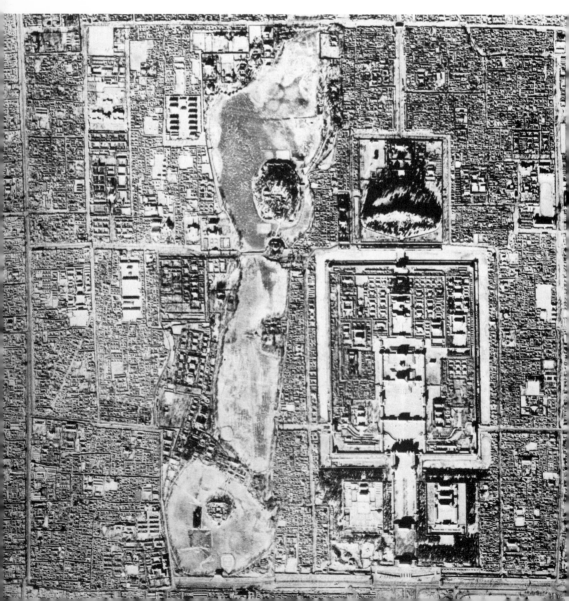

The Mongols themselves dated their Chinese Empire from the year 1263, when Kubilai mounted the throne and established his capital at Peking, which he called Khanbalig, 'the City of the Great Khan'. About twelve years later Marco Polo, then in the Emperor's service, wrote a vivid description of Cambaluc, as he called it, of its palaces, its hall that could dine six thousand people, and its park:

> Between the two walls of the enclosure which I have described there are fine parks and beautiful trees bearing a variety of fruits. There are beasts also of sundry kinds, such as white stags and fallow deer, gazelles and roebucks and fine squirrels of various sorts, with numbers also of that animal that gives the musk, and all manner of other beautiful creatures, insomuch that the whole place is full of them . . . and the Great Khan has caused this beautiful prospect to be formed for the comfort and solace and delectation of his heart.[1]

The architecture and art that Marco Polo is describing are purely Chinese – a magnificent creation of the styles of the Sung Dynasty by craftsmen who perhaps had in mind the glories of Hui-tsung's capital at Kaifeng. All that the Mongols contributed was the colossal scale. Recent excavations in Peking reveal that the Yüan capital was even larger than the Ming city established when the Emperor Yung-lo moved his seat of power back to Peking in 1417. A little Yüan work still survives, the remains of the Yüan city walls and gates have been traced, and the foundations of several noblemen's

The Three Great Halls, San Ta Tien, of the Imperial Palace, Peking, looking south.

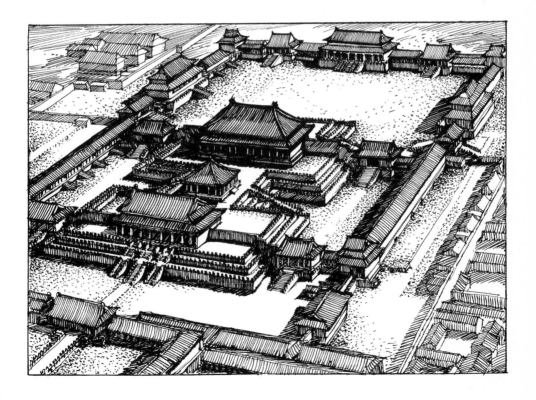

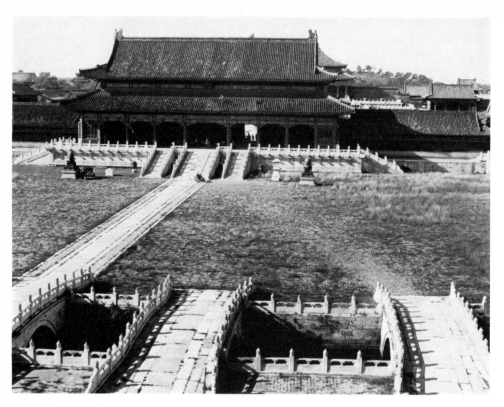

154 Peking: the Forbidden City, looking north from the Wu-men to the T'ai-ho-men. A corner of the T'ai-ho-tien is visible beyond. Ming and Early Ch'ing Dynasties.

mansions excavated, one containing a small hoard of blue and white porcelain.

The city that we see today is the work of Yung-lo and his Ming and Ch'ing successors. The Ming capital, which came to be called the 'Tartar City', after its occupation by the Manchus in 1644, is actually smaller than that laid out by the Mongols, though the total area was greatly increased again when the Manchus created to the south the 'Chinese City' for the native inhabitants. Peking consists of a city within a city within a city. Surrounded by a wall fifteen miles long, the Tartar City comfortably holds the 'Imperial City' (with a perimeter of six and a half miles), in the heart of which lies the 'Purple Forbidden City' – the Imperial Palace itself. At the extreme southern end of a north–south axis that stretches for seven and a half miles lie the three-tiered marble Altar of Heaven and the circular Ch'i-nien-tien, Hall of Annual Prayers – the 'Temple of Heaven', whose blue-tiled roofs are familiar to every visitor to Peking.

Ancient Chou ritual, to which the Ming and Ch'ing rulers rigidly conformed, had prescribed that the Son of Heaven should rule from 'three courts'. Accordingly, the heart of the Forbidden City is dominated by three great halls of state, the San Ta Tien, set one behind the other at the climax of the great vertical axis. The first from the south, and the largest, is the T'ai-ho-tien (Hall of Supreme Harmony), used by the Emperor for his grander audiences, raised on a huge platform and approached by marble stair-cases. Behind it lies the waiting hall, Chung-ho-tien (Hall of Middle Harmony), while beyond is the Pao-ho-tien (Hall of Protecting Harmony), used for state banquets. The private apartments, offices of state, palace workshops and gardens occupy the northern half of this vast enclosure. Not many of the palace buildings we see today are the original structures, however. The T'ai-miao (Grand Ancestral Shrine) is indeed Ming, having been rebuilt in 1464 after a fire; but the history of the T'ai-ho-tien is more typical. First built by Yung-lo in 1427, it was largely rebuilt on the same plan in 1645, while a further reconstruction was started in 1669 and not finished till thirty years later. It was again rebuilt in 1765, since when it has been frequently restored and repainted, though so conservative were the Ch'ing architects that it is unlikely that they departed much from the Ming original – which was itself a cautious repetition of the style of the fourteenth century. Indeed, from Yüan times onwards, Chinese architecture became less and less adven-turous. Gone are the daring experiments in quadripartite gables, spiral canopies and dynamic bracketing that give such interest and vitality to Sung architecture. Now each building is a plain rectangle. The eaves have become so heavily loaded with unnecessary carpentry that the architect has to place an extra colonnade under their outer edge to support the weight, thus making superfluous the elaborate canti-levered system of brackets and *ang*, which now shrinks away to a decorative and meaningless frieze or is masked behind a band of scroll-work suspended from the eaves. The splendour of the Forbidden City lies not in its details, but rather in its rich colour, the magnificently simple sweep of its roofs and the stupendous scale of its layout. These build-ings were all of timber. A few barrel-vaulted stone or brick temple halls were built in the late sixteenth century, but, as before, the use of the vault and dome was largely confined to tombs, a typical example being the tomb of the Wan-li Emperor in the Western Hills, the excavation of which, completed in 1958, occupied a large team of Chinese archaeo-logists for two full years.

Like other invaders before them, the Mongols supported the Buddhists as a matter of policy. They were particularly attracted to the esoteric and magical practices of the Tibetan Lamaists, who were encouraged to set up their temples in Peking. The Buddhist architecture, sculpture and painting produced by Chinese craftsmen under their patronage represents no real advance upon that of the Sung Dynasty, except perhaps in sheer scale and magnificence. The truly significant developments in the arts were the work of the literati who had retired from public life, and spent their enforced leisure in the writing of a new kind of fiction and drama, still popular today, which has permanently enriched Chinese literature. With few exceptions, the great painters

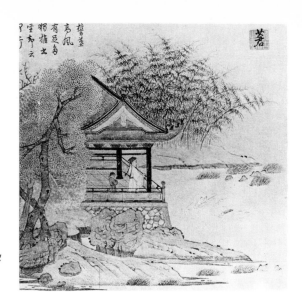

155 Ch'ien Hsüan (*c.* 1235–1301).
*The Fourth-century Calligrapher Wang
Hsi-chih Watching Geese.* Detail of a
handscroll. Ink and colour on paper.
Yüan Dynasty.

of the age also put themselves beyond their conquerors' reach.

Ch'ien Hsüan (*c.* 1235–after 1300), already middle-aged when the Sung Dynasty fell, lived out his life in seclusion. Two small album-paintings, of a squirrel and a sparrow, show him (if indeed they are his) as an exponent of Southern Sung *intimisme*; but in his gentle way he was a revolutionary too. For he was perhaps the first major Chinese painter, apart from the eccentric Mi Fu, who deliberately sought inspiration in the past. His choice of the archaic T'ang style for his charming handscroll of the calligrapher Wang Hsi-chih watching geese, and indeed of the very subject itself, may be seen both as a repudiation of the Sung culture that had betrayed itself, and as the beginning of the creative reinterpretation of the art of the past that was to become henceforward a major preoccupation of the scholar-painters.

It would be strange indeed if so splendid a court as that of Kubilai Khan had had in its service no painters of talent, and in Chao Meng-fu (1254–1322) the Emperor found a man ideally suited to bridge the gulf that lay between his régime and the Chinese educated class. Chao was a descendant of the first Sung Emperor, and had already served the old dynasty in a minor post for several years when Kubilai appointed him. His first job was the writing of memorials and proclamations, but he soon rose to the rank of Cabinet Minister, confidential adviser to the Emperor, and Secretary to the Hanlin Academy. Though he often regretted his decision to collaborate, it was men of his kind who civilized the Mongols and thus, indirectly, encompassed their eventual downfall. Chao Meng-fu was also a great calligrapher, versed in all the styles from the archaic 'old seal' script, through the clerical (*li*) style, the standard (*k'ai*) style, to the running draft character.

I have said little in this book about the eloquent and exacting art of calligraphy, an art whose finer points can only be appreciated with long study and training. 'Affection for the written word', wrote Chiang Yee, 'is instilled from childhood in the Chinese heart.' From the merchant who hoists up his newly written shop-sign with ceremony and incense to the poet whose soul takes flight in the brilliant sword-dance of the brush, calligraphy is revered above all other arts. Not only is a man's writing a clue to his temperament, his moral worth and his learning, but the uniquely ideographic nature of the Chinese script has charged each individual character with a richness of content and association the full range of which even the most scholarly can scarcely fathom.

The illustrations show the main stages in the development of the Chinese script from the earliest known writing, the crude pictographs and ideographs scratched on the oracle bones (*chia-ku-wen*) and sunk in the ritual bronzes (*chin-wen*) of the Shang Dynasty. After the fall of the Shang, this script, which most probably derived its forms from writing on clay with a stylus, evolved into the monumental 'big seal' (*ta-chuan*) script seen on the long bronze inscriptions of the Middle Chou period.

As China expanded and fragmented during the Warring States period a number of regional variants of the *ta-chuan* script inevitably evolved. These were standardized, with everything else, by the Ch'in Chief Minister Li Ssu in the form called 'small seal' (*hsiao-chuan*). This is still used for seal-carving today, but the strokes are too even and regular to be easily made with the brush. With the fall of Ch'in, the seal script went out of fashion (except for formal and ritual purposes), and was replaced by the 'clerical script' (*li-shu*), a style which for the first time really conveyed the supple rhythm of the Chinese brush, which was greatly improved during the Han Dynasty.

Some Chinese characters have as many as twenty and more strokes. According to tradition, it was the need for a script that could be written quickly in the heat of battle that gave birth to the highly cursive 'draft script' (*ts'ao-shu*). In fact, some such abbreviated script must have been in existence for some time for practical and commercial uses, but in the Han it developed into an art form in its own right. Indeed, in the turbulent post-Han period it became, in company with the 'intellectual Taoism' fashionable at the time, something of a cult among the literati. Meanwhile, the rather formal and angular Han *li-shu* was evolving naturally into the more flowing and harmonious 'regular script' (*k'ai-shu*, or *cheng-shu*) which has, with its variants, remained the standard form, learned by every child, up to the present day.

The great calligrapher Wang Hsi-chih, a contemporary of Ku K'ai-chih in Nanking, developed a suave and fluent *k'ai-shu*, and a more cursive form derived from it (the *hsing-shu*, 'running script'), in contrast to the northern style

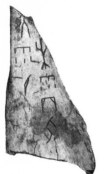

156 Oracle bone,
from Anyang.
Sung Dynasty.

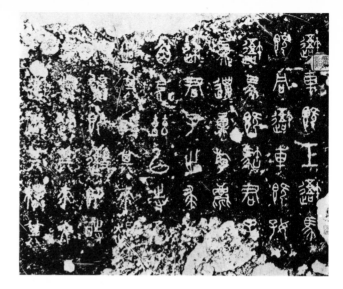

157 *Chuan-shu* script. Rubbing from one of the 'Stone Drums'.
Chou Dynasty.

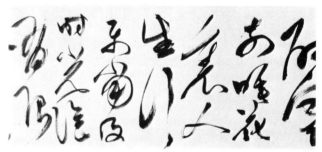

159 *Ts'ao-shu* script. Ch'en Shun (1483–1544): part of the inscription
on his *Studies from Life*, 1538. Handscroll. Ink on paper. Ming Dynasty.

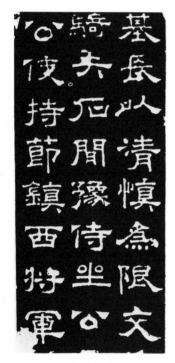

158 *Li-shu* script. Rubbing from a
stone slab.

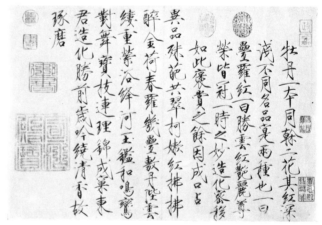

160 *K'ai-shu* script. The Emperor Hui-tsung (reigned 1101–25). Part
of his *Poem on the Peony*, written in the 'thin gold' (*shou-chin*) style.
Handscroll. Ink on paper. Sung Dynasty.

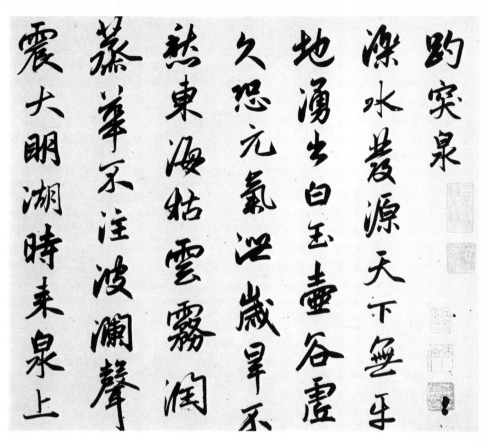

跑突泉
深水發源天下無乎
地湧出白玉壺谷靈
久恐元氣泄歲旱不
熱東海姑雲霧潤
蒸華不注波瀾聲
震大明湖時来泉上

161 *Hsing-shu* script. Chao Meng-fu (1254–1322): part of his *Pao-t'u Spring Poem*. Handscroll. Ink on paper. Yüan Dynasty.

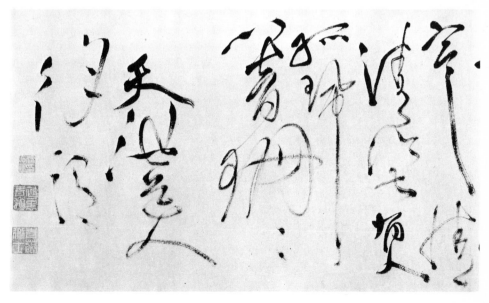

162 *K'uang-ts'ao-shu* script. Hsü Wei (1521–93): poem. Handscroll. Ink on paper. Ming Dynasty.

of the Wei Dynasty, which continued to preserve something of the strength and angularity of the old Han *li-shu*. Through the Six Dynasties the two traditions, southern and northern, suave and angular, developed side by side. When China was reunited under the Sui and T'ang some great calligraphers, notably Yen Chen-ch'ing, succeeded in reconciling the somewhat archaic power of the northern style with the elegant fluidity of the southern.

By this time the main traditional schools were well established. Beyond them lay the calligraphy of the individualists, Zen adepts, Taoist eccentrics and drunkards, each of whom created his own style of *k'uang-* (crazy) *ts'ao-shu*, in which energy, oddity and illegibility competed for the honours. A gentleman in Chao Meng-fu's position might admire writing of this kind, but he would be very unlikely to practise it himself.

CHAO MENG-FU   Chao Meng-fu's popular fame rests not only on his calligraphy, however, but also on his almost legendary skill in the art of painting horses, so much so that almost any good example with a respectable claim to antiquity is attributed to him. As Court Painter to the Mongols it would be surprising if his *œuvre* had *not* contained a number of pictures of the animal so dear to their hearts. But it is chiefly as a landscape-painter that Chao Meng-fu must be remembered. He might, indeed, have said of himself, with Cézanne, 'I am the primitive of the way I have discovered.' He occupies a pivotal position in the history of Chinese landscape-painting, for, living at a time when the Sung tradition had exhausted itself, or exploded into Zen gestures with the brush, he united a direct, spontaneous expression of feeling with a deep reverence for the antique. Looking back beyond the orthodox Sung styles, he rediscovered the poetry and the brushwork of the long-neglected 'southern' manner of Tung Yüan and Chü-jan. In doing so, he opened the way not only for the next generation of Yüan amateur painters –

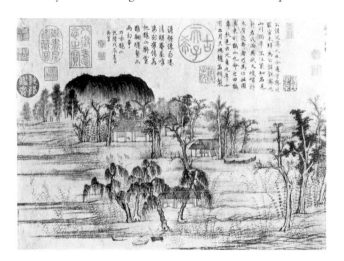

163 Chao Meng-fu (1254–1322). *The Autumn Colours on the Ch'iao and Hua Mountains*. Detail of a handscroll dated 1295. Ink and colours on paper. Yüan Dynasty.

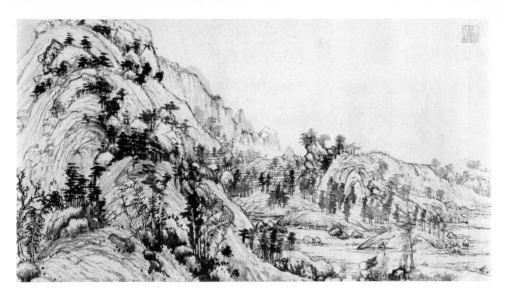

notably the 'Four Masters' discussed below – but for almost all subsequent scholarly landscape-painting up to the present day. In his most famous surviving landscape, painted for a friend to remind him of his homeland, Chao Meng-fu, with dry scholarly wit, combines references to the quaintly archaic landscape style of the T'ang Dynasty and to the broad, calm vision of Tung Yüan.

164 Huang Kung-wang (1269– 1354). *Living in the Fu-ch'un Mountains*. Detail of a handscroll dated 1350. Ink on paper. Yüan Dynasty.

The movement of which Chao Meng-fu was the initiator found its fulfilment half a century later in the work of the Four Great Masters of the Yüan Dynasty, Huang Kung-wang, Ni Tsan, Wu Chen and Wang Meng. The oldest was Huang Kung-wang (1269–1354), whose greatest, and perhaps only, surviving work, is the handscroll, *Living in the Fu-ch'un Mountains*, in the Palace Museum Collection, Taipei. Little is known about his career except that for a time he held a minor official post, and that he retired to a life of scholarship, teaching painting and poetry in his native Chekiang. His masterpiece was painted slowly, as the mood took him, over a period of three years, being finished in 1350. The treatment is magnificently broad, relaxed and unaffected, with not the least hint of the decorative silhouette, the 'one-corner composition' and other mannerisms of the Hangchow Academy. We feel that this is the painter himself speaking from the depths of his heart. Colophons by the Ming painters Shen Chou and Tung Ch'i-ch'ang both mention Tung Yüan and Chü-jan as having inspired him, but the spontaneity of his touch shows clearly that Huang Kung-wang has caught the spirit of antiquity without becoming its slave.

This noble simplicity of utterance was carried even further by Ni Tsan (1301–74), a wealthy country gentleman who, to escape ruinous taxation, spent his later years drifting in a houseboat through the lakes and hills of south-eastern

THE FOUR GREAT MASTERS OF LANDSCAPE-PAINTING

187

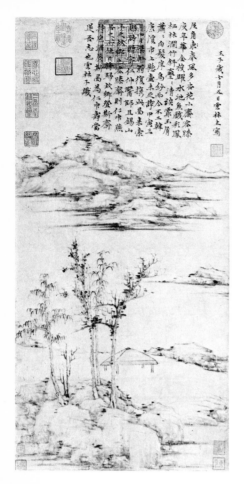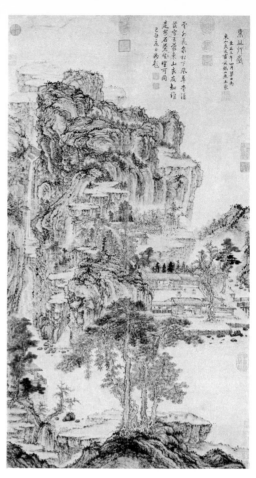

165 Ni Tsan (1301–74). *The Jung-hsi Studio*. Hanging scroll. Ink on paper. Yüan Dynasty.

166 Wang Meng (died 1385). *Thatched Halls on Mount T'ai*. Hanging scroll. Ink and colour on paper. Yüan Dynasty.

Kiangsu, lodging at monasteries and staying with friends. The establishment of the Ming Dynasty in 1368 enabled him to return to his old home and die in peace. To the Ming *wen-jen* he was the ideal type of the untrammelled scholar-painter. If Huang Kung-wang was austere, then what word can we use to describe Ni Tsan? A few bare trees on a rock, a few hills across the water, an empty pavilion; that is all. The forms are spare and simple. The ink is dry and of an even greyness, touched here and there by sparsely applied *tien* (dots) set down, very black, with the side of the brush: it was said of Ni Tsan that 'he was as economical of ink as if it were gold'. No concessions are made to the viewer; no figures, no boats or clouds enliven the scene, and nothing moves. The silence that pervades the picture is that which falls between friends who understand each other perfectly. The innumerable imitations of his style produced by later artists show clearly how much strength is hidden in his apparent weakness, how much skill in his fumbling with the brush, what richness of content in his emptiness.

Of quite a different type was Wang Meng, whose turbulent, congested landscapes seem to embody something of the violence of the times he lived in. He had held office under the Mongols, served as a magistrate after the Ming restoration, and died in prison in 1385. He was a master of a close-knit texture made up of tortuous, writhing lines and a rich variety of *ts'un*; but though he seems to leave nothing out, his touch is sensitive and his composition clearly articulated. He is one of the few Chinese painters – Shih-ch'i is perhaps another – who, though using a brush technique of restless intensity, can achieve an effect of monumental repose.

A gratifying number of great paintings of the Yüan Dynasty have survived to testify to the remarkable revolution by which these and other gifted men broke free from the conventions of Southern Sung and set Chinese painting upon a new path. Moreover, the divorce which occurred under the Mongols between the court and its patronage on the one hand and the scholar-painters on the other was to remain a feature of the painting of the Ming and Ch'ing Dynasties. It goes without saying that the divorce between the culture of the literati and that of the masses was even more complete, to the impoverishment of both. It is with the Yüan painters that the intensely intellectual and literary associations of landscape-painting come to the fore. Now it becomes customary for the painter himself to write a poem or inscription on the painting; this may be joined by others written by friends and later admirers till the picture is almost obliterated under inscriptions and seals which, far from ruining it in Chinese eyes, may greatly enhance its value.[2] From now on, also, painters of the literary school much prefer to paint, like the calligraphers, on paper, which is more absorbent than silk and consequently responds more readily to the touch of the brush.

It is not surprising that the difficult art of bamboo-painting should have found special favour in the Yüan Dynasty, for it was a natural subject for the proud and independent *wen-jen*, who lived out their secluded lives far from the Mongol court. To them, indeed, the bamboo was itself a symbol of the true gentleman, pliant yet strong, who maintains his integrity unsullied no matter how low the adverse winds of circumstance may bend him. The lithe grace of its stalk and the dashing swordpoint of its leaves offered the perfect subject to his brush; but, above all, the painting of bamboo in monochrome ink brought the painter closest to that most difficult of arts, calligraphy. In painting bamboo, the form and place of every leaf and stalk must be clearly adumbrated; the awkward junctures cannot be hid in mist, as in landscape-painting; the gradations from black ink in the near leaves to pale in the distance must be precisely judged, the balance of stalks to leaves, of leaves to empty space, exactly struck. Having achieved this, the painter must still know how the bamboo grows, and give to his own the springing movement of the living plant. A great bamboo-painting is a virtuoso performance of a very high order.

BAMBOO-PAINTING

The art had first become fashionable during the Six Dynasties,[3] when it was the custom, except when painting on a very small scale, to outline the stem and leaves in ink and fill them with body-colour. This painstaking technique was chiefly handed down by the academicians, though the Sung artist Ts'ui Po and the fourteenth-century master Wang Yüan also used it occasionally. Bamboo-painting seems to have gone somewhat out of fashion during the T'ang Dynasty (Hui-tsung had no T'ang specimens in his collection), but had become widely popular by the time of the Northern Sung, when its greatest exponents were Wen T'ung and the poet and calligrapher Su Tung-p'o. During the Yüan Dynasty several of the great literati were accomplished painters of bamboo in monochrome ink, notably Ni Tsan and Chao Meng-fu, although in this most exacting art the latter had a rival in his wife Kuan Tao-sheng, one of China's greatest woman painters. Li K'an (c. 1260–1310), who took as his master Wen T'ung, devoted his whole life to bamboo, which he studied both as an amateur botanist and as a painter. His illustrated manual on the bamboo, *Chu-p'u hsiang-lu*, became an essential tool in the hands of every practitioner, as well as providing the starting-point for all later writers on the subject. A more natural and spontaneous rendering of the subject than Li K'an ever achieved is the little album-leaf by Wu Chen which I have illustrated, remarkable for its economy of statement and subtle union of the twin arts of painting and calligraphy.

167 Wu Chen (1280–1354). *Bamboo.* Leaf from an album dated equivalent to 1350. Ink on paper. Yüan Dynasty.

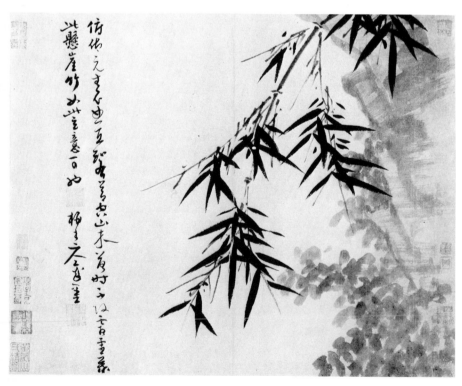

10 The Ming Dynasty

The ferment into which Central China had sunk as the Mongols lost control of the country was finally resolved when in 1368 Chu Yüan-chang, in turn shepherd, monk, bandit, war-lord and emperor, sent his armies north to occupy Peking, from which the last Yüan ruler had fled. He proclaimed himself Emperor of the Ming Dynasty, set up his capital in Nanking, and within four years had not only recovered much of the territory held by the T'ang at the height of their power, but had extended his control over the Trans-Baikal region and Manchuria as well. He built at Nanking a capital with a city wall twenty miles in circumference, the longest in the world, and under him and his successor Central and South China enjoyed a new importance and prosperity. But in 1417 the third Emperor, the usurper Yung-lo,[1] moved his capital back to Peking, whence he had received his chief support in his struggle for power, and it was he who rebuilt it on the scale we see today. But Peking, on two counts, was a bad site: it was situated too far to the north of China's new economic centre of gravity, the Yangtse Valley; it was also highly vulnerable. For China's northern enemies – now the Manchus – had only to cross the Great Wall to be at the gates of the city. The troubles that beset the Ming Dynasty throughout its subsequent history were largely due on the one hand to the remoteness of the capital from the parts of China that mattered most – the centre and south – and on the other to the constant tension along the Great Wall, which lay only forty miles from Peking. Yung-lo was aggressive and secured the frontier, but his successors were weak and corrupt, the victims of eunuchs at court and rebellions in the provinces, and before long the northern defences were left unguarded.

I have already drawn a parallel between the Warring States and classical Greece on the one hand and Han China and ancient Rome on the other. It is said that history never repeats itself, but the similar relationship of Ming China to Sung is too close to be passed over. For the mixture of power and corruption, grandeur and lack of imagination that characterized the Roman Empire was equally marked during the Ming Dynasty, which took as its model not the weak and dreamy Sung, whom they despised, but the splendour, the vigour – and, be it said, the occasional vulgarity – of T'ang. In the early fifteenth century Ming China was immensely powerful. Her navies roamed the southern seas under the remarkable Admiral Cheng Ho, a eunuch in high favour

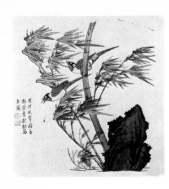

168 Colour woodblock print from the 'Kaempfer series'. Seventeenth century.

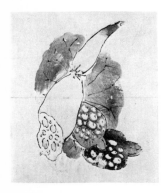

169 Colour woodblock print from the *Shih-chu-chai hua-p'u* (*Treatise on the Paintings and Writings of the Ten Bamboo Studio*). Ming period, early seventeenth century.

with the Emperor. But Cheng Ho was, characteristically, not bent on conquest; his five expeditions between 1405 and 1433 were for the purpose of showing the flag, making alliances and opening up trade-routes – and, incidentally, collecting curiosities for the entertainment of the court. China had no other interest in the outside world. Before the end of the century, however, Vasco da Gama had rounded the Cape of Good Hope; by 1509 the Portuguese were in Malacca and by 1516 in Canton, and China was finally forced to take account of the Western barbarians by reason of their atrocious conduct round her own shores.

The splendour of the Ming court concealed a creeping paralysis. Officials, selected by civil service examinations which centred round the stultifying complexities of the 'eight-legged essay', became increasingly conservative and conventional in outlook. The energies of savants at court were devoted less to original scholarship than to the preparation of such vast works as the *Yung-lo ta-tien*, an encyclopaedia in 11,095 volumes compiled between 1403 and 1407. The Sung emperors had been men of taste and education, able to inspire the best in their scholars and painters; the Ming emperors were for the most part ruffians, usurpers or weak victims of court intrigue. As a result, the palace tradition in painting petered out in a frozen academicism, and for significant developments we must look not to the court, but to the scholars, collectors and amateurs, many of them men of independent means, who carried on the tradition of the *wen-jen* of the Yüan Dynasty. This is the age of the gentleman's country estate, of garden-designing as a pastime for scholar and painter, of connoisseurship and of the great private collections such as those of Hsiang Mo-lin (1525–90) and of Liang Ch'ing-piao (1620–91), whose seal on a painting – if genuine – is often all that the modern collector requires to attest to its authenticity. It was these and other private collectors, rather than the Ming emperors, who preserved the remaining masterpieces of Sung and Yüan, some of which were to find their way back into the imperial collection in the eighteenth century.

COLOUR PRINTING

Bibliophiles also collected paintings, and repaired, remounted and annotated them, while the association between books and pictures became even closer with the development of wood-block illustrations in colour. The earliest colour printing known in China – indeed, in the world – is a two-colour frontispiece to a Buddhist *sūtra* scroll, dated 1346. Under the Ming, erotic books were illustrated in line blocks using up to five colours. One of the first books to include full-colour printing was the *Ch'eng-shih mo-yüan* (*Mr Ch'eng's Miscellany*), published in 1606, for which a few of the monochrome illustrations were copied from prints given to the author by the great Jesuit missionary Matteo Ricci.

The art of colour printing reached its peak in the rare group of anonymous seventeenth-century prints known as the 'Kaempfer Series', after an early collector of them, and in the *Shih-chu-chai shu-hua p'u* (*Treatise on the Paintings and Writings of the Ten Bamboo Studio*), published in 1633. Thereafter, handbooks on the art of painting as a pastime were to proliferate, the most famous being the *Chieh-tzu-yüan hua-chüan* (*Painting Manual of the Mustard Seed Garden*), first published in five parts in 1679, and still used as a technical primer by Chinese students and amateurs today.

At the Ming court there was no personality of the stature of Chao Meng-fu to mediate between the academicians and the literati, who kept their distance and made no attempt to influence court art for the better. The Ming emperors, following the T'ang model, made the Bureau of Painting a subdivision of the Hanlin Academy, but it was no longer the centre of culture and art that it had been in former times. It was set up in the Jen-chih Palace within the Imperial City, and a special office under the Directorate of Palace Eunuchs was established to control it. Painters were honoured with high military titles – to distinguish them from civil officials – and treated with great favour. This favour, however, depended upon absolute obedience to a rigid code of rules and regulations. Even though several of the emperors set out to rival Hui-tsung as patrons, and one, the Hsüan-te Emperor (Hsüan-tsung, 1426–35), was a gifted painter himself, the task of the academicians was simply to establish a new nationalistic art on the T'ang model. They lived, moreover, literally in terror of their lives. Chou Wei, a gentleman-painter, was executed through the slander of his colleagues; Sheng Chu, because in a wall-painting he inadvertently insulted the Emperor; while Tai Chin was dismissed, to die in poverty, because he had painted the garment of a fisher-man red, the colour reserved for officials. Under such circum-stances it is astonishing that any good work was produced at all.

The most talented of the court painters was Pien Wen-chin (*c.* 1400–40), who specialized in painting birds and flowers in the careful, decorative, outline-filled-with-colour style of the Five Dynasties master Huang Ch'üan. In his day he was considered one of the three greatest artists living; and, indeed, his works have a delicacy and perfection of drawing and colour which link him rather to Hui-tsung than to any of the host of decorators who turned out paint-ings by the hundred to adorn the innumerable rooms of the Palace. Of these the most gifted was the late fifteenth-century painter Lü Chi, whose magnificently decorative compositions, rich in colour, definite and precise in form, conservative in style, were exactly suited to the taste of his imperial patrons. In landscape, the models for the aca-demicians were Ma Yüan and Hsia Kuei, partly because they too had been academicians, partly because the basis of their work, like that of the flower-painters, was not self-expression but technique, and technique could be learnt. Ni

MING COURTLY AND
PROFESSIONAL PAINTING

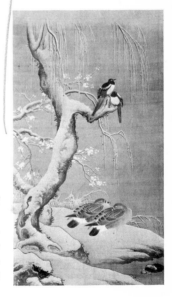

170 Lü Chi (late fifteenth to early sixteenth century). *A Pair of Wild Geese on a Snowy Bank.* Hanging scroll. Ink and colour on silk. Ming Dynasty.

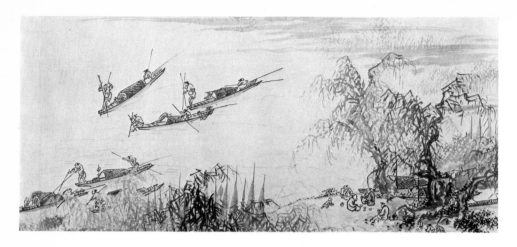

171 Tai Chin (*c.* 1390–1460). *Fishermen.* Detail of a handscroll. Ink and colour on paper. Ming Dynasty.

Tuan, for example, modelled himself on Ma Yüan, Chou Wen-ching on both Ma Yüan and Hsia Kuei, Li Tsai – who is said to have impressed the great Japanese landscape-painter Sesshu – on Ma Yüan and Kuo Hsi. In their works the element of mystery in the Sung romantics has hardened into a brilliant eclecticism.

Among the court painters in the early years of the fifteenth century was Tai Chin (Tai Wen-chin), who, like his colleagues, based his style on that of the Southern Sung Academy. But he was too gifted and independent a spirit to submit to official dictatorship, and retired to his native Chekiang, where he remained for the rest of his life, and where his influence was so wide as to give the name of his province to a very loosely connected group of professional landscape-painters. The Che school, as it was called, embodied the forms and conventions of the Ma-Hsia tradition but treated them with a quite unacademic looseness and freedom, as is shown for instance in the detail from Tai Chin's handscroll, *Fishermen*, in the Freer Gallery, Washington, D.C. Other outstanding artists of the Che school – who, however, had no connection with Tai Chin himself – were Wu Wei and Chang Lu, both of whom specialized in figures in a landscape setting. At the very end of the dynasty, the Che school enjoyed a brief final flowering in the elegant and eclectic art of Lan Ying (1578–1660).

PAINTING OF THE LITERATI: THE WU SCHOOL

Meanwhile, as during the Yüan Dynasty, the amateur tradition continued to flourish among the scholarly gentlemen of Kiangsu, notably those of Wu-hsien, which gave its name to an important school of landscape-painting, the Wu school. Although by no means the first of this group, Shen Chou (1427–1509) and Wen Cheng-ming (1470–1559) were its greatest ornaments. Shen Chou, who came of a family of scholars and painters, lived out his life in comfortable retirement, the very embodiment of the *wen-jen* ideal. He steeped himself in the spirit of the Northern Sung masters, but modelled his own style more particularly on Huang Kung-wang and Ni Tsan, whom he copied assiduously. His well-known landscapes in the manner of Ni Tsan are extremely revealing of the change that was coming over the literary men's art during the Ming Dynasty; for while Ni Tsan is almost forbiddingly plain and austere, Shen Chou is something of an extrovert, who cannot help infusing a human warmth into his paintings. He also worked with superb ease and confidence in the manner of Wang Meng and Wu Chen. But Shen Chou was no mere copyist. He distilled a style that is uniquely his own. Whether in long panoramic landscapes, tall mountain scrolls or small album-paintings, his brush-work, seemingly so casual, is in fact firm and confident, his detail crystal clear yet never obtrusive, his figures – like those of Canaletto – reduced to a kind of shorthand yet full of character, his composition open and informal yet perfectly integrated; and when he uses colour he does so with an exquisite freshness and restraint. It is not surprising that he became so popular, not only with the literati of his own time but also with modern connoisseurs. His debt to Huang Kung-wang is subtly evoked both in the style of the album-leaf which I have illustrated and in the subject, a self-portrait, *Returning Home from the Land of the Immortals*, with, as his companion, a crane who might be the spirit of Crazy Old Huang himself. Above, Shen Chou writes:

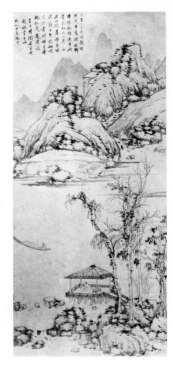

172 Shen Chou (1427–1509). *Landscape in the Manner of Ni Tsan.* Hanging scroll. Ink on paper. Ming Dynasty, 1484.

> With crane and lute aboard, I am homeward bound across
> the lake;
> White clouds and red leaves are flying together.
> My home lies in the very depths of the mountains,
> Among the bamboos, the sound of reading, a tiny couch
> and a humble gate.[2]

Such album-leaves are full of a very human charm, and it is only when we compare Shen Chou with Huang Kung-wang or Wu Chen that we realize that something of their grandeur and breadth of vision is lost. But it was Shen Chou who transformed their lofty style into a language which other less gifted painters could use, and his influence is still at work today.

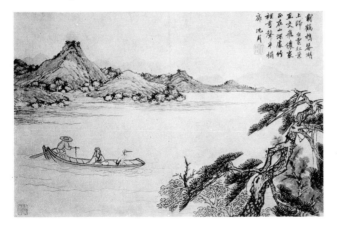

173 Shen Chou. *Returning Home from the Land of the Immortals.* Album-leaf mounted as a handscroll. Ink and colour on paper. Ming Dynasty.

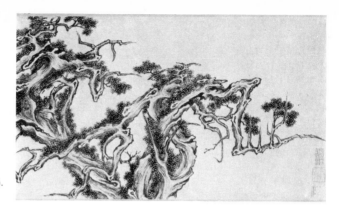

174 Wen Cheng-ming (1470–1559).
The Seven Junipers. Album-leaf.

We cannot, unfortunately, linger over the many gifted painters working in the new 'literary' style who followed in his footsteps, though we must not neglect his pupil Wen Cheng-ming, who sat for the civil service examinations regularly for twenty-eight years in the hope of becoming an official. He was for some time *tai-chao* in the Hanlin Academy but later returned to Soochow, where, during his declining years, he painted a remarkable series of gnarled old trees, in pure monochrome ink, which in their rugged, twisted forms seem to symbolize the noble spirit of the aged *wen-jen* himself. He was a noted calligrapher, and a tireless and influential teacher, with a wide range of styles and techniques at his command. His son Wen Chia and his nephew Wen Po-jen were also gifted painters in the Wu tradition, while among his numerous pupils and followers were Lu Chih (1496–1576) and Ch'en Shun (Ch'en Tao-fu, 1483–1544), both specialists in landscapes and in flower-painting, and Ch'ien Ku (1508–after 1574), who also worked in the manner of Tai Chin.

T'ANG YIN AND CH'IU YING   Two painters active in the first half of the fifteenth century cannot be classified as belonging to either the Che or the Wu school. T'ang Yin (1479–1523) ruined a promising career when he became involved in a scandal over the civil

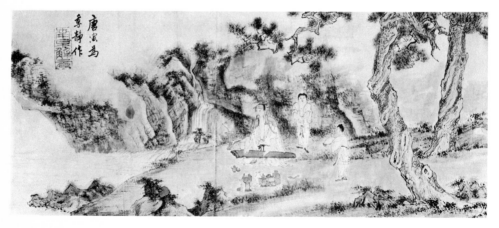

175 T'ang Yin (1479–1523). *Gentleman Playing the Lute in a Landscape*. Detail of a handscroll. Ink and slight colour on paper. Ming Dynasty.

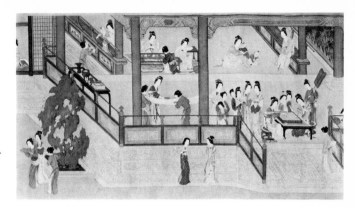

176 Ch'iu Ying (*fl.* 1520–40). *Spring Dawn in the Han Palace*. Detail of a handscroll. Ink and colours on silk. Ming Dynasty.

service examinations; he could thus no longer be considered a gentleman, and spent the rest of his life between the brothels and wine-shops of Soochow on the one hand and the seclusion of a Buddhist temple on the other, painting for a living. He was a pupil of Chou Ch'en, and his true teachers were Li T'ang, Liu Sung-nien, Ma Yüan and the great Yüan masters. He was also a friend of Shen Chou and Wen Cheng-ming, and because of this is often classed with the Wu school. But his towering mountains, painted in monochrome ink on silk, are a re-creation of the forms and conventions of the Sung landscapists, though with a hint of mannerism and exaggeration. The *Gentleman Playing the Lute in a Landscape* (Palace Museum, Taipei) is a good example of his work – scholarly in content, professional in style. It is these conflicting qualities in his style and social position that make him so hard to place and have caused a Japanese scholar to label him 'neo-academic'. Into the same class falls Ch'iu Ying (*fl.* 1520–40), a man born also in Wu-hsien, but of lowly origins, who was neither court painter nor *wen-jen*, but a humble professional, idealizing in his pictures the leisurely life of the gentry whose equal he could never be, and happiest if one of the great literati would condescend to write an eulogy on one of his paintings. He is also famous for his long handscrolls on silk, depicting with exquisite detail and delicate colour such popular themes as the 'Peach Blossom Garden', life at the court of Ming Huang, or the activities devised by the palace ladies to occupy their time. As a landscapist he was the last great exponent of the green and blue style, though he worked also in the ink washes of the Wu school. His delightful pictures are widely appreciated both in China and in the West, and next to Wang Hui he is probably the most-forged painter in the history of Chinese art.

In the development of the literary school no man played a more significant part than the scholar-painter Tung Ch'i-ch'ang (1555–1636), who rose to high office under Wan-li. For not only did he embody, in his paintings, the aesthetic ideals of his class, but he also gave them theoretical formulation

TUNG CH'I-CH'ANG AND THE NORTHERN AND SOUTHERN SCHOOLS

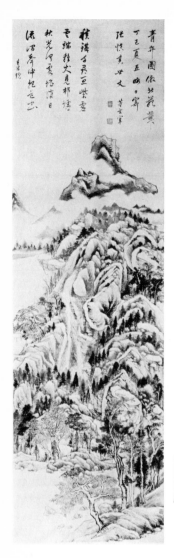

177 Tung Ch'i-ch'ang (1555–1636). *Dwelling in the Ch'ing-pien Mountains.* Hanging scroll. Ink and colour on paper. Ming Dynasty.

through his critical writings. Tung Ch'i-ch'ang was himself a noted calligrapher and a painter of landscapes in monochrome ink, but though he worked freely in the manner of the great masters of the past, he was not content merely to paraphrase. His creative reinterpretations of earlier styles are animated by a passion for pure form, an expressive distortion, which few of his followers understood. They preferred to take his theories more literally, to the detriment of scholarly painting during the ensuing three centuries. For it is as a critic that Tung Ch'i-ch'ang is most famous. It was he, borrowing an idea first put forward by the poet-painter Tu Ch'iung in the fifteenth century, who formulated the theory of the northern and southern schools for the express purpose of demonstrating the superiority of the *wen-jen* tradition over all others. It was primarily through landscape-painting, he maintained, that the scholar and gentleman expressed his understanding of the working of the moral law in nature, and hence his own moral worth. The *wen-jen*, indeed, was the only kind of man who could do this successfully, for only he was free both from the control of the Academy on the one hand and the necessity to make a living on the other; moreover, as he was a scholar, his wide reading in poetry and the Classics gave him an understanding of the nature of things, combined with an epicurean nobility of taste, which the lower orders of professional painters could never hope to acquire. In the spontaneous play of ink and brush, in his freedom to select, omit, suggest, the *wen-jen* had at his command a language capable of conveying the subtlest ideas.

The tradition of the independent scholar-painter was called by Tung Ch'i-ch'ang the 'southern school', because he saw in it an analogy to the southern school of Ch'an Buddhism in the T'ang Dynasty, which had held that enlightenment came of itself, spontaneously and suddenly, as opposed to the northern or gradual school, which had maintained that it could only be attained by degrees, after a lifetime of preparation and training. To Tung Ch'i-ch'ang all the great gentleman-painters were members of the southern school, beginning in the T'ang Dynasty with his hero Wang Wei – for a genuine work from whose hand he spent a lifetime searching – and passing down through the great Northern Sung masters Tung Yüan, Chü-jan, Li Ch'eng and Fan K'uan, through Mi Fei (another ideal 'southern' type) to the Four Great Masters of Yüan, ending in his own time with Shen Chou and Wen Cheng-ming. To the northern school he relegated all academic and court painters, beginning with Li Ssu-hsün and his followers in the green and blue style, including among them Li T'ang and Liu Sung-nien, Ma Yüan and Hsia Kuei. He had some difficulty with Chao Meng-fu. As a scholar, calligrapher and landscapist Tung admired him greatly, but he could never bring himself to include Chao among the 'southern' painters, because he had compromised himself in the eyes of the literati by taking office under the Mongols.

This arbitrary scheme has dominated, and bedevilled, Chinese art criticism for three centuries, while its obvious inconsistencies have caused endless confusion. Moreover, it has been extended to cover not only landscape but also bamboo and bird-and-flower painting as well. What Tung Ch'i-ch'ang objected to in the painters he dubbed 'northern' was on the one hand a careful academic realism making use of clearly defined forms and strong decorative colour, such as we see in the work of the followers of Chao Po-chü, and on the other the tendency towards brilliant mannerist effects and a conventional romanticism latent in the style of Ma Yüan and Hsia Kuei. We may discount Tung Ch'i-ch'ang's prejudices and refuse to accept his classification in individual cases, but his division into northern and southern schools (which, as must by now be obvious, has nothing whatever to do with geography), does in fact represent a just division between two kinds of painting – the one in its purest manifestations academic, eclectic, precise and decorative, the other free, calligraphic, personal, subjective. At the same time, the doctrine of the two schools is a reflection of the feelings of the scholars themselves at this time. The corrupt Ming Dynasty was approaching its downfall, and men of integrity were once again withdrawing from public service into obscurity. Amateur painters found comfort and reassurance in the belief that they were the élite, upholding the Confucian virtues, while painters and scholars in the service of the Emperor were prostituting their talents. However vague or inaccurate it might be as an interpretation of the history of Chinese painting, the doctrine is important as a symptom of the predicament of the Late Ming literati – a predicament that is also reflected in their own painting.

The court by now was hopelessly corrupt, and no longer the focus of loyalty and enlightened patronage. Intellectuals withdrew in despair, a few courageous spirits forming semi-secret protest groups such as the Tung-lin Society, with which Tung Ch'i-ch'ang was loosely connected. Yet the decay of the dynasty produced no real closing of the ranks, and the literati were often divided and isolated. Soochow, Sung-chiang and Nanking were only the chief among many centres of artistic activity, and it has been said that there were now as many schools as there were painters.

But, to compensate, the breakdown also loosened the traditional restraints upon originality. While many artists still followed in the footsteps of Shen Chou and Wen Cheng-ming, others broke free, even if their new direction was only into a reinterpretation of some aspect of the tradition itself. In Soochow, for example, Sheng Mao-yeh and Chao Tso turned back to the Northern Sung for inspiration, Ch'en Hung-shou gave an ironic twist to the ancient figure-painting style that derived from Ku K'ai-chih, Wu Pin produced fantastic distortions of the classic styles of Li Ch'eng and Fan K'uan whose realism was for a time influenced by European engravings brought by the first Jesuit missionaries.

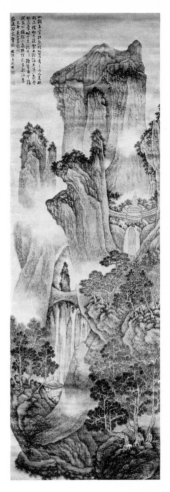

178 Wu Pin (c. 1568–1626). Fantastic landscape. Dated 1616.

Some artists defended the Ma-Hsia school, and one even went so far as to denigrate the immaculate Ni Tsan. In such a chaotic and crumbling world, in which a painter's search for style, an attitude, a place in the tradition was at the same time a search for his own identity, it is easy to see how a dominating personality such as Tung Ch'i-ch'ang could take command of all but the most independent painters, and sweep them along behind him down the path to a new orthodoxy.

SCULPTURE AND THE
DECORATIVE ARTS

To many people 'Ming' means not painting – for it is only recently that Ming painting has come to be appreciated outside China – but the decorative arts. Before I discuss them, however, I should say a word about sculpture. As, during the Sung and Yüan Dynasties, Buddhism gradually loosened its hold over the mind and heart of China, so did Buddhist sculpture decline. Under the Ming 'revival', what it lacks in spiritual content it makes up for in vigour – a vigour shown, for example, in the colossal guardian figures of officials, warriors and animals which line the 'spirit way' leading to the tombs of the Ming emperors outside Nanking and Peking. The casting of large figures in iron had developed during the Sung Dynasty, as a substitute for more precious bronze. The finest of these figures have a simplicity and compactness of modelling that make them extremely impressive. Far greater freedom of movement was possible in ceramic sculpture, which now lent an air of gaiety and splendour to the roof-ridges of palaces and temples, already glittering with yellow, blue and green tiles. The boldly conceived figure of a man in green and brown glazed terracotta (called *liu-li*) which I have illustrated is a splendid example of the confident manner in which Ming craftsmen revived and transformed the style of the T'ang Dynasty.

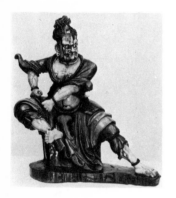

179 Yen-lo-wang (Yama). Pottery decorated with coloured glazes (*liu-li*). Ming Dynasty.

TEXTILES

The Ming love of colour and of all that made for luxurious living was satisfied by the cloisonné enamel, the lacquer, and the richly woven textiles which were worn both by officials and by the wealthier members of the middle class. Figured silks, embroideries and brocades have a long history in China: examples of all types going back to the T'ang Dynasty and earlier have been found in the dry desert sand of Chinese Turkestan, and are more perfectly preserved in the Shōsōin Repository at Nara. Many T'ang motifs were still in use during the Sung Dynasty, to be revived once again during the Ming and continued, with some modifications, during the Ch'ing. The great achievement of the Sung weavers had been the perfecting of *k'o-ssu*, a form of tapestry woven from silk, using a needle as a shuttle. This technique had been invented in Central Asia, possibly by the Sogdians, improved by the Uighurs, and finally passed on to the Chinese early in the eleventh century. The term *k'o-ssu*, translatable as 'cut silk', is descriptive of the vertical gaps between adjacent areas of colour visible when it is held up to the light, but other variants suggest that *k'o-ssu* is probably a transliteration of the Persian *qazz* or Arabic *khazz*, referring to silk and silk products. After the débâcle of 1125–27 the art was taken to the Southern Sung court at Hangchow, where a historian records that *k'o-ssu* was used for mounting paintings and binding books in the imperial collection. It was also used for robes, decorative panels and, most astonishingly, for translating paintings and calligraphy into the weaver's art. We can form some idea of its microscopic fineness when we realize that whereas the finest Gobelins tapestry has 8 to 11 warp threads to the centimetre, Sung *k'o-ssu* has up to 24, and 116 weft threads per centimetre of warp as against the 22 of Gobelins. During the Yüan Dynasty, when trade across Central Asia was probably easier than at any other period in history, panels of *k'o-ssu* were exported at enormous expense to Europe, where they were incorporated into the vestments of the cathedrals in Danzig, Vienna, Perugia and Regensburg, while splendid examples have also been found in Egypt. Hung-wu, the spartan and ferocious first Emperor of the Ming, forbade its manufacture, but it was revived early in the fifteenth century under Hsüan-te.

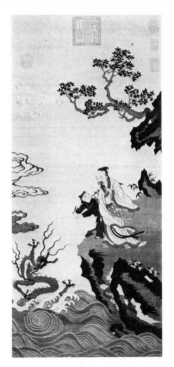

180 *Magician Changing a Bamboo Walking-stick into a Dragon. K'o-ssu silk tapestry. Ming Dynasty.*

Little Sung *k'o-ssu* has survived until today, but we may get an impression of the splendour of the weaver's art from the court robes of the Ming Dynasty. These include both the ceremonial robes made for the imperial sacrifices and decorated with the Twelve Emblems – sacred symbols which go back to hallowed antiquity and are described in the early Chou *Classic of History* (*Shu-ching*) – and the so-called 'dragon robes', a term used to describe a long semi-formal robe worn by courtiers and officials from Ming times onwards, embroidered with a number of motifs of which the chief, and most conspicuous, was the dragon. If we are to judge from surviving paintings, dragons with three claws had been a principal motif on T'ang robes, and became an established institution under the Yüan. Strict sumptuary laws introduced in the fourteenth century permitted a robe with four-clawed dragons (*mang-p'ao*) to lesser nobles and officials, while restricting to the emperor and royal princes dragons with five claws. The Ming emperors wore robes decorated with both the dragons and the Twelve Symbols. Dragon robes became extremely popular under the Ch'ing, when the regulations of 1759 confined the Twelve Symbols, at least in theory, to the emperor's personal use.

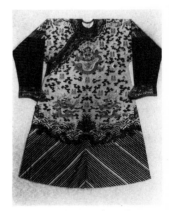

181 *Imperial Dragon robe. Woven silk tapestry. Ch'ing Dynasty, Yung-cheng period.*

The Ming and Ch'ing official robes were further embellished with 'Mandarin squares', badges of rank which had already been used decoratively during the Yüan Dynasty and were first prescribed for official dress by the sumptuary laws of 1391. The Ming squares were broad, and made in one piece, generally from *k'o-ssu* tapestry. The Manchus, who were content with embroidery, used them in pairs back and front, splitting the front panel down the centre to fit the open riding-jacket. Official regulations prescribed bird motifs (symbolizing literary elegance) for civilian officials, animals (suggesting fierce courage) for the military; the emblems were precisely graded, from the fabulous monster *ch'i-lin* (for dukes, marquesses and imperial sons-in-law), through the white crane or golden pheasant (for civil officials of the first and second ranks), down to the silver pheasant (for the fifth to ninth ranks). Military ranks had a corresponding animal scale. Though these woven and embroidered robes vanished from the official world with the passing of the Manchus in 1912, they may still be seen today, lending their glitter and pageantry to the traditional theatre.

LACQUER

Lacquer, as we have seen, was already a highly developed craft during the Warring States and Han periods. At that time, decoration was restricted to painting on a ground of solid colour or incising through one colour to expose another beneath it. During the Yüan Dynasty there started the practice of applying lacquer in many layers and then, before it had completely hardened, inlaying it with mother-of-pearl, carving it in floral designs, or carving through alternating layers of contrasting colours, a technique known by its Japanese name, *guri*. Genuine Sung pieces, nearly all in simple, unadorned shapes, are rare, but by the Yüan period decorated lacquer had become very popular, and the names of several master-craftsmen of the Early Ming period are recorded. Nevertheless, lacquer is easy to imitate, and many of the 'signed' pieces of the fifteenth century, and those bearing Ming reign-titles (*nien-hao*), may well be later Chinese or Japanese forgeries. Indeed, by the fifteenth century the Japanese had become so expert in lacquer-work that Chinese craftsmen were journeying to Japan to learn the art.

The typical Chinese lacquer of the Ming period was carved in red, with rich floral or pictorial designs (*t'i-hung*); these were either modelled in full relief, or the background was cut away, leaving the design in flat relief, as on many Han engraved stones. By the Chia-ching period two styles, one

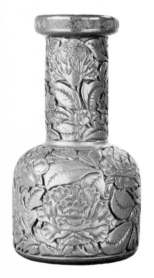

182 Vase in the form of a paper-beater. Red lacquer carved with floral patterns. Ming Dynasty, early fifteenth century.

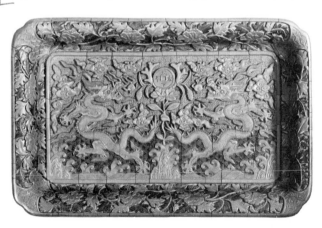

183 Rectangular dish. Red, greenish-black and yellow lacquer, carved with a design of dragons amid clouds and waves. Ming Dynasty, Wan-li period (1573–1620).

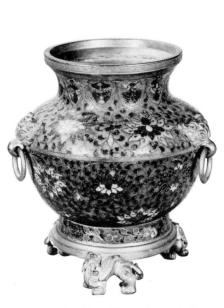

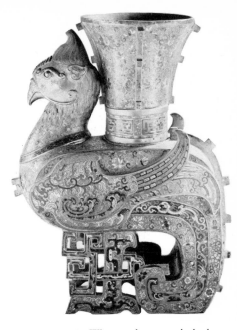

184 Jar on three lions. Cloisonné enamel. Ming Dynasty, fifteenth century.

185 Wine vessel, *tsun*, on the back of a phoenix. Cloisonné enamel. Ch'ing Dynasty, eighteenth century.

sharp-edged, the other more rounded, can be identified. The vase decorated with peonies which I have illustrated is a richly carved example of the full relief style, modelled in a shape that imitates the *kinuta* celadon vases of the Southern Sung period.

CLOISONNÉ ENAMEL

The earliest known reference to cloisonné enamel in China occurs in the *Ko-ku yao-lun*, a collectors' and connoisseurs' miscellany first published in 1387 or 1388, where it is referred to as Ta-shih (Muslim) ware. No authentic examples of fourteenth-century Chinese enamel-work have yet been identified, though it is quite possible that pieces were being made for ritual use in the Lama temples of Peking during the latter part of the Yüan Dynasty.[3]

This art, which permits of such rich and vibrant colour effects, came into its own during the Ming Dynasty, and the oldest positively datable pieces have the Hsüan-te reign-mark (1426–35). They include incense-burners in archaic shapes, dishes and boxes, animals and birds, and pieces for the scholar's desk. In the Early Ming pieces the *cloisons* are not perfectly filled and the surface has a certain roughness; but the designs are bold, vigorous and endlessly varied. Unfortunately, as the technique improved these qualities were lost, till we come to the technically perfect yet lifeless and mechanical enamel-ware of the time of Ch'ien-lung. Identical shapes and designs were produced through the nineteenth century, while today the reappearance of these same designs bears eloquent witness to the archaistic revival of traditional arts under the People's Republic.

It used to be thought that the ceramic art in China declined, if it did not actually come to a standstill, during the Yüan Dynasty. The Yüan rulers in Peking were not men of refined taste, and their patronage must have been a sad anticlimax after the challenge set by the Sung emperors. A splendid jar in the British Museum, decorated with the 'baby among floral scrolls' design in brown reserved on a white slip, is dated 1305 and shows that the Tz'u-chou tradition was still vigorous, though it was never to recapture the beauty of form and drawing of the Sung pieces. But now the focus of the ceramic industry shifts permanently to the centre and south. The kilns at Lung-ch'üan and Li-shui in Chekiang continued to produce celadons on a large scale – indeed, production must have increased to keep pace with the demand for exports to the Near East which the *Pax Tartarica* had stimulated. A baluster vase dated 1327 in the Percival David Foundation, London, is typical of the more 'baroque' preferences of the period, being elaborately and somewhat tastelessly decorated with floral scrolls moulded in relief under the glaze. More daring was the technique of leaving the central decorative motif on a dish, such as a dragon, unglazed in relief. Sometimes these reliefs were modelled by hand, but the presence in the Percival David Foundation of a celadon dish and a flask bearing identical dragons (the former unglazed and the latter glazed) indicates that moulds were also used. It is possible that spotted celadon (*tobi-seiji*) may also have been a Yüan innovation. There are signs, however, that by the mid fourteenth century the quality of Lung-ch'üan wares was beginning to decline, probably on account of the competition from the factories at Ching-te-chen in Kiangsi.

During the Sung Dynasty the finest products of the Ching-te-chen kilns had been white porcelains, chiefly *ch'ing-pai* ware and an imitation of the northern Ting-yao. But by the beginning of the fourteenth century new techniques were already being explored. The *Annals of Fou-liang*, written before 1322, notes that at Ching-te-chen 'they have experts at moulding, painting and engraving'. Painting I shall consider in a moment. Moulding and engraving can be seen in the so-called *shu-fu* (privy council) wares. It seems likely that the *shu-fu* was the first ware to be made at Ching-te-chen to official order. It comprises chiefly bowls and dishes with incised, moulded or slip decoration – generally consisting of flower sprays, lotus leaves, or phoenixes amid clouds – under a bluish-white (*ch'ing-pai*) glaze. Sometimes the characters *shu-fu* are included, or other auspicious words such as *fu* (happiness), *shou* (long life) or *lu* (emolument). Closely related to these are the stem-cups, ewers, bottles and jars whose decoration consists of applied reliefs (often in zones separated by pearl-beading), and the figurines, chiefly of *bodhisattvas*, used in domestic shrines, of which several fine examples have recently been excavated from sites of the Yüan period.

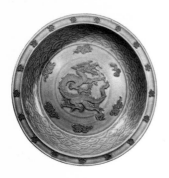

186 Dish. Porcelain covered with celadon glaze, leaving the dragon and clouds in biscuit relief. Yüan Dynasty.

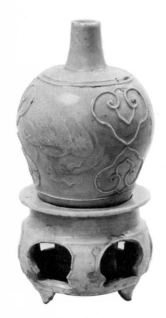

187 Vase and stand. *Ch'ing-pai* porcelain with relief and pearl-bead decoration. Yüan Dynasty.

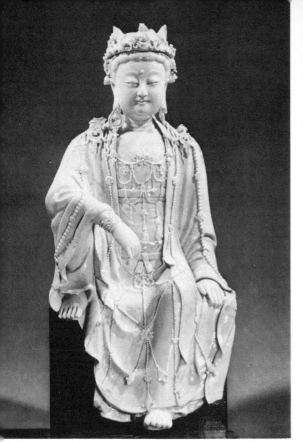

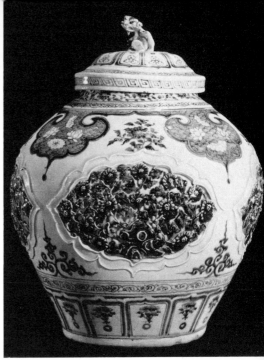

188 (*left*) *Bodhisattva*. *Ch'ing-pai* porcelain. Excavated at Yüan capital, Peking. Yüan Dynasty.

189 (*right*) Wine-jar. White porcelain decorated with open-work panels and painting in underglaze red and blue. Excavated at Pao-ting, Shensi. Yüan Dynasty.

UNDERGLAZE RED AND BLUE

Another of the innovations at Ching-te-chen which may have occurred before the middle of the fourteenth century was painting in copper-red under the glaze. It is not known where this technique was invented. It is certainly not Near Eastern and may possibly, as some Japanese scholars have suggested, have originated in Kŏrea in the Koryŏ period at the end of the twelfth or beginning of the thirteenth century. Some of the most attractive early Chinese examples are the bottles with graceful pear-shaped body and flaring lip, decorated with sketchily drawn flower-sprays or clouds. During the Ming Dynasty the designs become more elaborate, but the copper-red had a dull colour and a tendency to run, and was consequently abandoned in the fifteenth century in favour of the more manageable underglaze cobalt-blue. This defect is very apparent in a superb fourteenth-century jar decorated with flower-sprays in an underglaze red so intense that it is almost black, which is believed to have been taken from one of the Thirteen Imperial Tombs (Shih-san Ling) of the Ming emperors outside Peking, and is now in a private collection in Japan. The decoration is very similar to that of Yüan blue and white, and indeed the two families are intimately related. Occasionally underglaze blue and red are combined, as on the handsome jar in the Percival David Foundation, London.

In the whole history of ceramics probably no single ware has been so much admired as Chinese blue and white. It has been imitated in Japan, in Indochina and Persia, and it was the inspiration of the pottery of Delft and other European factories; its devotees have ranged from the head-hunters of Borneo and New Guinea to Whistler and Oscar Wilde, and its enchantment is still at work. Perhaps Chinese potters had begun to paint in cobalt under a transparent glaze in South China late in the thirteenth century, but there is no written record of the art before the slighting reference in the *Ko-ku yao-lun* (1387 or 1388), which, speaking of the products of the Jao-chou factories, says 'there are blue-and-white and five-colour wares but they are very vulgar'. Painting in underglaze blue and black was already practised in Persia during the thirteenth century, while in Mesopotamia painting in cobalt on a tin glaze goes back to the ninth century. We have already noted crude underglaze painting in Changsha in the T'ang Dynasty, and more advanced techniques in the Tz'u-chou wares of the Sung Dynasty, so the application of underglaze painting to the white porcelain of Ching-te-chen during the Yüan Dynasty is not at all surprising. In some of the earliest pieces underglaze blue painting is combined with relief or incised decoration of the *shu-fu* type, and there is no doubt that an intimate relationship existed between them. Cobalt had been one of the coloured glazes used on the splashed T'ang wares, but as these went out of fashion during the Sung Dynasty, when the Near Eastern sources of cobalt were no longer accessible, there is no historical connection between these T'ang coloured glazes and painting in blue under a transparent glaze. Perhaps the idea of painting in cobalt came from the Near East; but the shapes of the vessels, the technique of painting and the motifs employed were for the most part Chinese.

The pieces which can now be dated with confidence in the first half of the fourteenth century are mostly stem-cups, pear-shaped vases with flaring lip and small covered jars, decorated with dragons, lotus or chrysanthemum scrolls and narrower bands of petals. The famous dated temple vases of 1351 in the Percival David Foundation, London mark the transition to decoration on a bolder and more confident scale. By the time these monumental pieces were made, the potters and painters at Ching-te-chen had fully mastered their art, and the vases and dishes of the next hundred years are unequalled for their splendour of shape and beauty of decoration. The drawing is free and bold, yet delicate, the blue varying from almost pure ultramarine to a dull greyish colour, and with a tendency to clot and turn black where it runs thickest – a fault which was eradicated by the sixteenth century and cleverly imitated in the eighteenth. The climax was reached in the Hsüan-te period (1426–35), to which belong the earliest pieces bearing genuine reign-marks. In addition to dishes there are stem-cups, jars and flattened 'pilgrim flasks', in which an earlier tendency to crowd the surface with flowers, waves, tendrils and other motifs set in ogival panels has given way to a delicate play of lotus scrolls,

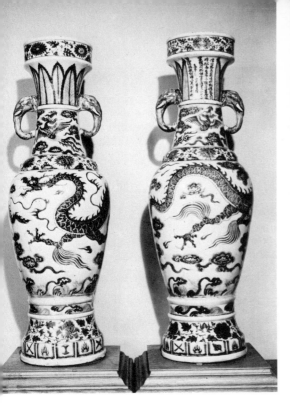

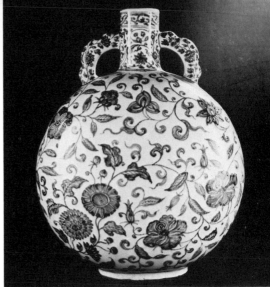

191 Flask. Porcelain decorated in underglaze blue. Ming Dynasty, Yung-lo period.

190 Temple vases, dated equivalent to 1351. Porcelain decorated in underglaze blue. Yüan Dynasty.

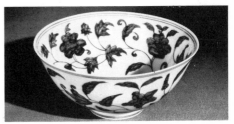

192 Bowl. Porcelain decorated in underglaze blue. Ming Dynasty, Ch'eng-hua period.

vines or chrysanthemums over a white surface. The influence of courtly bird-and-flower painting on porcelain decoration is very evident in the lovely blue and white flask which I have illustrated.

The blue and white of each reign has its own character, which the connoisseur can readily recognize. The Hsüan-te style continued in the Ch'eng-hua era, though beside it there now appeared in the so-called 'palace bowls' a new style more delicate and less sure in its drawing and consequently easier for the eighteenth-century potter to imitate. In the Cheng-te period (1506–21) there was a great demand among the Muslim eunuchs at court for the so-called 'Mohammedan wares', consisting mostly of brush-rests, lamps, boxes and other articles for the writing-table, whose decoration incorporated inscriptions in Persian or Arabic. The pieces of the reigns of Chia-ching (1522–66) and Wan-li (1573–1620) show a change from the old floral decoration to more naturalistic scenes, while in the former reign the Taoist leanings of the court made popular such auspicious subjects as pine trees, immortals, cranes and deer.

The imperial wares of the Wan-li period closely follow those of Chia-ching, but there now begins a general decline in quality, the result of mass production, rigidity in the requirements of the palace, and the exhaustion of the fine-quality clay-beds at Ching-te-chen. The most pleasing and vigorous blue and whites of the last hundred years of the

Ming are wares made in the numerous commercial kilns. These are of two kinds: those made for domestic consumption (*min*: literally 'people's'), and the even more roughly modelled and painted export wares, made for sale or barter to the countries of South-east Asia, to which I shall refer again. Soon after 1600 a particular type of thin, brittle Wan-li export blue and white began to reach Europe. This ware, called *kraak* porcelain because it had formed part of the cargo of two Portuguese carracks captured on the high seas by the Dutch, caused a sensation when it appeared on the market in Holland, and was soon being imitated in the painted faience of Delft and Lowestoft. In spite of intense efforts on the part of European potters, however, it was not until 1709 that the Dresden potter Johann Böttger, an alchemist in the service of Augustus the Strong of Saxony, succeeded for the first time in making true porcelain – more than a thousand years after it had been perfected in China.

CHING-TE-CHEN By the middle of the fifteenth century Ching-te-chen had become the greatest ceramic centre in China. It was ideally situated near the Poyang Lake, whence its products could go by lake and river to Nanking and by the Grand Canal to Peking. An apparently inexhaustible supply of china-clay lay in the Ma-ch'ang Hills near by, while just across the river at Hu-t'ien was to be found the other essential ingredient in the manufacture of porcelain, namely 'china-stone' (*tz'u-shih*, often called *pai tun-tzu* when in its prepared form). By this time there had evolved out of the nearly white *ch'ing-pai* and *shu-fu* wares of Sung and Yüan a true white porcelain, which was perhaps already being made at the imperial factory for the Hung-wu Emperor. The most beautiful pieces, however, were those made in the Yung-lo period (1403–24), most of which are decorated with motifs incised or painted in white slip under the glaze – a technique aptly called *an-hua*, 'secret decoration', for it is scarcely visible unless the vessel is held up to the light. From the technical point of view, the eighteenth-century white glaze is perhaps more perfect, but it lacks the luminous warmth of the Ming surface. In some Yung-lo bowls the porcelain body is pared down to paper thinness, the vessel thus appearing to consist of nothing but glaze: these are the so-called 'bodiless' (*t'o-t'ai*) pieces. Almost as beautiful are the other monochromes produced at Ching-te-chen, notably the dishes, stem-cups and bowls decorated in 'sacrificial red' (*chi-hung*), or with dragons under a yellow or blue glaze.

TE-HUA WARES Ching-te-chen, though the largest, was by no means the only Ming factory producing monochrome wares. A white porcelain was being made at Te-hua in Fukien as early as the Sung Dynasty. The Fukien wares, indeed, form a race apart. They never bear reign-marks, and are extremely difficult to date accurately, while they range in quality from the finest porcelain with a luminous, warm and lustrous glaze,

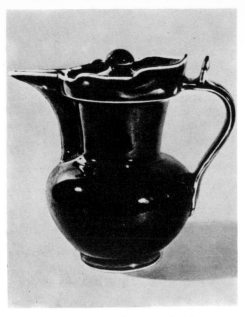

193 'Monk's hat' jug. Porcelain covered with
pao-shih-hung 'precious stone red' glaze. Ch'ien-lung
inscription of 1775 engraved in the base. Ming Dynasty,
Hsüan-te period (1424–1535).

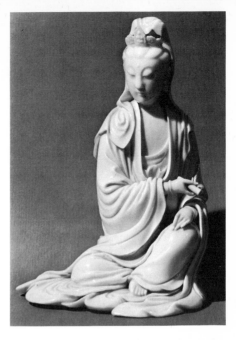

194 Kuanyin. Fukien ware; white porcelain. Early
Ch'ing Dynasty, seventeenth or eighteenth century.

with a brownish tint where it runs thick, to the more
metallic products of the last hundred years. In addition to
vessels and ceremonial objects such as incense-burners and
other bronze shapes, the Te-hua potters modelled figurines
in white porcelain, a lovely example being the Kuanyin
from the Barlow Collection at the University of Sussex.
Here the subtle turn of the body and the liquid flow of the
drapery show how much ceramic modelling was influenced
by the sweeping linear rhythms of figure-painting. From
the seventeenth century onwards Te-hua ware was shipped
from Amoy to Europe, where, as 'blanc-de-Chine', it had a
considerable vogue and was widely imitated.

Robust Ming taste is more typically expressed in the so-
called *san-ts'ai*, 'three-colour' wares. The exact origin of this
family is not known, though there is reason to believe that
it may have been produced in stoneware at Chün-chou in
Honan, where the kilns were still active in the sixteenth
century, while it was also, and more perfectly, made in
porcelain at Ching-te-chen. The colours are generally more
than three in number, but the ware takes its name from the
rich turquoise, dark blue and aubergine which predominate.
They are thickly applied in bold floral motifs, and separated
by raised ridges which perform the same function as the
cloisons on Ming enamels. Occasionally the turquoise glaze
was used alone, as on a vase in the Percival David Foundation,
London, inscribed on the shoulder 'For general use in the
Inner Palace'. Although this ware follows the range of
shapes made earlier in Chün ware – storage-jars, flower-pots
and bulb-bowls – the vigour of the shapes and the strong,

ENAMELLED WARES

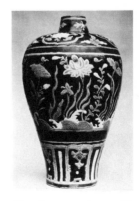

195 Vase. Stoneware decorated in
san-ts'ai (three-colour) enamels.
Ming Dynasty.

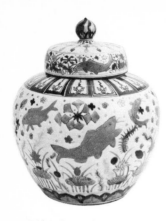

196 'Fish jar'. Porcelain decorated in *wu-ts'ai* (five-colour) glazes. Ming Dynasty, Chia-ching period (1522–66).

rich-coloured glazes show how much closer in feeling Ming art often comes to that of the T'ang Dynasty than to that of the Sung.

Another important Ming family comprises the five-colour wares (*wu-ts'ai*), a name given to the white porcelain painted with enamel colours, an art which was perfected by Chinese potters, possibly in the reign of Hsüan-te or slightly earlier. The colours were prepared from the materials of lead glaze, applied over the glaze or directly 'on the biscuit', and the vessel was fired again at a lower temperature. Some of these pieces are small and 'bodiless', the clay being pared down to paper-thinness between the outer and inner glaze, the painting – chiefly vines, flower-sprays and flowering branches – being disposed with perfect taste and a subtle balance over the white ground. Sometimes, as in the *tou-ts'ai* ware, the enamels were combined with underglaze blue, but this phrase, which means 'contesting colours', hardly does justice to their delicate harmony. The five-colour enamels of the Ch'eng-hua period were never surpassed for their purity of form and decoration; they were already being copied in the Wan-li period, while even to the expert the finest of eighteenth-century copies are almost indistinguishable from them.

EXPORT WARES

Beside these exquisite enamels the sixteenth century saw the appearance of a more full-blooded style, often decorated with *genre* scenes chiefly in red and yellow; this style was to be echoed in the *wu-ts'ai* wares made for export in the South China kilns – known generally by the misleading term 'Swatow' ware. No pottery was made at Swatow itself, but some of these rough and vigorous porcelains (both blue and white and five-colour enamels) were made up-river at Chao-chou and probably at Shih-ma in Fukien, while a kiln producing blue and white export ware has recently been found in Ch'üan-chou, Marco Polo's Zayton. Swatow, however, was most probably the main port of dispatch.

China's export trade to the Nan-hai ('South Seas') was already flourishing during the Sung and Yüan Dynasties. Early Ming wares, including celadon, Ching-te-chen white porcelain, Tz'u-chou, *ch'ing-pai* and Te-hua, have been found in huge quantities over an area extending from the Philippines to East Africa. These export wares had a profound influence on the native pottery of South-east Asia: blue and white was not only successfully imitated in Japan (Imari ware), but also in Annam and, less successfully because they lacked the cobalt, by the Thai potters at Sawankalok, although the Siamese kilns succeeded in producing a beautiful celadon of their own. Before the end of the Ming Dynasty, the Chinese factories were also making porcelain on order for European customers, notably through the Dutch 'factory' established at Batavia (Jakarta) in 1602; but this trade, which was to play so great a part in the contacts between Europe and China, I must leave to the next chapter.

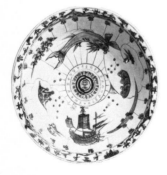

197 Dish. Porcelain decorated with underglaze blue and overglaze red. 'Swatow ware', probably from Shih-ma, Fukien. Late Ming Dynasty.

11 The Ch'ing Dynasty

The Ming Dynasty was brought down by the same inexorable laws of decay which had operated on previous occasions in Chinese history: corruption and the power of the eunuchs at court, leading to breakdown of the administration, large-scale banditry in the provinces, and enemies on the northern frontier patiently awaiting their opportunity to pounce. In 1618 the Manchu nation had been founded on the banks of the bleak Sungari River. Seven years later the Great Khan, Nurhachi, set up his capital in Mukden, calling his new dynasty Ch'ing ('pure') to parallel the Chinese Ming ('bright'). Their moment came when in 1644 the Chinese General Wu San-kuei appealed to them for help to expel the rebel leader Li Tzu-ch'eng, who had forced his way into Peking. The Manchus promptly accepted, drove Li out of the city and, while Wu San-kuei was pursuing him into the west, quietly occupied the capital and proclaimed the rule of the Ch'ing Dynasty. Their unexpected success left the Manchus momentarily exposed, but Wu San-kuei waited ten years before attempting to dislodge them, and then it was too late. But for nearly four decades he and his successors held South China, which was not finally secured for the Manchus until the capture of Kunming in 1682. As a result of this long civil war there grew up a bitter hostility between north and south. Peking became increasingly remote and suspicious, the south ever more rebellious and independent.

It would be wrong to picture the Manchus as barbarous and destructive. On the contrary, they felt an intense admiration for Chinese culture and leaned heavily on the Chinese official class. But the more independent-minded of the Chinese intelligentsia were a potential source of danger to the régime, and the Manchu trust of the literati did not extend to a sympathetic consideration for the 'new thought' of the eighteenth century. Having few cultural traditions of their own, they clung to the most reactionary forms of Confucianism, becoming more Chinese than the Chinese themselves, and strenuously resisting up to the end every one of the attempts at reform which were made by the literati, some of whom were responsible and far-seeing men. This hidebound refusal to recognize the inevitability of change eventually brought about the collapse of the dynasty. But for the first century and a half, China basked in the sunlight of her restored power and prosperity, which was due largely to the work of the second Emperor, K'ang-hsi

(Sheng-tsu), who ruled from 1662 to 1722. It was he who pacified all China and restored her to a paramount position in Asia.

During the seventeenth century and the first half of the eighteenth China was treated with enormous respect by the European powers; admiration for her principles of government filled the writers of the Enlightenment, while her arts gave birth to two waves of *chinoiserie*, the first late in the seventeenth century, the second at the height of the eighteenth. During this period, indeed, China had far more influence upon the thought, art, and material life of Europe than had Europe on China. Western influence was confined to court, where, ever since the arrival of the Jesuit missionary Matteo Ricci in 1601, the emperors and their immediate entourage of officials and savants had been in close touch with Western art and learning. But apart from Adam Schall's reform of the calendar and Verbiest's ordnance factory, the arts and techniques brought by the Jesuits were treated by all but a tiny minority of scholars as mere curiosities. This was not true of painting, however. For while the literati completely ignored European art, some academicians at court made strenuous efforts to master Western shading and perspective in the interests of greater realism.

The most characteristic intellectual achievement of the Ch'ing Dynasty was, like that of the Ming, not creative so much as synthetic and analytical; indeed, in the production of such works as the huge anthology *Ku-chin t'u-shu chi-ch'eng* (1729), and the *Ssu-k'u ch'üan-shu*, an encyclopaedia in thirty-six thousand volumes begun in 1773 and completed nine years later, the Ch'ing scholars far surpassed their Ming forbears in sheer industry. Characteristically, also, the latter work was compiled not primarily in the interests of scholarship, but as a means of seeking out all books whose contents might reflect upon the legitimacy of the Manchu Dynasty. Nevertheless, this enormous compilation contains many otherwise unknown texts and the fruits of much scholarly research. For this was an antiquarian age, when, as never before, men looked back into the past, burrowing into the Classics, dabbling in archaeology, forming huge collections of books and manuscripts, paintings, porcelain and archaic bronzes. Most famous among the collectors of paintings were Liang Ch'ing-piao, whom I have already referred to, and the salt magnate An I-chou (*c.* 1683–*c.* 1740), many of whose treasures were later acquired by the Ch'ien-lung Emperor. Ch'ien-lung, who had succeeded the able but ruthless Yung-cheng in 1736, possessed a prodigious enthusiasm for works of art, and in his hands the imperial collection grew to a size and importance it had not seen since the days of Hui-tsung.[1] His taste, however, was not always equal to his enthusiasm, and he could not resist the temptation to write indifferent poems all over his most treasured paintings and stamp them with large and conspicuous seals. His abdication in 1796 (because he considered it unfilial to occupy the throne longer than his illustrious grandfather) marks the end of the great days of the Ch'ing Dynasty. To the familiar story of internal dissolution was added the aggressive advance of the European powers, whose original admiration had now given way to hostility, provoked by impatience at irksome trade restrictions. We need not linger over the tragic history of the nineteenth century, the shameful Opium Wars, the failure of the Taiping rebels to regenerate China, and her final abasement after 1900. This was not a time for greatness either in politics or in the arts. Though a few of the literati maintained a certain independence of spirit, the educated class as a whole took its lead more and more from the reactionary attitude of the Manchus.

The architecture of the Ch'ing Dynasty was, in the main, a tame and cautious continuation of the style of the Ming – with one notable exception. To the north-west of the capital the K'ang-hsi Emperor laid out an extensive summer palace, in emulation of the great hunting-parks of the Han and Liang emperors. It was enlarged by Yung-cheng, who gave it the name Yüan-ming-yüan, and again by Ch'ien-lung, who added to the many palaces already built in it a huge assembly of pleasure pavilions designed by the Italian Jesuit missionary and court painter Guiseppe Castiglione (1688–1766) in a somewhat sinified version of Italian eighteenth-century Baroque. These extraordinary buildings were set about with fountains and water-works devised by Father Benoît, a French Jesuit who had familiarized himself with the fountains at Versailles and Saint-Cloud. Every detail down to the furniture was specially designed (much of it copied from French engravings), and the walls were hung with mirrors and Gobelins tapestries sent out by the French court in 1767. The total effect must have been bizarre in the extreme. But the heyday of the Yüan-ming-yüan was brief. Before the end of the eighteenth century the fountains had long ceased to play, and Ch'ien-lung's successors so neglected their transplanted Versailles that by the time the European allies destroyed the Western-style buildings and looted their treasures in 1860, the Yüan-ming-yüan had already fallen into a sad autumnal state of disrepair. But we can obtain some idea of what it looked like in its prime from the engravings made by Castiglione's Chinese assistants in 1786. The last great architectural achievement – if it deserves the name at all – of the Manchus was the summer palace built by the Dowager Empress Tzu-hsi on the shore of the Po-hai to the north-west of the capital with funds raised by public subscription to construct a navy. Although she was condemned at the time for her extravagance, it has since been observed that had she built a fleet it would certainly have been sunk by the Japanese in the War of 1895, while the summer palace will endure for centuries.

Less pretentious and far more appealing among the Late Ch'ing buildings is the Ch'i-nien-tien, Hall of Annual

ARCHITECTURE

198 The Po-hai and the Summer Palace, Peking.

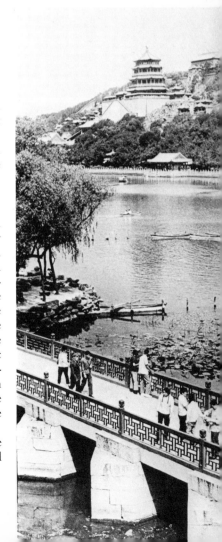

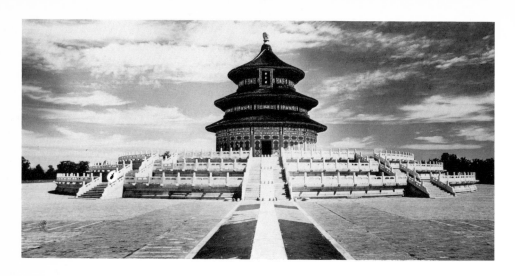

Prayers, erected near the Altar of Heaven in the southern
quarter of the city late in the nineteenth century. Its gleaming
marble terraces, its richly painted woodwork and the deep
blue of its tiles dazzle the eye. But we need only to glance at
the poverty of its detail, and its reliance upon paint rather
than imaginative carpentry, to realize that, fairy-like as is
its total effect, the Hall of Annual Prayers marks the final
exhaustion of a great tradition.

EUROPEAN INFLUENCE ON
COURTLY ART

In a corner of the Forbidden City, K'ang-hsi set aside a
courtyard known as the Ch'i-hsiang-kung as a studio and
repair-shop, where Chinese and Jesuit artists and mechanics
worked side by side, painting, engraving and repairing
clocks and musical instruments. The court painter, Chiao
Ping-chen, studied perspective there under the Jesuits and
embodied what he learned in forty-six illustrations to the
famous agricultural work *Keng-chih-t'u*, while his pupil
Leng Mei was noted for delightful but over-elegant paintings of court ladies, generally in a garden setting, which
showed some knowledge of Western perspective.
Castiglione, who had arrived in Peking in 1715, was already
an accomplished painter. He soon mastered the academic
manner of his Chinese colleagues, and proceeded to create a
synthetic style in which a Chinese medium and technique
are blended with Western naturalism, aided by a subtle use
of shading. He was a favourite at court, where his still-life
paintings, portraits and long handscrolls depicting horses in
a landscape or scenes of court life (signed, very carefully,
with his Chinese name Lang Shih-ning) were greatly
admired. He had numerous pupils and imitators, for the
decorative realism of his style was particularly suited to the
kind of 'furniture-painting' which the palace required in
such quantities to decorate its endless apartments. Castiglione,
however, no more affected the general trend of Chinese
painting in his time than did the Chinese artists working for

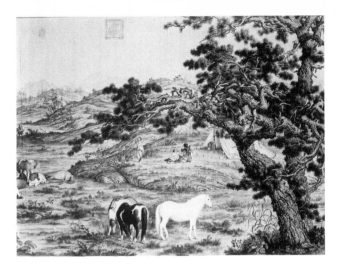

the Europeans in Canton and Hongkong. Tsou I-kuei (1686–1772), a court artist to Ch'ien-lung noted for the painstaking realism of his flower-paintings (an art in which he probably influenced the style of his colleague Castiglione), much admired Western perspective and shading. 'If they paint a palace or a mansion on a wall,' he wrote, 'one would almost feel induced to enter it.' But he makes it clear that these are mere technicalities, to be kept in their proper place: 'The student should learn something of their achievements so as to improve his own method. But their technique of strokes is negligible. Even if they attain perfection it is merely craftsmanship. Thus foreign painting cannot be called art.'[2]

The most interesting and neglected of the Ch'ing professional painters, however, were the group centred round Li Yin and Yüan Chiang, both of whom were working in prosperous Yangchow between about 1690 and 1725, after which the latter, like his son(?) Yüan Yao, became a court painter. They are chiefly noted for having given a violent twist to the long moribund 'northern' tradition by applying to the style and composition of Early Sung masters such as Kuo Hsi the fantastic distortions of the Late Ming 'expressionists'. The blend of fantasy and mannerism in their work can be seen in the meticulously painted landscape by Yüan Chiang in the de Young Museum, San Francisco.

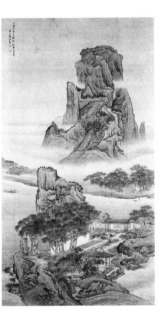

201 Yüan Chiang (first half of the eighteenth century). *Gentlemen Conversing in a Landscape*. Hanging scroll. Ink and colours on silk. Ch'ing Dynasty.

The literati shared none of the academicians' admiration for European painting, for they now felt themselves to be the custodians of a tradition infinitely more precious than anything the West had to offer. Through the sheer force of his personality, Tung Ch'i-ch'ang had given a new interpretation to the style of Tung Yüan and Chü-jan, but his less gifted followers during the Ch'ing Dynasty took his injunction to restore the past, *fu ku*, too literally, and in most of the work of the Four Wangs and their followers, the free

WEN-JEN HUA: THE FOUR WANGS;
WU LI AND YÜN SHOU-P'ING

unfettered styles of the Ming literati froze into a new academicism. But even if they played the same tune over and over again, they played it beautifully.

The earliest of the four was Wang Shih-min (1592–1680), who had learned to paint from the hand of Tung Ch'i-ch'ang himself. Like his master, he deeply admired the broad, relaxed manner of Huang Kung-wang, and his great series of landscapes in the manner of the Yüan recluse, painted in his seventies, are among the noblest achievement of the Ch'ing literati. Wang Chien (1598–1677), his close friend and pupil, was an even more conscientious follower of the Yüan masters. More gifted was Wang Hui (1632–1717), who as a poor student had been introduced to Wang Shih-min, whose pupil he became. He devoted much of his talent to the imitation of early masters, and his huge *œuvre* consists chiefly of variations on the styles of the great classical masters as they had been successively reinterpreted by Huang Kung-wang, Tung Ch'i-ch'ang and Wang Shih-min. The Palace Museum Collection in Taipei contains a number of clever pastiches of tenth-century and Northern Sung landscapes which are almost certainly his work.

Of the four Wangs, Wang Yüan-ch'i (1642–1715) was the most gifted and original. The grandson of Wang Shih-min, he rose to high office under the Manchus, becoming Chancellor of the Hanlin Academy and Vice-President of the Board of Finance. He was a favourite of K'ang-hsi, who frequently summoned him to paint in his presence, and he was appointed one of the editors of the great anthology of painting and calligraphy, *P'ei-wen-chai shu-hua-p'u*, published by imperial order in 1708. But Wang Yüan-ch'i was no academician. Although he drew his themes from the Yüan masters and his curious angular forms and gaunt trees from Tung Ch'i-ch'ang, he had an obsession with form, unique in a Chinese painter, which has caused some Western writers to liken him to Cézanne. With deep concentration, he would, as it were, pull apart and reassemble the elements in his landscapes like a Cubist, to achieve a semi-abstract order of reality of great purity and serenity that recalls Ni Tsan and is utterly different from the mannered distortions of Yüan Chiang and his school.

Chinese art historians like to classify painters in groups, and the 'Four Wangs', together with Wu Li and Yün Shou-p'ing (1633–90), make up the 'Six Great Masters of the Ch'ing Dynasty'. Yün Shou-p'ing (commonly known as Yün Nan-t'ien) was the son of an ardent Ming loyalist and consequently had to live in partial obscurity in the Soochow-Hangchow region, far from the capital, where he supported himself by his painting and calligraphy. He had aspirations as a landscape-painter, but, feeling himself unable to compete in this field with his close friend Wang Hui, he turned to flower-painting, chiefly in the 'boneless' style. He is at his best in the intimate art of painting fans and album-leaves, and his pictures have become deservedly popular for

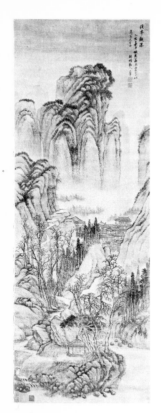

202 Wang Hui (1632–1717). *Landscape in the Manner of Fan K'uan*, dated equivalent to 1695. Hanging scroll. Ink and slight colour on paper. Ch'ing Dynasty.

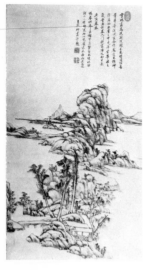

203 Wang Yüan-ch'i (1642–1715). *Landscape in the Manner of Ni Tsan*. Hanging scroll. Ink and slight colour on paper. Ch'ing Dynasty.

216

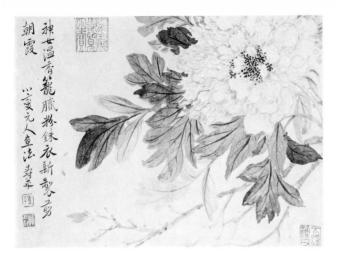

204 Yün Shou-p'ing (1633–90). *Peony*. Leaf from an album of flower studies. Ink and colour on paper. Ch'ing Dynasty.

the beauty of their colour and the skill of their brushwork and arrangement. Wu Li, born in 1632, is of unusual interest because he came under the influence of the Jesuits, was baptized, spent six years studying theology in Macao, where he was ordained in 1688, thereafter devoting the rest of his life to missionary work in Kiangsu. However, his conversion in no way changed his style of painting. A pupil of Wang Chien and an intimate friend of Wang Hui, he called himself Mo-ching Tao-jen, the Taoist of the ink-well (in the literal sense of Alice's treacle-well), continuing, after an unproductive period following his conversion, to paint in the eclectic manner of the Early Ch'ing *wen-jen*, without a hint of European influence, until his death in 1718.

No account of seventeenth-century painting should omit the name of Hung-jen, one of the 'Four Masters of Anhui', a Buddhist monk who died young in 1663 after painting a small number of spare, dry, exquisitely sensitive, yet monumental landscapes, closer in spirit to Ni Tsan than to any of his contemporaries. Another important group of the period was the 'Eight Masters of Nanking' who included several minor landscapists of great sensibility, such as Kao

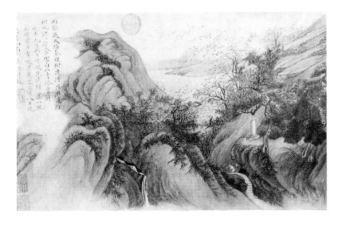

205 Wu Li (1632–1718). *White Clouds and Green Mountains*. Detail of a handscroll. Ink and colour on silk. Ch'ing Dynasty.

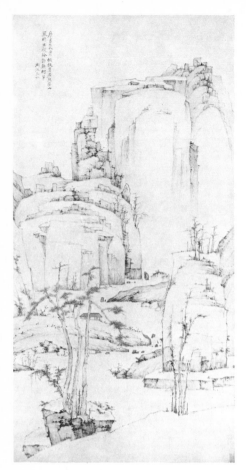

206 Hung-jen (1610–63). *The Coming of Autumn.* Hanging scroll. Ink on paper. Ch'ing Dynasty.

207 Kung Hsien (*c.* 1620–1689). *A Thousand Peaks and a Myriad Rivers.* Hanging scroll. Ink on paper. Ch'ing Dynasty.

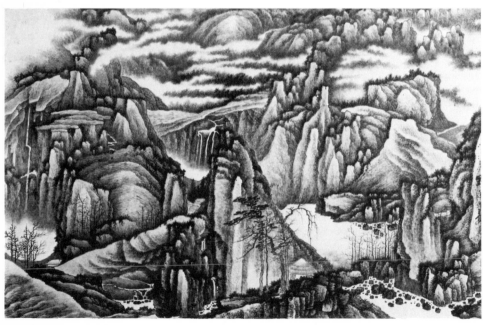

Ts'en and Fan Ch'i, and one major figure – Kung Hsien (c. 1620–89), one of whose strange, silent landscapes I have illustrated. The ominous stillness, produced by a brush that barely moves, the chiaroscuro and dense texture, suggest that Kung Hsien and his circle may have seen European engravings brought to Nanking by the Jesuits. Though a dour recluse, Kung Hsien was an influential teacher, and his pupil Wang Kai was the chief compiler of the *Painting Manual of the Mustard Seed Garden*, referred to on page 193.

An example of the growing eclecticism of the eighteenth century is Hua Yen (1682–after 1755), or Hsin-lo Shan-jen, whose *œuvre* included 'boneless' bird and flower paintings, bamboo-paintings, echoes of the misty impressionism of Kao K'o-kung, as well as landscapes in the literary style of

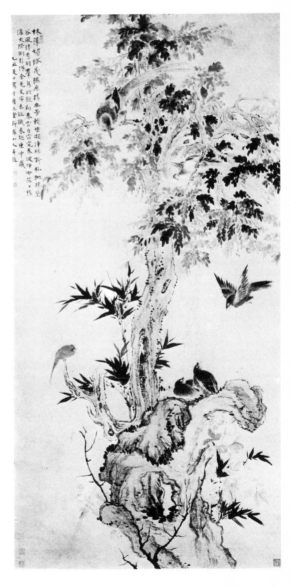

208 Hua Yen (1682–after 1755). Birds, tree and rock. Dated equivalent to 1745. Hanging scroll. Ink and colour on paper. Ch'ing Dynasty.

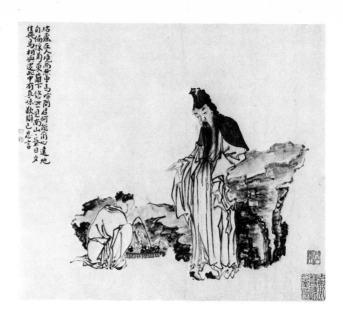

209 Huang Shen (1687–after 1768).
*The Poet T'ao Yüan-ming enjoys the
Early Chrysanthemums*. Album-leaf.
Ink and colour on paper. Ch'ing
Dynasty.

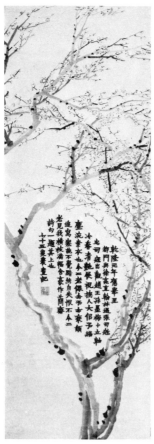

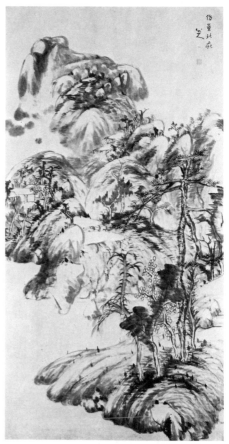

210 Chin Nung (1687–1764). Plum
blossom. Hanging scroll. Ink on
paper, 1736.

211 Chu Ta (Pa-ta Shan-jen, 1625–c. 1705).
Landscape in the Manner of Tung Yüan.
Hanging scroll. Ink on paper.

Wang Hui and Shen Chou and in the old green and blue style. Hua Yen was one of the 'Eight Eccentrics of Yangchow', who also included among their number Lo P'ing (1733–99), Huang Shen (1687–after 1768), the element of caricature in whose paintings made him especially popular in Japan, and Chin Nung (1687–1764), who did not begin to paint his odd, vigorous and highly individual landscapes, and bamboo- and flower-paintings, until he was fifty.

Groupings such as the 'Four Wangs', the 'Eight Masters of Nanking' and the 'Eight Eccentrics of Yangchow' have little foundation in fact. Where, for instance, does individualism stop and eccentricity begin? These terms cannot be defined. Does the name involve some links within the group? Not necessarily. Were there really eight masters in Nanking, eight eccentrics in Yangchow? It all seems too pat. Some of these men were friends, others not; some were outstanding, others quite obscure. But the traditional groupings are helpful, as much to Chinese as to Western readers, in reducing the bewildering number of Ch'ing painters to some sort of order.

The careers and work of some of the Yangchow Eccentrics point to a change in the status of the so-called 'amateur' painter in China. Ideally, he was an official or a man of means who painted for pleasure in his spare time. But among the Ch'ing gentlemen-painters were many who were not officials and had no private income and so were forced – although this was not openly acknowledged – to paint for a living. Wang Hui, for example, painted industriously for the patrons in whose mansions he lodged for months at a time, while competition for the patronage of the rich Yangchow salt merchants forced artists such as Huang Shen and Chin Nung to cultivate a deliberate oddity to attract their attention. The repetitiveness of Wang Hui and the eccentricity of Huang Shen were due in part at least to sheer economic necessity. The miracle is that the discipline and sensitivity of their brushwork is so seldom compromised.

By now it must be clear that painters such as Hung-jen, Kung Hsien and Hua Yen were by no means orthodox members of the literary school. They belong rather in the company of the Individualists, whose achievement made the first sixty years of the Ch'ing Dynasty one of the most creative periods in the history of Chinese painting. The greatest of the Early Ch'ing Individualists were Chu Ta (1625–c. 1705), K'un-ts'an (Shih-ch'i, c. 1610–c. 1670) and Shih-t'ao (Tao-chi, 1641–c. 1717).

Chu Ta, or Pa-ta Shan-jen, as he generally signed himself, was a distant descendant of the Ming royal house who on the advent of the Manchus became a monk. When his father died, he was struck dumb and would only shout and laugh, the butt of the children who ran after his ragged figure in the streets. He turned his back not only upon the world but upon the art of painting as practised in his time. His brush style

THE INDIVIDUALISTS

appears careless and slapdash and yet, like that of the Ch'an eccentrics who were his spiritual ancestors, it is incredibly sure and confident. His landscapes, executed in a dashing shorthand, carry Tung Ch'i-ch'ang's creative distortion of the southern tradition to a pitch that must have shocked the orthodox disciples of the Late Ming master. Perhaps his peculiar genius shows best in his swift album-sketches, in which a small, angry-looking bird perches upon a rock in an infinity of space, or in his studies of fish-like rocks and rock-like fishes, drawn in a few brilliant sweeping lines of the brush. This is 'ink-play' at its most unrestrained; yet it is no mere empty virtuosity, for Pa-ta's deceptively simple style captures the very essence of the flowers, plants and creatures he portrays.

Shih-t'ao and Shih-ch'i are linked together by Chinese art historians as the 'Two Stones' (*Erh Shih*), yet there is no positive evidence that they were close friends. Shih-ch'i (K'un-ts'an) was a devout Buddhist who spent all his life as a monk and his later years as abbot of a monastery at Nanking, an austere and unapproachable recluse. The texture of his landscapes, painted with a dry, scrubby brush, has the groping, almost fumbling quality that we find in Cézanne, and, as in Cézanne, this very awkwardness, this refusal to make concessions to the viewer, bear witness to the painter's integrity. Yet the final effect – in the beautiful autumn landscape in the British Museum, London, for example – gives an impression of grandeur and serenity.

Shih-t'ao, whose family name was Chu Jo-chi, was a lineal descendant of the founder of the Ming Dynasty, which fell when he was a boy of fourteen. He thereupon joined the Buddhist community on Lu-shan, taking the monastic name Tao-chi. But he was no recluse, and never a real monk. In 1657 he went to live in Hangchow, and thereafter spent much of his life wandering about China, visiting sacred mountains in the company of monks, scholars, and painter friends such as Mei Ch'ing, and spending three years in Peking (where he and Wang Yüan-ch'i collaborated on a picture *Bamboo and Rocks*). Finally he settled in Yangchow, where he often painted in company with Pa-ta Shan-jen till the latter's death in c. 1705. He himself died perhaps twelve years later. A chronicle of Yangchow, a city famous for its gardens, says that one of his favourite hobbies was 'piling up stones' – that is, designing gardens, among which his Garden of Ten Thousand Rocks, laid out for the Yü family, was considered his masterpiece. It may be that some of his little album landscapes were actually suggestions for garden designs.

Though Shih-t'ao was a Buddhist by training, he was a Taoist at heart. His aesthetic philosophy is contained in the *Hua-yü-lu*, a series of notes on painting written at different times, put together and published after his death. Like Kung Hsien, he has no doubts about his own powers, though, unlike Kung Hsien, we may be sure he had his tongue in his

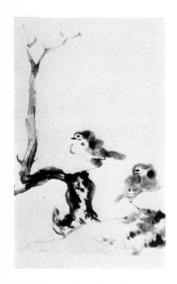

212 Chu Ta. *Two Birds*. Album-leaf. Ink on paper. Ch'ing Dynasty. Detail.

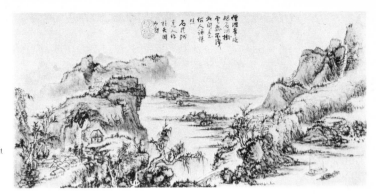

213 Shih-ch'i (K'un-ts'an, c. 1710–93). *Autumn Landscape*. Dated equivalent to 1666. Handscroll. Ink and slight colour on paper. Ch'ing Dynasty.

cheek when he wrote, 'If it happens that my work approaches that of some old painter, it is he who comes close to me, not I who am imitating him.' The core of his doctrine is the supreme importance of the *i-hua* – literally, the 'one line'. There has been much speculation as to what this means, but perhaps it had already been explained by the Sung writer Kuo Jo-hsü, commenting on a remark of Chang Yen-yüan's about Lu T'an-wei. 'His meaning,' wrote Kuo, 'was not that a whole page of writing or the depiction of an entire object can be carried out with a single brushstroke; but rather that from beginning to end the brush is kept responsive, with continuity and interrelationship, and no "break in flow of spirit".'[3] It is by means of the *i-hua* that form is made to emerge out of undifferentiated chaos, and only when he understands this can the painter begin to represent nature. It is essential, moreover, that he be deeply versed in the old masters, though this does not mean that he should imitate their methods, for, as Shih-t'ao said in the *Hua-yü-lu*, 'The method which up till now has not been a method is the painter's best method.' Shih-t'ao's concept of the ecstatic union of the artist with nature is not new, but nowhere in the whole of Chinese art will we find it expressed with so much spontaneous charm. Whether in a long handscroll, such as the delightful illustration of T'ao Yüan-ming's *The Peach*

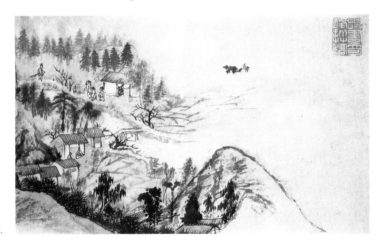

214 Shih-t'ao (1641–c. 1717). *The Peach Blossom Spring*. Detail of a handscroll. Ink and colour on paper. Ch'ing Dynasty.

Blossom Spring in the Freer Gallery, Washington, D.C., or in a towering landscape, such as the magnificent view of Mount Lu in the Sumitomo Collection, Oiso, or in his album-leaves, his forms and colours are ever fresh, his spirit light, his inventiveness and wit inexhaustible.

The art of Shih-t'ao, and indeed that of all the Individualists, represents a private protest against the new academicism of the literati. But as the Ch'ing settled deeper into that stagnation which seems to have been the fate of every long-lived dynasty in Chinese history, the lamp of individualism burned more and more dimly. During the nineteenth century the growing foreign menace produced not action but paralysis at the centre, and patronage shrank to almost nothing. A handful of literati kept the tradition alive, however, until in the twentieth century there took place a revolution in Chinese painting over which the artists themselves had little control.

CERAMICS The astonishing work of the seventeenth-century Individualists was produced during a long period of confusion, banditry and civil war which began after the death of the Wan-li Emperor in 1620 and was not finally resolved until the time of K'ang-hsi. These years of political and economic chaos had a serious effect upon the gigantic ceramics industry at Ching-te-chen. Already before the end of the Ming Dynasty the imperial wares had sharply declined in both quality and quantity. The reign of T'ien-ch'i is noted for a coarse, brittle blue and white prized in Japan as *tenkei* ware, but marked pieces of his successor Ch'ung-chen are very rare and of poor quality. During these years China lost to Japan the great market she had built up in South-east Asia and Europe, and did not fully recover it again till Wu San-kuei had been defeated and South China had been brought once more under the control of the central government. Consequently the so-called 'transitional wares' of the mid seventeenth century, being for the most part continuations of earlier styles, are not always easy to identify. The most characteristic of them are strongly built blue and white jars, bowls and vases decorated with figures in landscapes, rocks and flowers (especially the 'tulip', possibly based on a European motif) in a thick violet glaze which Chinese collectors call 'ghost's-face blue' (*kuei–mien–ch'ing*) and Western connoisseurs 'violets in milk'. Many of them were made primarily for export, and, like the export blue and white of Chia-ching and Wan-li, have a freedom of drawing that gives them considerable appeal.

CHING-TE-CHEN No abrupt change at Ching-te-chen followed the establishment of the new dynasty. The imperial factory was still functioning after a fashion in the 1650s, and pieces produced during these unsettled years represent, as we would expect, a continuation of the style of the Wan-li period. Between 1673 and 1675 Kiangsi was laid waste by Wu San-kuei's rebel horde and in the latter year the imperial factories at Ching-te-chen were destroyed. They were rebuilt a few years later. In 1682 K'ang-hsi appointed as Director of the Imperial Kilns Ts'ang Ying-hsüan, a Secretary in the Imperial Parks Department. Ts'ang, who arrived at Ching-te-chen early in the following year, was the first of three great directors whose names are linked to this supreme moment in the history of Ching-te-chen. It is not known precisely when Ts'ang retired. In 1726 Yung-cheng appointed Nien Hsi-yao, who in turn was succeeded in 1736 by his assistant T'ang Ying, who held the office until 1749 or 1753. Thus Ts'ang's directorship corresponds roughly to the K'ang-hsi period, Nien's to Yung-cheng, and T'ang Ying's to the first years of Ch'ien-lung.

Two Chinese works give us useful information on the Imperial Kilns and their output, though both were written after the factory had begun to decline. Chu Yen published his *T'ao-shuo* in 1774, while the *Ching-te-chen t'ao-lu*, written by Lan P'u, did not appear till 1815. The most valuable description, however, is that contained in two letters written by the French Jesuit Père d'Entrecolles, who was in China from 1698 to 1741, and not only had influential friends at court but also many converts among the humble artisans in the factories at Ching-te-chen. These letters, dated 1712 and 1722, give a vivid picture of the whole process of manufacture, of which he was an intelligent observer:[4] a recent Chinese writer has called him an 'industrial spy'. He recounts how the *petuntse* (china-stone) and *kaolin* (china-clay) are quarried and prepared, and the enormous labour involved in kneading the clay. He describes a degree of specialization among the decorators so minute that it is a wonder the painting has any life at all: 'One workman does nothing but draw the first colour line beneath the rims of the pieces; another traces flowers, while a third one paints. . . . The men who sketch the outlines learn sketching, but not painting; those who paint [that is, apply the colour] study only painting, but not sketching,' all in the interests of absolute uniformity. Elsewhere he says that a single piece might pass through the hands of seventy men. He speaks of the hazards of the kiln and of how a whole firing is often lost by accident or miscalculation. He tells how the Emperor would send down Sung Dynasty *kuan*, Ju, Ting and Ch'ai wares to be copied, and of the gigantic fish-bowls ordered by the palace which took nineteen days to fire. The greatest challenge, however, was set by the agents of the European merchants at Canton, who demanded open-work lanterns, table-tops, and even musical instruments in porcelain. As early as 1635 the Dutch were forwarding, via Formosa, wooden models of the shapes of vessels required. We can get some idea of the extent of the foreign trade from the fact that in 1643 no less than 129,036 pieces of porcelain were sent via Formosa to the Dutch Governor-General of Batavia for shipment to Holland. Most of it must have been made at Ching-te-chen.

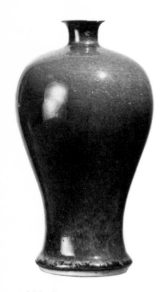

215 Mei-p'ing vase. Porcelain, with ox-blood (*Lang-yao*) glaze. Ch'ing Dynasty, K'ang-hsi period.

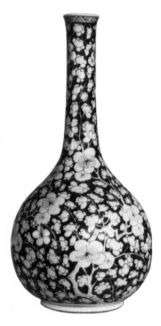

216 Bottle. Porcelain, decorated with plum blossoms in underglaze blue. Ch'ing Dynasty, K'ang-hsi period.

The most beautiful K'ang-hsi wares, and those which have been most admired both in China and the West, are not the oddly shaped and extravagantly decorated pieces made for the export market, but the small monochromes, which in their classic perfection of form, surface and colour recapture something of the subtlety and restraint of the Sung. The *T'ao-lu* says that Ts'ang Ying-hsüan's clays were rich, his glazes brilliant, his porcelain thin-bodied, and that he developed four new colours – eel-skin yellow, spotted yellow, snake-skin green and turquoise-blue. He also perfected a mirror black which was often decorated with gold, an exquisite soft red shading to green known as 'peach-bloom' and used, it seems, for a very small range of vases and vessels for the scholar's desk, an 'imperial yellow', and a clear powder-blue, blown on through a bamboo tube and then often painted with arabesques in gold. These pieces were especially admired in France, where it was the fashion to mount them in *ormolu*. The most splendid effect was a rich red produced from copper, known in Europe as *sang-de-bœuf* ('ox-blood') and in China as *Lang-yao*; several members of the Lang family have been suggested as possible candidates for the honour of having had this ware named after them – the most likely being Lang T'ing-chi, who, as Governor of Kiangsi from 1705 to 1712, took an active interest in the kilns at Ching-te-chen. The glaze was probably applied by spraying and ran down the sides of the vase, stopping miraculously short of the foot – a degree of control which was lost in the Ch'ien-lung period and has only recently been recovered; while a beautiful effect appears round the rim where the colour has failed to 'develop' and the glaze has a pale greenish tinge. The K'ang-hsi potters also copied the beautiful white 'egg-shell' bowls of Yung-lo, their versions being more flawless than the Ming originals, and made a fine imitation of the classical Ting ware of the Sung period.

These monochromes appealed chiefly to cultivated taste. Much more widely appreciated were the underglaze blue and enamelled wares, for which there was a huge demand both in China and abroad. Most K'ang-hsi blue and white was produced by the mass-production methods of which Père d'Entrecolles gives so depressing a picture, and as a result has a technical perfection combined with a dead uniformity only partly redeemed by the magnificent quality of the cobalt itself, which has a vivid, intense luminosity never equalled before or since. It had a great vogue in Europe in the first half of the eighteenth century, particularly popular being the 'ginger jars' decorated with blossoming prunus on a blue ground reticulated with lines suggesting ice-cracks. Thereafter it was largely replaced in favour by the brightly coloured enamelled wares. Between 1667 and 1670 an imperial edict had been issued forbidding the use of the K'ang-hsi reign-mark. It is not known how long the ban remained in force, but there are comparatively few genuine pieces with the K'ang-hsi mark, and a correspondingly large number to which the potters added the fictitious marks of the Ming emperors Hsüan-te and Ch'eng-hua.

The great achievement of the potters working under Ts'ang Ying-hsüan, however, was in the enamels, of which two kinds had been developed by the end of the Ming Dynasty: *wu-ts'ai* (five colours) enamelled over the glaze, and *san-ts'ai* (three colours) applied directly 'on the biscuit'. In the K'ang-hsi *wu-ts'ai*, overglaze violet-blue replaces the underglaze blue of Wan-li, but the dominating colour is a transparent jewel-like green, which led its European admirers in the nineteenth century to christen it *famille verte*. Most of these pieces are vases and bowls, made purely for ornament, and decorated with birds or butterflies amid flowering branches, disposed with an exquisite and subtle sense of balance which strongly suggests that these designs were inspired by paintings. The revived *san-ts'ai* enamel-on-biscuit was used chiefly for reproductions of archaic bronzes, and for figurines of Buddhist and Taoist divinities, children, birds and animals. Also enamelled directly on the biscuit is the so-called *famille noire*, whose polychrome floral decoration is set off against a background of a rich black made almost iridescent by being washed over with a transparent green glaze. Until recently this spectacular ware had an enormous vogue among foreign collectors, and, like certain other Ch'ing enamels, still commands prices out of all proportion to its aesthetic worth. Examples of both *famille verte* and *famille noire* were sometimes adorned with Ch'eng-hua reign-marks to show how highly their makers regarded them. Towards the end of the K'ang-hsi period the robust vigour of the *famille verte* began to yield to a new style dominated by a delicate rose-pink, which is known in Europe as *famille rose* and which the Chinese call *yang-ts'ai* (foreign colour). It had been invented, in about 1650, by Andreas Cassius of Leyden, who succeeded in producing a rose-red from gold chloride. A saucer dish, dated 1721, in the Percival David Foundation, London, must be one of the earliest Chinese examples of the use of this colour, which was probably introduced by the Jesuits.

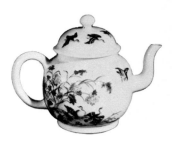

217 Teapot. *Famille verte* porcelain decorated with enamels in *Ku Yüeh* style. Mark and period of Ch'ien-lung. Ch'ing Dynasty.

The feminine elegance of *famille rose* came to its full flowering with the appointment of Nien Hsi-yao as Director of the Imperial Kilns in 1726. Nien's directorship is chiefly famous for its 'imitation of the antique and invention of novelties'. As a typical example of the former we have his exquisite copies of classical Sung wares, so perfect that a Ju ware bottle now in the Percival David Foundation was for many years accepted as a genuine Sung piece by the Palace Museum authorities in Taipei, until its concealed Yung-cheng mark was discovered. Indeed, many Yung-cheng pieces had the reign-mark ground away so that they might be passed off as Sung when they were illicitly sold out of the palace collection. Nien's 'novelties' included the 'tea-dust' glaze, made

WARES OF THE YUNG-CHENG
PERIOD

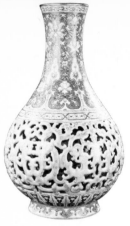

218 Double vase, *t'ao-p'ing*. Porcelain, the inner vessel decorated in underglaze blue, the outer, with pierced sides, in *fen-ts'ai* enamels. Ch'ing Dynasty, Ch'ien-lung period

WARES OF THE CH'IEN-LUNG PERIOD

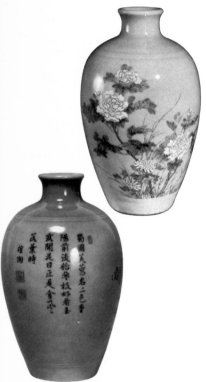

219 Vase. Porcelain, decorated with flowers in *famille rose* enamels and a poem by T'ang Ying. Eighteenth century, Ch'ien-lung period.

by blowing green enamel on to an iron yellow-brown glaze, an improvement on the exquisite pale-blue glaze known in Europe as *clair-de-lune*, and such Rococo effects as painting in ink-black flecked with gold, or in greenish-blue flecked with red. Already in 1712 d'Entrecolles had been asked by the officials at Ching-te-chen for curious European objects which might be copied in porcelain and sent to court, and during the Yung-cheng period – and increasingly under Ch'ien-lung – this taste for extravagant forms and new effects was to absorb the energies of the potters at the cost of real refinement of taste. Its most lamentable results can be seen in the decline of *famille rose*, which early in the Yung-cheng period had had an exquisite, feminine delicacy; it was spoilt by the foreign demand for rich and garish decoration, finally degenerating into the livid salmon-pink of the nineteenth century.

In point of sheer craftsmanship the Ch'ien-lung period is supreme, and the finest of the enamelled wares produced under the directorship of T'ang Ying are unsurpassed. T'ang lived and worked with his potters, had complete mastery of their techniques and was continually experimenting with new effects, reproducing the colour and texture of silver, grained wood, lacquer, bronze, jade, mother-of-pearl and even cloisonné. He copied Italian faience drug-pots, Venetian glass, Limoges enamels and even Delft painted pottery and Japanese 'old Imari' ware, which were themselves copies of Late Ming blue and white. T'ang Ying also reproduced all the familiar Sung wares (his rather glassy copies of Lung-ch'üan celadon being particularly fine), while his versions of the robust Canton wares were considered a great improvement on the originals. But the most beautiful of the porcelains produced under his direction are the enamelled egg-shell vessels and bowls, such as the lovely lavender vase, decorated with mallow flowers and chrysanthemums and bearing a poem believed to be by T'ang Ying himself. In recent years fashion has swung away from these exquisite objects to the more free and vital wares of T'ang and Sung, in which we can see and feel the touch of the craftsman's hand, but nothing can surpass the finest of these Ch'ien-lung pieces for sheer perfection of finish.

The influence of European taste on the decoration of Ching-te-chen porcelain, which had been growing since the end of the K'ang-hsi period, is nowhere more clearly seen than in a small and choice group of *famille rose* enamelled pieces known as *Ku-yüeh-hsüan*.[5] Indeed, many of them are decorated with European scenes, and even the Chinese flower motifs have a foreign quality in the realistic drawing, shading and handling of perspective. They generally bear poems followed by red seals, while the *nien-hao* on the base is in embossed enamel.

A few words should be said on the subject of the porcelain made for the European market during the seventeenth and eighteenth centuries. Already in the sixteenth century the South China potters were decorating dishes with Portuguese coats of arms, and the Dutch trade vastly increased the demand in the seventeenth century. It was the Dutch who chiefly furnished the 'porcelain rooms' in the great houses of France and Germany, of which the unfinished 'Japanese Palace' of Augustus the Strong, King of Prussia and Elector of Saxony, was the most ambitious. Augustus is reputed to have bartered a regiment of grenadiers for a set of *famille verte* vases, while it was he at whose order Johann Böttger made the first European porcelain in Dresden in 1709. During the seventeenth century European enthusiasts had been quite content to receive Chinese shapes decorated in the Chinese taste, but by the end of the century the practice was growing of sending out to Canton not only specimen shapes but also subjects for decoration, in response to which Ching-te-chen sent white porcelain 'in the blank' down to Canton, where it was painted under the supervision of the European agents. The motifs included armorial bearings, *genre* scenes, figure subjects, portraits, hunting scenes, pictures of ships (taken chiefly from engravings), and religious subjects such as the Baptism, Crucifixion and Resurrection – the so-called 'Jesuit China'. Towards the end of the eighteenth century, however, the enthusiasm for things Chinese began to wane, since Europe was now beginning to supply her needs from her own porcelain factories. The great days of the export trade were over, and the so-called 'Nankeen ware' (enamelled porcelain) of the nineteenth century bears eloquent witness to its decay.

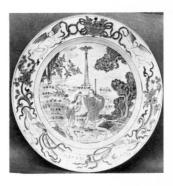

220 'Jesuit China' dish. Porcelain, decorated in underglaze blue with a Crucifixion scene after a European engraving. Ch'ing Dynasty.

Although the Imperial Kilns continued to flourish until the end of the eighteenth century, their great era ended with the departure of T'ang Ying. Thereafter the decline was slow but steady. At first we see an even greater ingenuity and elaboration in the manufacture of such freakish objects as boxes with porcelain chains and perforated and revolving vases. But after the beginning of the nineteenth century the decay is more rapid, and though some of the wares of the reign of Tao-kuang (1821–50) are of fine quality, the industry suffered a crippling blow when Ching-te-chen was sacked by the Taiping rebels in 1853. Thereafter there was a revival under T'ung-chih (1862–74), and a further revival has taken place in the twentieth century. Today the factories at Ching-te-chen are run on modern industrial lines, but care is being taken to preserve the skills and techniques of the traditional potters.

While the Imperial Kilns were concentrating on an ever greater technical perfection, it was the provincial factories in the south which most successfully maintained their vigour and vitality. Of the scores of these kilns we can only mention a few. I-hsing in Kiangsu specialized in the production of

NINETEENTH–CENTURY AND PROVINCIAL WARES

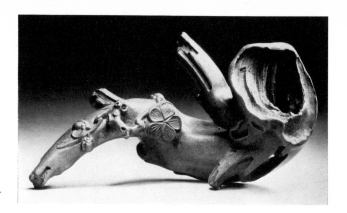

little vessels, made of red stoneware, for the scholar's table, most ingeniously fashioned in the form of plants, tree-trunks, beetles, rats and other creatures, and in the manufacture of teapots. Te-hua continued to make the fine white porcelain developed during the Ming Dynasty. Other provincial wares were made either for local use or for shipment to regions less exacting in their demands than the Europeans. This applies particularly to the vulgar but vigorous brown stonewares made at Shekwan, near Fatshan in Kwangtung, consisting chiefly of ornamental pieces, figurines and large jars decorated with a thick blue glaze streaked and flecked with grey and green, which since the Ming Dynasty had both gratified local taste and had been exported in quantity to the Nan-hai ('South Seas').

DECORATIVE ARTS:
JADE, LACQUER, GLASS

In about the year 1680 K'ang-hsi set up workshops in the palace precincts for the manufacture of porcelain, lacquerware, glass, enamel, furniture, jade and other objects for court use. The porcelain project, intended to replace distant Ching-te-chen, was found impracticable and was soon abandoned, but the other workshops turned out a variety of decorative arts of superb quality and continued in production for the rest of the dynasty. The finest pieces of jade-carving are often assigned, with very little reason, to the reign of Ch'ien-lung. Carved jade is extremely difficult to date, and work of the highest quality has been produced right up to the present day.

Other factories supplied the needs of the wealthy middle class and of the export market. Peking and Soochow, for example, specialized in carved lacquer, Foochow and Canton in the painted sort. The Canton products were considered inferior both in China and abroad because they were often made hastily to meet the demands of European merchants who were only permitted to reside in Canton for a few months of the year. The Foochow lacquer folding-screens and cabinets, with their bold carving and rich colours embellished with powdered gold, were exported not only to Europe but also to Russia, Japan, Mecca and India. So many were transhipped from the Coromandel Coast of

222 Carp leaping out of the water. Carved green jade. Ch'ing Dynasty.

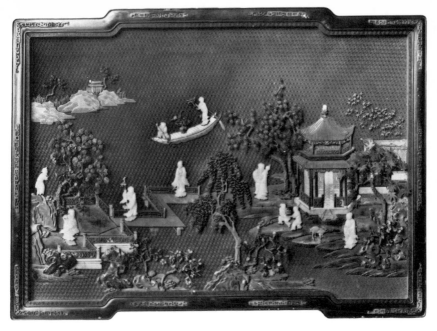

223 Taoist Paradise. Carved red lacquer inset with jade, lapis lazuli and gilt metal. Ch'ing Dynasty, eighteenth century.

South India that this kind of lacquer became known in eighteenth-century England as 'Coromandel ware'.

K'ang-hsi's glass factory produced a wide variety of coloured glass bottles and vases, the speciality being an opaque glass laminated in layers of several contrasting colours, through which the designs were carved by the intaglio method. 'Snuff-bottles' (originally made for medicine during the Sung and Yüan Dynasties) were carved in glass and painted with enamel colours. They were also made in an endless variety of semi-precious substances such as lacquer, jade, crystal, coral, agate and enamel, all of which were imitated in porcelain at Ching-te-chen. In the eighteenth century the art of 'back-painting' on glass was introduced from Europe into China. It was said to have been practised by Castiglione in Peking, and soon became popular for painting delightful *genre* scenes on the backs of mirrors. The application of this technique to the decoration of the inside surface of transparent snuff-bottles, first attempted in about 1887, represents the last effort of the dying arts of the Ch'ing Dynasty to venture into new fields.

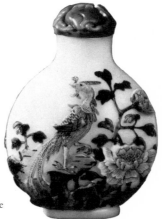

224 Snuff-bottle. Enamelled glass, inscribed *Ku-yüeh-hsüan* on the base Ch'ing Dynasty.

12 The Twentieth Century

It was towards the end of the nineteenth century that China began to stir once more into life, roused by the aggressive penetration of the Western powers. But it was to be decades before her response to Western art was anything more than passive or reluctantly imitative. China's rulers, unlike their Japanese counterparts of the Meiji period, did not see the arts of Europe as an aid to modernization and reform. If they had any attitude at all to Western culture, as opposed to Western guns and machines, it was one of hostility and contempt, and the problems of the cultural confrontation, as far as the arts were concerned, were left to take care of themselves.

ARCHITECTURE   From the mid nineteenth century onwards, Western-style commercial buildings, schools and churches were rising wherever the foreigners penetrated. If those put up by the foreigners were bad, the Chinese imitations of them were even worse. A hybrid style, combining Chinese and Western elements, soon came into being, but until well into the present century, practising architects knew too little about traditional building methods to be able to adapt them successfully to modern materials, and the results were generally disastrous.

In 1930 a group of architects founded the Chinese Architectural Research Society to remedy this defect, and to explore new ways of adapting traditional forms to modern needs. It was joined in the following year by Liang Ssu-ch'eng, who became the dominating influence in Chinese architecture for three decades. The results of their work, and of that of foreign architects such as Henry K. Murphy, can be seen in government and university buildings erected in Nanking, Shanghai, Peking and elsewhere during the few peaceful years before the Japanese invasion of 1937. Attractive as some of these are, they are still essentially Western buildings 'sinified' with a traditional curved roof and enriched with detail translated from timber into painted concrete. A recent, deplorable example of this style is the National Palace Museum in Taipei, beloved of tourists. These architects had not yet discovered the truth, long before grasped by the Japanese, that the essence of their traditional architecture lies not in the curved roof, lovely as it is, but in the post and frame structure which, unlike the roof, is readily adaptable to modern needs and materials.

After Liberation in 1949, Chinese official architecture came for a time under the influence of the Soviet wedding-

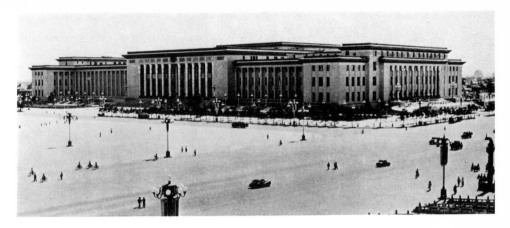

cake style, which left its mark on a group of public buildings put up in the 1950s, notably the Military Museum of the Chinese People's Revolution. This style has since been repudiated on economic no less than ideological grounds. Movement towards acceptance of what is loosely called the 'international modern style' has been slow and cautious. Beginning with the Peking Children's Hospital (1954), it has been most successful where a major structural challenge had to be met – for instance, in the Peking Workers' Gymnasium (1961) and the Capital Gymnasium (1971). The Great Hall of the People in Peking, seating ten thousand and completed in 1959 in the astonishingly short time of eleven months, is less remarkable for its style, which is conservative, than for its vast size, the classical dignity of its proportions, and its success as a symbol of the enduring strength of the new China.

225 The Great Hall of the People, Peking. 1959.

DECORATIVE ARTS

The decorative arts of the last hundred years reveal the same unresolved conflict between new alien styles and stagnant traditional ones. Although the level of craftsmanship remained high, the porcelain, lacquer and carved jade produced before 1950 was derivative and uninspired. Liberation, however, brought with it a vigorous revival of traditional crafts, fostered initially by the Peking Handicrafts Research Institute. To take but one example, in the Peking Jade Studios alone there are today fifteen hundred carvers at work; young apprentices learn secrets once jealously guarded by old master craftsmen, and together they are producing work of a technical quality probably higher than at any time since the reign of Ch'ien-lung.

Much of the output of these workshops is produced for the export market, which demands chiefly traditional designs. But at the same time, the needs of a socialist society in process of rapid industrialization are met, in jade- and ivory-carving for example, by idealized revolutionary themes, and increasing demand is met by mechanization, notably in some of the great ceramics factories at Ching-te-chen. The design problems that arise during transition from handicraft to industrial mass-production have yet to be completely solved; but this should cause no surprise when we remember how long this process took in Europe.

PAINTING The painting of the last hundred years presents perhaps the most vivid illustration of the tensions between old ideas and new, native styles and foreign, that are shaping modern China. By the nineteenth century the court painters, once so highly honoured, had sunk to a status hardly higher than that of palace servants, and even their names are not known. The literati, too, were victims of the growing paralysis of Ch'ing culture, and there were few outstanding amateur painters. In the first half of the century Tai Hsi (1801–60) and T'ang I-fen (1778–1853) were typically orthodox followers of the academic literary style of Wang Hui. But after the middle of the nineteenth century there came a gradual change. The style of Jen I (Jen Po-nien, 1840–95), the most interesting of the Late Ch'ing artists, owed part of its vigour to an infusion from popular art, part to the new restless spirit that was then abroad in the prosperous coastal cities.

For in Shanghai, where Jen Po-nien lived, the impact of European civilization was beginning to be felt. It showed itself in painting less in any change of style than in a new energy and boldness, which was perhaps the unconscious answer of the literati to the challenge of Western art. This new spirit burst forth in a handful of late followers of the Wu school, such as Chao Chih-ch'ien (1829–84), a distinguished scholar noted for his paintings of vines and flowers amid rocks, whose compositions and brush techniques were to influence the modern master Ch'i Pai-shih. Chao's follower Wu Ch'ang-shih (1842–1927) was a prolific painter chiefly of bamboo, flowers and rocks, which he combined with calligraphy in compositions of considerable power. The heavy, emphatic ink and strong colour that these artists employed come as a refreshing contrast to the timid good manners of the earlier generation.

Among the twentieth-century artists who may have been provoked into a reassertion of traditional styles were Huang Pin-hung (1864/5–1955) and Ch'i Pai-shih (1863–1957). Huang Pin-hung was one of the last of the great Wu school landscape-painters. He led the busy life of a 'professional amateur' between Shanghai and Peking, as painter, teacher, art historian and connoisseur, developing a style that became more and more daring and expressionistic as he approached old age. From a very different milieu came Ch'i Pai-shih, son of a small tenant-farmer in Hunan, who by talent and sheer determination became a dominating figure among painters in Peking, expressing himself with great boldness and simplicity. In his sixties he painted some very original landscapes, but he is best known for his late paintings, chiefly of birds and flowers, crabs and shrimps, which he reduces to essentials while miraculously preserving their inner life.

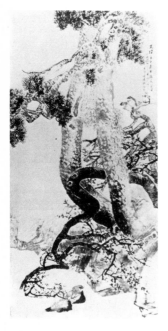

226 Jen Po-nien (1840–95). *Pine Tree and Mynah Birds*. Hanging scroll. Ink and colour on paper.

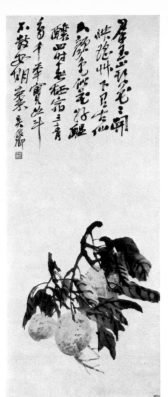

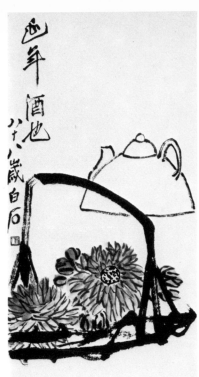

227 Wu Ch'ang-shih
(1842–1927). *Lychee Nuts.*
Hanging scroll. Ink and
colour on paper. Late
nineteenth to early
twentieth century.

228 Ch'i Pai-shih
(1863–1957). *The Thing
for Prolonging Life is Wine!*
Hanging scroll, 1951. Ink
and colour on paper.

In contrast to these thoroughly traditional masters is
Chang Ta-ch'ien (Chang Dai Chien), born in Szechwan in
1899 and trained in the Late Ch'ing literary style. Although
in dress and manner seemingly a survival from an earlier age,
he has responded to a wide range of influences, even including that of Abstract Expressionism, a movement that has had
a stimulating effect on countless Far Eastern painters since
1950. After moving to Brazil in 1949, Chang Ta-ch'ien
finally settled in California, where his robed and bearded
figure has become a familiar sight amid the pines of Carmel.

It might be thought that Westernization in the first half of
the twentieth century would have dealt Chinese traditional
art the same crippling blow that had struck Japanese art in
the nineteenth. This did not happen, partly because of the
overpowering strength of the tradition itself and the cultural
self-confidence of the educated class, partly because 'fine art'
was in the custody of amateurs and was kept separate from
their professional lives. Their work and milieu might change,
but when they took up the brush, it was still to express themselves in the language of Tung Ch'i-ch'ang and Wang Hui.
Such was their belief in the validity of the tradition, moreover, that for the most part they could take what they
wanted from Western art without surrendering to it. When,
much later, Chairman Mao exhorted artists to 'make foreign
things serve China', and to 'make the past serve the present',
he was pointing a path forward that they found easy to
follow, and one, indeed, that had already been taken by some

artists, notably Hsü Pei-hung (Ju Péon, 1895–1953), a decade earlier. In spite of the artistic controversies that enlivened the 1920s and 1930s, Chinese artists on the whole avoided such violent oscillations between acceptance and rejection of the West as had shaken Japanese art since the Meiji Restoration of 1868.

After tentative beginnings here and there in the coastal cities, the modern movement in Chinese art was launched in 1916 by Kao Chien-fu, who had recently returned from Japan. While in Tokyo, he had come under the influence of the Nihonga movement, dedicated to the revival of the Japanese tradition by introducing Western techniques such as shading and chiaroscuro, and contemporary subject-matter: one of Kao Chien-fu's most famous early hanging scrolls depicted a tank and an aeroplane. The work of Kao Chien-fu's Ling-nan p'ai (Cantonese school), as it was called, was too Japanese in feeling, and too deliberately synthetic, to command a wide following, but it showed that the traditional medium could be adapted to modern themes. Since 1949, shorn of its somewhat slickly decorative texture, the style created by the Ling-nan p'ai has been developed in China as one solution to the problem of expressing realistic, revolutionary content in the traditional medium.

The first modern art school in the Orient had been founded in 1876 in Tokyo. But no developments took place in China until 1906, when Nanking High Normal School and the Peiyang Normal School in Peking each opened a Department of Fine Art on the Western pattern. They were soon followed in Shanghai by several private studios modelled upon romantic notions of the typical Paris *atelier* which had

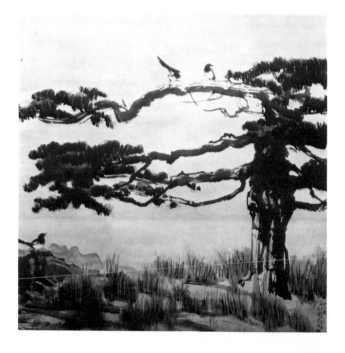

229 Hsü Pei-hung (Ju Péon, 1895–1953). *Magpies on an Old Tree*. Ink on paper. *c.* 1944.

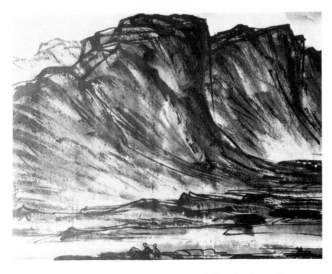

230 Lin Feng-mien (born 1906). *The Yangtse Gorges*. Ink and colour on paper.

been acquired, very much at second hand, from Japanese artists who had studied in France. Soon after the end of the First World War, art schools were being opened in Peking and Shanghai, Nanking and Hangchow, while the more fortunate students were flocking to Paris, where they came under the influence of the Post-Impressionists, Picasso, and Matisse.

By the middle 1920s Hsü Pei-hung had returned to Nanking, Liu Hai-su to Shanghai, Lin Feng-mien to Hangchow, and there was beginning to flourish in the big coastal cities an art which was for the most part just as academic as that of the traditional painters, the only difference being that now the medium was not Chinese ink but oil-paint. The French Concession in Shanghai became a little Montmartre, the centre of a transplanted Bohemianism that was inevitably quite out of touch with the feelings and aspirations of the mass of the Chinese people.

In the early 1930s, however, as the menace of Japanese aggression rose on the horizon, the atmosphere began to change. In Shanghai, the cosmopolitan Société des Deux Mondes, founded by the modern painter P'ang Hsün-ch'in, was dissolved, and the Storm Society took its place. Artists and writers became involved in bitter debates about their responsibility to society: the Bohemians proclaimed a doctrine of art for art's sake, the Realists urged a shift to the left and a closer identity with the people.

Finally, all doubts about the place of the artist in modern China were resolved by the Japanese attack on Peking in July 1937. Three years of steady retreat brought the painters and intellectuals close to the heart of the real China, and the later work of P'ang Hsün-ch'in, of the realists such as Hsiao Ting, and of the best of the wood-engravers, is full of a sense of discovery – not only of their own people, but also of their own land, for they had been driven by the war far into the Interior, to come for the first time face to face with the

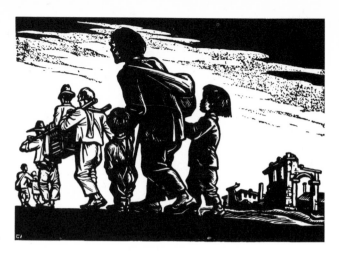

Li Hua. Refugees. Woodcut, c. 1939.

beauty of the western provinces, as yet untouched by the hybrid culture of the Treaty Ports. As the war dragged on, however, artists with a social conscience became bitterly disillusioned by the moral decay and corruption on the home front. Some joined the woodcut movement, which had been founded by the great writer Lu Hsün in the 1920s and was now being promoted as a weapon of socialist propaganda; others turned in protest to political cartooning or, to outwit the censor, to an elaborate and indirect form of social symbolism.

The Japanese surrender in 1945 left China exhausted and longing for peace. But hardly had the firing died away when this unhappy land was plunged into civil war, and all hopes of peaceful reconstruction were shattered. The art of the last years before the fall of the Kuomintang régime was marked by anger and bitterness on the part of the Realists, or by an almost defiant lyricism in the work of P'ang Hsün-ch'in, the wood-engraver Huang Yung-yü, and Chao Wu-chi (Zao Wou-ki), a young student of Lin Feng-mien at the Hang-chow Academy who had emerged from the obscurity of the Japanese occupation with a highly sensitive and original style which seemed to point the way to a new direction in Chinese painting. In 1948 Zao Wou-ki went to Paris, where he has since acquired an international reputation. Perhaps the most remarkable metamorphosis occurred in the art of Tseng Yu-ho, who, from being a competent academic painter in the manner of her master P'u Ch'in in post-war Peking, has, since she went to live in Honolulu, come under the influence of some of the most advanced movements in Western art.

For two decades, Chinese artists living outside the People's Republic have been making a significant contribution to the international movement in modern art. While the first Asian response to Abstract Expressionism took place in Japan in the 1950s, the Chinese painters who embraced the movement in the 1960s gave it a new depth, for their response was at the same time a rediscovery of the abstract, calligraphic

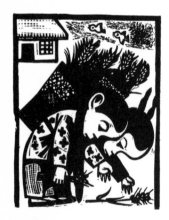

Huang Yung-yü. Harvest. Woodcut, 1948.

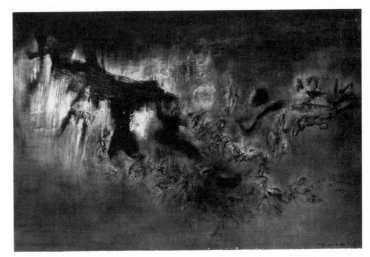

231 Chao Wu-chi (Zao Wou-ki, born 1920). *Mistral*, 1957. Oil on canvas.

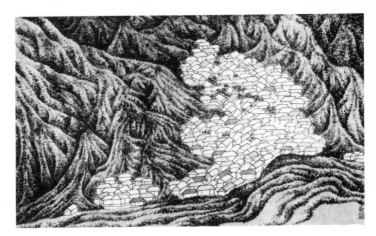

232 Tseng Yu-ho (born 1923). *Hawaiian Village*, 1955. Ink on paper.

233 Chuang Che. Abstraction.

roots of their own tradition, and not merely, as it had been for some Japanese artists, a skilful adoption of yet another new style from abroad. Yet even when their work appears most abstract it is, like that of the Late T'ang 'expressionists', never entirely divorced from the natural world, and the fact that we can 'read' their abstractions as landscapes gives them an added, and very Chinese, dimension. The pioneers were Liu Kuo-sung and Chuang Che, who in 1956 founded the 'Fifth Moon' group in Taipei, Lü Shou-k'un (Lui Shou Kwan), and members of the lively 'Circle' and 'In Tao' groups in Hongkong, which included Han Chi-fen (Hon Chi Fun), Chiang Yee (Cheung Yee) and Laurence Tam. Notable among Chinese artists in South-east Asia, Chung Ssu-pin (Choong Soo-pieng) in Singapore, before he became an abstract painter, was responding to the exotic beauty of the tropics with a style refreshingly free from the obvious influence of Gauguin.

ART IN CHINA SINCE
LIBERATION Meanwhile, within the People's Republic the total mobilization of hands and minds to the task of transforming China into a great modern power has had a profound effect upon the arts. Chairman Mao's exhortations to creative artists to serve the people, and to take both from foreign art and from their own tradition what China could use, have borne fruit most spectacularly not so much in painting as in a group of operas and ballets created in the 1960s, such as *The White-Haired Girl* and *The Red Detachment of Women*. In their novel combination of Chinese and Western techniques these dramatic works are certainly experimental, but they convey their meaning much too explicitly to be considered *avant-garde* in the usual Western sense of the term.

The same blending of old and new forms, and of Chinese and Western techniques, can be seen in the work of painters such as Li K'o-jan, Shih Lu, Ch'ien Sung-yen and T'ao I-ch'ing, who in their scrolls combine a skilful use of the traditional medium with some degree of Western realism, to celebrate the achievements of the new society and the eternal beauty of the Chinese landscape. There is today no room, in any walk of Chinese life, for the individualist. Not only has orthodoxy been re-established from above, but the artists themselves are anxious to communicate with a public still largely uneducated in the arts. To them, modern Western movements which push the frontiers of art to new limits, or require a commentary to be comprehensible at all, have no appeal.

The Great Proletarian Cultural Revolution of 1966–69 launched a devastating attack upon current trends in education, scholarship and the arts. Universities and art schools were closed, museums shut their doors, there were no more art exhibitions, and in June 1966 publication of all the art and archaeological journals abruptly ceased. Almost everyone engaged in these activities was criticized for bourgeois 'revisionist' attitudes, and some individuals were publicly

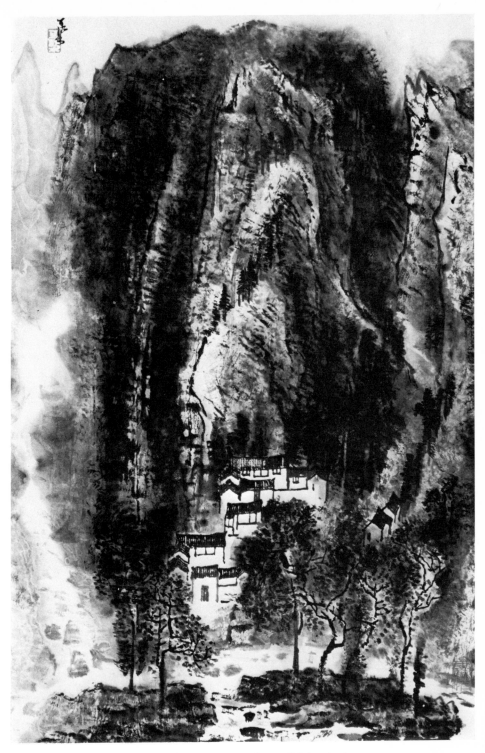

234 Li K'o-jan (born 1907). *Village in the Mountains*. Hanging scroll. Ink and colour on paper.

humiliated. The impression formed abroad was that all scholarly and artistic activity had come to an end – an impression which the Chinese authorities themselves did nothing to dispel.

Then, in 1971, reports began to spread of sensational discoveries made during the previous five years – some at the height of the Cultural Revolution – which were confirmed when in 1972 publication of the archaeological journals was resumed. It then became clear that rumours circulating abroad about the destruction of works of art and ancient monuments by extremist elements in the Red Guard had been greatly exaggerated, and that, even though the museums were closed to the public, archaeology and conservation had continued at the high level they had attained after 1949.

During the turbulent years of the Cultural Revolution painters and sculptors tended to sink their individuality in anonymous group projects such as *The Rent Collection Courtyard*, which, although completed in 1965, was praised by the leaders of the Cultural Revolution as a model and was widely copied. This is a dramatic tableau of life-size figures in clay plaster, which re-creates round the courtyard of a rapacious former landlord in Szechwan a harrowing scene that had been only too familiar to the local tenant-farmers before Liberation. By 1972 some artists of whom nothing had been heard for six years were found to be quietly going on with their work, and in May of that year the first major exhibition of contemporary Chinese painting

235 Anonymous team of sculptors. *The Rent Collection Courtyard*, 1965. Detail of a life-size tableau in clay-plaster, in a former landlord's mansion at Ta-yi, Szechwan.

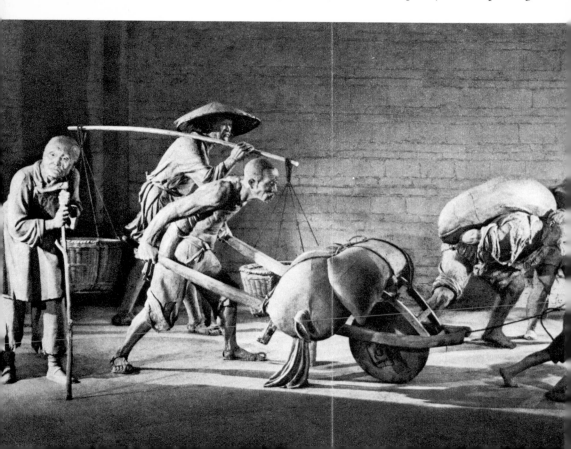

since 1966 was held in Peking. It was noted that a number of the pictures in that exhibition once again bore the signatures and seals of the artists themselves.

Earlier editions of this book ended with the suggestion that the storms of the previous fifty years were over, and that Chinese civilization had resumed its steady flow into the future. The upheaval of 1966–69 has left us wondering whether the flow was quite as steady as it had appeared. For to maintain the mood of intense idealism and dedication generated by the Cultural Revolution demands constant and unrelenting effort. That the remnants of the old intelligentsia have been under heavy pressure is undeniable. Readers of this book brought up in the Western liberal tradition may well ask, has it been worth it? Has not the improvement in the lot of the masses been bought at too great a cost? Does not the playing down of individual creative achievement in the arts lead to the stifling of the human spirit, and so to the death of art itself?

To these questions the new China answers a resounding 'no'. Indeed, there is a deep creative satisfaction to be got from serving and helping to educate one's fellow men, from writing poems and painting pictures that move them, a sense of being wanted by society which some Western artists, driven to exploit a personal idiosyncracy to gain any attention at all, may well envy.

The Chinese, moreover, take now, as they have always taken, a very long view. The time to talk about the freedom

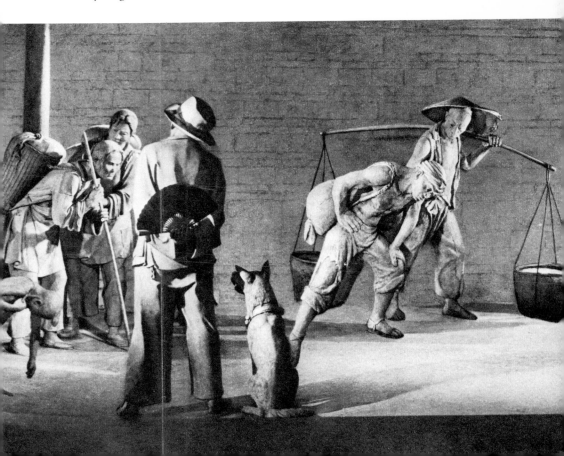

of the individual, they say, will come when the basic conditions of security and a livelihood for all have been fulfilled. They feel that at this moment in their history they are faced with but two alternatives: to create, as in the old days, for an élite and lose touch with the masses, or to work for the masses and so raise the level of Chinese culture as a whole; and they have decisively chosen the latter course. Some artists, musicians and writers made the choice entirely voluntarily, others only after thorough and agonizing 're-education'. What choices will be open when the general standard of creation and appreciation in the arts has been raised remains to be seen. But unless, as seems extremely unlikely, 'revisionism' once more gains the upper hand, and Chairman Mao's philosophy is repudiated, the guiding principle for creative artists and craftsmen must surely continue to be to 'serve the people'.

Notes to the text

CHAPTER 1

1 Kwang-chih Chang (Chang Kwang-chih), *The Archaeology of Ancient China*, 2nd ed. (New Haven, Connecticut, 1968), page 148.

CHAPTER 2

1 Mizuno Seiichi, *Bronzes and Jades of Ancient China* (1959), pages 8–9.

2 Some years ago Bernhard Karlgren, studying the form and decoration of a large number of Shang bronzes, divided them into two distinct styles, A and B. He could not explain, however, why there should be two styles. Recently, however, Chang Kwang-chih has suggested a simple solution to the problem. He has shown that the Shang rulers had a dualistic system whereby the succession went to two different groups of the royal house alternately; there were two traditions of the oracle-bone scripts, two parallel rows of royal ancestral halls, two clusters of royal tombs. It is reasonable to suppose, therefore, that the two bronze styles may have been associated with the two lines of succession of the royal family. See Kwang-chih Chang, *The Archaeology of Ancient China*, 2nd ed. (New Haven, Connecticut, 1968), page 255.

CHAPTER 3

1 Arthur Waley, *The Book of Songs* (London, 1937), pages 282–3.

2 Hsia Nai, 'Tracing the Thread of the Past', *China Reconstructs* 8, 10 (October 1959), page 46.

CHAPTER 4

1 It was Arthur Waley in his *An Introduction to the Study of Chinese Painting* (London, 1923, pages 21–23) who first pointed out the importance of Ch'u in the emergence in ancient China both of creative art and of a consciousness of the power of the artistic imagination. More recently David Hawkes has discussed the contribution of Ch'u in his *Ch'u Tz'u, The Songs of the South* (Oxford, 1959). He ends his General Introduction (page 19) with these words: 'As we begin to learn from the archaeologists something of the art of that great but ill-fated Kingdom of Ch'u, it becomes apparent that what we have in the earlier poems of *Ch'u Tz'u* is not an isolated and unaccountable literary phenomenon, but the full flowering of a remarkable and fascinating culture.'

2 David Hawkes, *op. cit.*, page 108. The phrase *hsi-pi*, indicating the Western origin of these buckles, may be derived from the Turkic-Mongol word for a garment hook, *Särbe*.

3 See Su T'ien-chun, 'Report on the Excavation of a Warring States Tomb at Sung-yüan-ts'un, Ch'ang-p'ing District, Peking', *Wen Wu* 9, 1959, pages 53–55 (in Chinese). These remarks, written in 1966, are borne out by a thermoluminescence test on twenty-two typical 'Hui-hsien' pieces, chiefly from well-known English and American collections, all of which were proved to be modern. See S.J. Fleming and E.H. Sampson, 'The Authenticity of Figurines, Animals and Pottery Facsimiles of Bronzes in the Hui Hsien Style', *Archaeometry* 14, 2 (1972), pages 237–44.

CHAPTER 5

1 David Hawkes, *Ch'u Tz'u, The Songs of the South* (Oxford, 1959), pages 105–7. Hawkes suggests (page 103) that this poem may have been written in 208 or 207 BC.

2 B. Karlgren, 'Early Chinese Mirror Inscriptions', *B.M.F.E.A.* 6 (1934), page 49.

3 As fresh discoveries increase the number of known kilns – only a very few of which are mentioned in this book – the problem of nomenclature becomes more and more acute. But until Chinese ceramics experts produce a new definitive classification it would not be helpful to the reader to depart too far from accepted names for well-known wares.

CHAPTER 6

1 There are a number of delightful stories about him in his official biography and in that fascinating collection of gossip, *Shih-shuo hsin-yü*. See Arthur Waley's account of him in his *An Introduction to the Study of Chinese Painting* (London, 1923), and Ch'en Shih-hsiang's translation of the official life, No. 2 in the University of California's translations of Chinese Dynastic Histories (Berkeley, 1953).

2 A Late Sung version of the *Lieh-nü t'u* in Peking is illustrated in *Wen-wu ts'an-k'ao tzu-liao*, 1958, 6, pages 22–24. The copyist has made effective use of the shading technique for drapery (visible also in the bed-hangings of the *Admonitions* scroll), which seems to have been a peculiarity of Ku's style, and suggests possible foreign influence.

3 This motive was frankly admitted in an edict of one of the barbarian rulers of Later Chao (*c.* 335): 'We were born out of the marches,' he declared, 'and though We are unworthy, We have complied with our appointed destiny and govern the Chinese as their prince. . . . Buddha being a barbarian god is the very one we should worship.' See Arthur Wright, 'Fo-t'u-teng, A Biography', *Harvard Journal of Asiatic Studies II* (1948), page 356.

4 The caves were first documented by Sir Aurel Stein, who visited them in 1907 and brought away with him a large collection of manuscripts and paintings from a sealed library. In the following year the great French sinologue Paul Pelliot systematically photographed and numbered the caves. His numbers, totalling nearly three hundred, are familiar to Western readers, and appear in my text in brackets preceded by the letter P. A second system of numbering was used by the noted painter Chang Ta-ch'ien, who with his assistants copied some of the frescoes during the Second World War. A third system was adopted by the National Art Research Institute of Tunhuang, which since 1943 has been actively engaged in preserving, restoring and copying the painting under the directorship of Ch'ang Shu-hung. This organization has now identified 492 caves and niches, and I have used their system in this book.

CHAPTER 7

1 It was probably the demands of Mahāyāna Buddhism for the endless multiplication of icons, diagrams, spells and texts that brought about the rapid development of block-printing during the T'ang dynasty. The earliest printed text yet discovered is a Buddhist charm dated equivalent to AD 770, found at Tunhuang by Sir Aurel Stein. It is likely, however, that the Chinese and Tibetans had been experimenting with block-printing since the middle of the sixth century, while the use of seals in Shang China and the practice of taking rubbings of inscriptions engraved on stone (made possible by the Han invention of paper) point to the existence of printing of a sort at a far earlier date.

2 *Aḥbār aṣ-Ṣīn Wa I-Hind.* Trans. and ed. Jean Sauvaget (1948), 16, Section 34.

3 The Ting ware kilns at Chien-tz'u-ts'un in Hopei were already producing a fine white porcelain, which may have been the elusive Hsing-yao.

4 See *Chinese Tomb Pottery Figurines* (Hong Kong, 1953), page 9.

5 From the *Compendium of Deities of the Three Religions, San chiao sou shen ta chuan*, quoted in Lu Hsün, *A Brief History of Chinese Fiction*, trans. Yang Hsien-yi and Gladys Yang (Peking, 1959), pages 21–22.

CHAPTER 8

1 *The Art and Architecture of China* (London, 1968), pages 97–98.

2 This passage has been slightly adapted from Tsung Pai-hua, 'Space-consciousness in Chinese Painting', *Sino-Austrian Cultural Association Journal I* (1949), page 27 (trans. Ernst J. Schwartz). Chinese theorists distinguish between three kinds of perspective in Chinese painting: *kao yüan* ('high distance') depicts the mountains as they would be seen by someone who was looking upwards from below; *shen yüan* ('deep distance') presents a bird's-eye view over successive ranges to a high and distant horizon, while *p'ing yüan* ('level distance') involves a continuous recession to a rather low horizon, such as we most often encounter in European landscape-painting.

3 This passage has been slightly adapted from Naitō Tōichirō, *The Wall-Paintings of Hōryuji*, trans. William Acker and Benjamin Rowland Jr (Baltimore, 1943), pages 205–6.

4 *The Awakening of Japan* (1905), page 77.

CHAPTER 9

1 *The Book of Ser Marco Polo*, trans. Sir H. Yule (London, 1903).

2 This scarcely applied to the inscriptions penned by the Ch'ien-lung Emperor on paintings in his collection. He had added no less than fifty-four to a Wang Meng landscape in the imperial collection before he could bring himself to write,

'Hereafter when this painting is unrolled for my pleasure, never again will I inscribe it.'

3 Chang Yen-yüan in the *Li-tai ming-hua-chi* mentions three bamboo-paintings executed before AD 600, and bamboo can be seen in the murals in several of the Six Dynasties caves at Tunhuang.

CHAPTER 10

1 Yung-lo is not, properly speaking, the name of the Emperor, but an auspicious title which he gave to his reign-period as a whole, thus doing away with the old system of choosing a new era-name every few years. The custom continued during the Ch'ing dynasty. K'ang-hsi, for example, is the title of the reign-period of the Emperor Sheng-tsu, Ch'ien-lung that of Kao-tsung. But because these reign-titles have become so well known in the West, chiefly through their use as marks on Chinese porcelain, I shall continue to use them in this book.

2 Adapted from Richard Edwards, *The Field of Stones: A Study of the Art of Shen Chou* (Washington, 1962), page 40.

3 See Sir Percival David, *Chinese Connoisseurship: the Essential Criteria of Antiquities* (London, 1971), pages 143–4.

CHAPTER 11

1 The catalogue of the Ch'ien-lung collection, *Shih-ch'ü pao-chi*, was compiled in three volumes between 1745 and 1817. Buddhist and Taoist works were catalogued separately. A survey made by the Palace Museum authorities in 1928–31 showed the vast scale of the collection: nine thousand paintings, rubbings and specimens of calligraphy, ten thousand pieces of porcelain, over twelve hundred bronze objects (including mirrors), and a large quantity of textiles, jades and minor arts. Some of the finest pieces had been sold or given away by the last Manchu emperor, P'u-i, during the twenty years following the Revolution of 1911. All but a fraction of the remainder were shipped to Taiwan by the Kuomintang before they quit China in 1949.

2 Europe, at this time, felt much the same way about China. 'In *Painting*', wrote Alvarez de Semedo in 1641, 'they have more curiositie, than perfection. They know not how to make use of either *Oyles* or *Shadowing* in the Art. . . . But at present there are some of them, who have been taught by us, that use *Oyles*, and are come to make perfect pictures.' Sandrart, in his *Teutsche Akademie* (1675), expressed a similar view. Cf. my article 'Sandrart on Chinese Painting', *Oriental Art*, I, 4 (spring 1949), pages 159–61.

3 See A. C. Soper, *Kuo Jo-hsü's Experiences in Painting* (Washington, 1951), page 16.

4 They were originally published in the Jesuit miscellany *Lettres édifiantes et curieuses*, vols XII and XVI (1717 and 1724), reprinted in S. W. Bushell, *Description of Chinese Pottery and Porcelain* (Oxford, 1910), and translated in part in Bushell, *Oriental Ceramic Art* (New York, 1899). Some interesting passages are quoted by Soame Jenyns in his *Later Chinese Porcelain* (London, 1951), pages 6–14.

Books for reference and further reading

GENERAL WORKS ON CHINA

Raymond Dawson, ed., *The Legacy of China* (Oxford, 1964)
Wolfram Eberhard, *A History of China* (London, 1960)
C.P. Fitzgerald, *China: A Short Cultural History* (third rev. ed., London, 1961)
L. Carrington Goodrich, *A Short History of the Chinese People* (rev. ed., London, 1959)
Joseph Needham, *Science and Civilisation in China*, vol. I (Cambridge, 1954)

GENERAL WORKS ON CHINESE ART

S. Howard Hansford, *A Glossary of Chinese Art and Archaeology* (rev. ed., London, 1961)
Sherman E. Lee, *A History of Far Eastern Art* (London, 1964)
Laurence Sickman and A.C. Soper, *The Art and Architecture of China* (rev. ed., London, 1968)
Michael Sullivan, *Chinese Art in the Twentieth Century* (London, Berkeley and Los Angeles, 1959); *Chinese and Japanese Art* (vol. IX of 'Great Art and Artists of the World', New York, 1966); *The Meeting of Eastern and Western Art* (London and New York, 1973); *Chinese Art, Recent Discoveries* (London and New York, 1973)

EXHIBITIONS AND GENERAL COLLECTIONS

Royal Academy of Arts, *The Chinese Exhibition: A Commemorative Catalogue of the International Exhibition of Chinese Art in 1935–36* (London, 1936)
S. Howard Hansford, *Chinese, Central Asian and Luristan Bronzes and Chinese Jades and Sculptures* (Vol. I of 'The Seligman Collection of Oriental Art', London, 1957)
R.L. Hobson and W.P. Yetts, *The George Eumorfopoulos Collection* (9 vols, London, 1925–32)
Sherman E. Lee and Wai-Kam Ho, *Chinese Art under the Mongols: The Yüan Dynasty (1279–1368)* (Cleveland, 1969)
Nils Palmgren, *Selected Chinese Antiquities from the Collection of Gustav Adolf, Crown Prince of Sweden* (Stockholm, 1948)
Michael Sullivan, *Chinese Ceramics, Bronzes and Jades in the Collection of Sir Alan and Lady Barlow* (London, 1963)

ARCHAEOLOGY

Terukazu Akiyama and others, *Arts of China, Neolithic Cultures to the T'ang Dynasty: New Discoveries* (Tokyo and Palo Alto, 1968)
J.G. Andersson, *Children of the Yellow Earth* (London, 1934)

Anon., *Historical Relics Unearthed in New China* (Peking, 1972)
Kwang-chih Chang, *The Archaeology of Ancient China* (rev. ed., New Haven, Connecticut, and London, 1968)
Cheng Te-k'un, 'Archaeology in China:' vol. I, *Prehistoric China* (Cambridge, 1959); vol. II, *Shang China* (Cambridge, 1960); vol. III, *Chou China* (Cambridge, 1966); *New Light on Prehistoric China* (Cambridge, 1966)
H.G. Creel, *The Birth of China* (rev. ed., New York, 1954)
Li Chi, *The Beginnings of Chinese Civilisation* (Seattle, 1957)

BRONZE

Noel Barnard, *Bronze Casting and Bronze Alloys in Ancient China* (Canberra and Nagoya, 1961)
Bernhard Karlgren, *A Catalogue of the Chinese Bronzes in the Alfred F. Pillsbury Collection* (Minneapolis, 1952); many important articles in the *Bulletin of the Museum of Far Eastern Antiquities* (Stockholm)
J.E. Lodge, A. Wenley, and J.A. Pope, *A Descriptive and Illustrative Catalogue of Chinese Bronzes* (Washington, 1946)
Max Loehr, *Chinese Bronze Age Weapons* (Ann Arbor, 1956); *Ritual Vessels of Bronze Age China* (New York, 1968)
J.A. Pope and others, *The Freer Chinese Bronzes* (2 vols, Washington, 1968)
Mizuno Seiichi, *Bronzes and Jades of Ancient China* (in Japanese with English summary, Kyoto, 1959)
William Watson, *Ancient Chinese Bronzes* (London, 1962)

PAINTING AND CALLIGRAPHY

James Cahill, *Chinese Painting* (New York, 1960); *The Restless Landscape: Chinese Painting of the Late Ming Period* (Berkeley, 1971)
Chiang Yee, *Chinese Calligraphy* (London, 1954)
Lucy Driscoll and Kenji Toda, *Chinese Calligraphy* (second ed., New York, 1964)
Richard Edwards, *The Field of Stones: A Study of the Art of Shen Chou* (Washington, 1962)
Basil Gray and John B. Vincent, *Buddhist Cave Paintings at Tun-huang* (London, 1959)
R.H. van Gulik, *Chinese Pictorial Art as Viewed by the Connoisseur* (Rome, 1958)
Kuo Hsi, *An Essay on Landscape Painting*, trans. S. Sakanishi ('Wisdom of the East' series, London, 1936)
Sherman E. Lee, *Chinese Landscape Painting* (rev. ed., Cleveland, 1962)
S. Sakanishi, *The Spirit of the Brush* ('Wisdom of the East' series, London, 1939)

Osvald Sirén, *The Chinese on the Art of Painting*
(New York, 1963); *Chinese Painting: Leading
Masters and Principles* (7 vols, London, 1956 and
1958)
A. C. Soper, *Kuo Jo-hsü's Experiences in Painting,
T'u-hua chien-wen chih* (Washington, 1951)
Laurence Sickman, ed., *Chinese Painting and
Calligraphy in the Collection of John M. Craw-
ford Jr* (New York, 1962)
Michael Sullivan, *The Birth of Landscape Painting
in China* (Berkeley, Los Angeles and London,
1961)
Tseng Yu-ho Ecke and Jean Gordon Lee, *Chinese
Calligraphy* (Philadelphia, 1971)
Arthur Waley, *An Introduction to the Study of
Chinese Painting* (London, 1923; more fully
illustrated ed., 1958)

SCULPTURE

Leroy Davidson, *The Lotus Sutra in Chinese Art*
(New York, 1954)
Mizuno Seiichi and Nagahiro Toshio, *Unko
Sekkutsu: Yun-kang, The Buddhist Cave Temples
of the Fifth Century* AD *in North China* (16 vols,
in Japanese with English summary, Kyoto,
1952–55); *Chinese Stone Sculpture* (Tokyo,
1950); *Bronze and Stone Sculpture of China: From
the Yin to the T'ang Dynasty* (in Japanese and
English, Tokyo, 1960)
Alan Priest, *Chinese Sculpture in the Metropolitan
Museum of Art* (New York, 1954)
Richard Rudolf, *Han Tomb Art of West China*
(Berkeley and Los Angeles, 1951)
Osvald Sirén, *Chinese Sculpture from the Fifth to the
Fourteenth Centuries* (4 vols, London, 1925)
A. C. Soper, *Literary Evidence for Early Buddhist
Art in China* (Ascona, 1959)
Michael Sullivan and Dominique Darbois, *The
Cave Temples of Maichishan* (London, Berkeley
and Los Angeles, 1969)

ARCHITECTURE

Andrew Boyd, *Chinese Architecture and Town
Planning* (London, 1962)
J. Prip-Møller, *Chinese Buddhist Monasteries*
(Copenhagen and London, 1937)
Osvald Sirén, *The Walls and Gates of Peking* (Lon-
don, 1924); *The Imperial Palaces of Peking* (3
vols, Paris and Brussels, 1926); *Gardens of
China* (New York, 1949)

CERAMICS

John Ayers, *Chinese and Korean Pottery and Porce-
lain* (vol. II of 'The Seligman Collection of
Oriental Art', London, 1964); *The Baur Collec-
tion* (2 vols, London, 1972)
Stephen Bushell, *Description of Chinese Pottery and
Porcelain: Being a Translation of the T'ao Shuo*
(Oxford, 1910)
Sir Harry Garner, *Oriental Blue and White* (Lon-
don, 1954)

G. St G. M. Gompertz, *Chinese Celadon Wares*
(London, 1958)
A. L. Hetherington, *Chinese Ceramic Glazes* (Lon-
don, 1948)
R. L. Hobson, *Chinese Pottery and Porcelain* (Lon-
don, 1915); *The Wares of the Ming Dynasty*
(London, 1923); *A Catalogue of Chinese Pottery
and Porcelain in the Collection of Sir Percival
David* (London, 1934)
W. B. Honey, *The Ceramic Art of China and Other
Countries of the Far East* (London, 1945)
Soame Jenyns, *Ming Pottery and Porcelain* (London,
1953); *Later Chinese Porcelain* (rev. ed., London,
1965)
John A. Pope, *Fourteenth-century Blue and White:
A Group of Chinese Porcelains in the Topkapu
Sarayi Musesi, Istanbul* (Washington, 1952);
Chinese Porcelains from the Ardebil Shrine (Wash-
ington, 1956)
G. D. Wu, *Prehistoric Pottery in China* (London,
1938)
See also under EXHIBITIONS AND GENERAL COL-
LECTIONS

JADE AND MINOR ARTS

Schuyler Cammann, *China's Dragon Robes* (New
York, 1952)
Martin Feddersen, *Chinese Decorative Art* (London,
1961)
Sir Harry Garner, *Chinese and Japanese Cloisonné
Enamels* (London, 1962)
S. Howard Hansford, *Chinese Jade Carving* (Lon-
don, 1950); *Chinese Carved Jades* (London, 1968)
Soame Jenyns and William Watson, *Chinese Art:
The Minor Arts* (London, 1963)
George N. Kates, *Chinese Household Furniture*
(London, 1948)
Berthold Laufer, *Jade: A Study in Chinese Archaeo-
logy and Religion* (New York, 1912)
Alfred Salmony, *Chinese Jade through the Wei
Dynasty* (New York, 1963)
Pauline Simmons, *Chinese Patterned Silks* (New
York, 1948)

PERIODICALS

Archives of Asian Art, formerly *Archives of the
Chinese Art Society of America* (New York,
1945–)
Ars Orientalis (Washington and Ann Arbor,
1954–)
Artibus Asiae (Dresden, 1925– ; Ascona, 1947–)
Bulletin of the Museum of Far Eastern Antiquities
(Stockholm, 1929–)
China Reconstructs (Peking, 1950–)
Far Eastern Ceramic Bulletin (Boston, 1948–50; Ann
Arbor, 1951–60)
Oriental Art (Oxford, 1948–51, New Series,
1955–)
Ostasiatische Zeitschrift (Berlin, 1912–43)
Revue des Arts Asiatiques (Paris, 1924–39)
Transactions of the Oriental Ceramic Society (Lon-
don, 1921–)

List of Illustrations

The diagrams and maps, which are not included in the numbered sequence of illustrations, are listed separately at the end of this section.

55 Detail of a tile from a tomb-shrine. Ht 19 cm. Boston.

56 Painted banner. Silk. Detail. From Ma-wang-tui, Changsha, Hunan.

57 Covered square-section jar, *fang-hu*. Ht 50·5 cm. From a tomb at Ma-wang-tui, Changsha, Hunan.

58 Paragons of filial piety. Lacquer painting on basket-work box. Ht of figures about 5 cm. From Lo-lang, Korea. National Museum, Seoul.

59 Fairy mountain incense-burner, *Po-shan hsiang-lu*. Bronze inlaid with gold. Ht 26 cm. From the tomb of Liu Sheng at Man-ch'eng, Hopei.

60 'TLV'-type mirror. Bronze. Diam. 18 cm. Seligman Collection, Arts Council of Great Britain, London.

61 Mirror. Bronze. Diam. 13·7 cm. Brundage Collection.

62 Head and shoulders of a horse. Jade. Ht 18·9 cm. Victoria and Albert Museum, London.

63 Woven silk textile. From the tomb at Ma-wang-tui, Changsha, Hunan.

64 Figured silk fabric from Noin-Ula, Mongolia. Hermitage Museum, Leningrad.

65 Jar, *hu*. Ht 36·5 cm. Nelson Gallery.

66 Watch-tower. Ht 84 cm. Freer Gallery.

67 Dog. Pottery. Ht 35·5 cm. From Changsha, Hunan. Brundage Collection.

68 Coin-tree or lamp-stand. Pottery. Ht 33·9 cm. From a tomb at Nei-chiang, Szechwan.

69 Tray with figures of acrobats, dancers, musicians and spectators or attendants. Painted pottery. L. 67·5 cm. From a tomb at Tsinan, Shantung.

70 Basin. Stoneware, Yüeh ware. Diam. 28·8 cm. Walker Art Center, Minneapolis.

71 After Ku K'ai-chih. The Emperor with one of his concubines. Illustration to *The Admonitions of the Instructress*. Detail of a handscroll. Ht 25 cm. British Museum.

72 Filial piety scenes. Panel from a wooden screen painted in lacquer. Ht of panel 81·5 cm. From a tomb at Ta-t'ung, Shansi.

73 After Ku K'ai-chih. Illustration to *The Fairy of the Lo River*. Detail of a handscroll. Ht 24 cm. Freer Gallery.

74 The story of the Filial Shun. Detail of an engraved stone slab from a sarcophagus. Ht 61 cm. Nelson Gallery.

75 Śākyamuni Buddha. Gilt-bronze. Brundage Collection.

76 Twelve-sided pagoda of Sung-yüeh-ssu on Mount Sung, Honan.

77 Mai-chi-shan, general view from the south-east. Photograph Dominique Darbois.

78 Śākyamuni Buddha with attendant Buddha, perhaps Maitreya, Yünkang. Ht of seated figure 13·7 m.

79 Interior of Cave VII, Yünkang.

80 Buddha group, south wall of Pin-yang-tung Cave, Lungmen. Ht of main figure 13·83 m.

81 The Wei Empress in procession with court ladies. Restored relief panel from Pin-yang-tung Cave, Lung-men. Ht 198 cm, w. 277 cm. Nelson Gallery.

82 Stele illustrating scenes from the Life of the Buddha and the Teachings of the *Lotus Sūtra*. Stone. In Cave 133, Mai-chi-shan, Kansu. Photograph Dominique Darbois.

83 Prabhūtaratna and Śākyamuni. Gilt-bronze. Ht 26 cm. Musée Guimet, Paris.

84 *Bodhisattva*. Stone. Ht 188 cm. University of Pennsylvania Museum, Philadelphia.

85 Worshippers. Fragment of a Buddhist stone relief from Wan-lo-ssu. Ch'iung-lai, Szechwan.

86 Buddha preaching the law. Wall-painting in Cave 249 (Pelliot 101), Tunhuang.

87 The Buddha incarnate in a golden gazelle (the Rūrū Jatakā). Wall-painting in Cave 257 (Pelliot 110), Tun-huang. Photograph Dominique Darbois.

88 Hunting scene on the lower part of the ceiling of Cave 249 (Pelliot 101), Tunhuang.

89 Chimera. Stone. University of Pennsylvania Museum, Philadelphia.

90 Dragon. Gilt-bronze. L. 19 cm. Fogg Museum of Art, Cambridge, Massachusetts.

91 Vase. Stoneware. Ht 23 cm. From a tomb at Anyang, Honan.

92 Flask. Stoneware. Ht 19·5 cm. From a tomb at Anyang, Honan.

93 Horse. Painted pottery. Ht 24·1 cm. Said to be from a tomb near Loyang, Honan. Royal Ontario Museum, Toronto.

94 Water-container in the form of a lion (or dog?). Stoneware, Yüeh ware. L. 12·1 cm. Brundage Collection.

95 'Chicken ewer'. Stoneware, Yüeh ware. Ht 33 cm. Musée Guimet, Paris.

96 Brick pagoda of Hsing-chiao-ssu, Sian, Shensi.

97 Charger and his groom. Stone relief from the tomb of the Emperor T'ai-tsung. L. 152 cm. University of Pennsylvania Museum, Philadelphia.

98 Vairoćana Buddha flanked by Ānanda, Kāśyapa, and attendant *bodhisattvas*. Stone sculpture. Ht of main figure 13·37 m. From Feng-hsien-ssu, Lungmen, Honan.

99 Torso of standing Buddha. Udyāna type. White marble. Ht 145 cm. From Hsiu-te Pagoda near Ch'ü-yang, Ting-chou, Hopei. Victoria and Albert Museum, London.

100 Seated Buddha (head restored). Stone. Ht 11·5 cm. From Cave XXI, north wall, T'ien-lung-shan, Shansi. Fogg Art Museum, Cambridge, Massachusetts.

101 The sage Vimalakīrti. Detail of a wall-painting in Cave 103 (Pelliot 137M), Tunhuang.

102 The Paradise of Amitābha. Detail of a wall-painting in the Kondō (Golden Hall) of Hōryūjï, Nara, Japan.

103 Pilgrims and travellers in a landscape. Wall-painting in Cave 217 (Pelliot 70), Tunhuang. Photograph Dominique Darbois.

104 Yen Li-pen. Detail of the handscroll of the Thirteen Emperors from Han to Sui. Ht 51 cm. Boston.

105 Female attendants. Wall-painting from the tomb of Princess Yung-t'ai near Sian, Shensi.

106 Han Kan. Painting of Light of the Night. Detail of a handscroll. Ht 29·5 cm. Mrs John D. Riddell, London.

107 Style of Wang Wei (?). *Riverside under Snow*. Part of a handscroll (?). Formerly Manchu Household Collection.

108 Anonymous. *Ming Huang's Journey to Shu*, or *An Imperial Excursion in the Hills*. Hanging scroll. Ht 55·9 cm. Taipei.

109 Covered jar with swing handle. Ht 24 cm. Excavated at Ho-chia-ts'un, Sian.

110 Octagonal wine-cup. Ht 6·5 cm. Excavated at Ho-chia-ts'un, Sian.

111 'Lion and grape' mirror. Mr and Mrs Myron S. Falk, New York.

112 Phoenix-head ewer. Ht 24·75 cm. Royal Ontario Museum, Toronto.

113 Jar. Ht 17·8 cm. Brundage Collection.

114 Vase, Hsing ware (?). Ht 23·5 cm. Brundage Collection.

115 Lobed bowl, Yüeh ware. Diam. 19 cm. Victoria and Albert Museum, London.

116 Seated woman. Earthenware. From a tomb at Loyang, Honan.

117 Tomb guardian trampling on a demon. Earthenware. Brundage Collection.

118 Camel carrying a band of musicians. Earthenware. Ht about 70 cm. From a tomb at Sian, Shensi.

119 Twelve-sided pagoda of Fu-kuang-ssu, Ying-hsien, Shensi.

120 Interior of the Buddha Hall of Upper Hua-yen Monastery, Ta-t'ung, Shansi.

121 Lohan. Earthenware. Ht 105 cm. From I-chou, Hopei. Metropolitan Museum of Art, New York, Hewitt Fund, 1921.

122 Kuanyin. Sculpture in wood and gesso. Ht 225 cm. Nelson Gallery.

123 Soul suffering the torments of Hell. Stone relief sculpture on a cliff at Ta-tsu, Szechwan. Ht about 50 cm.

124 In the manner of Shih K'o. *Two Minds in Harmony*. Part of a handscroll. Ht 44 cm. National Museum, Tokyo.

125 Attributed to Ku Hung-chung. *A Night Entertainment of Han Hsi-tsai*. Detail of a handscroll. Ht 29 cm. Palace Museum, Peking.

126 Attributed to Li Lung-mien. *A Horse*. One of five tribute horses. Detail of a handscroll. Ht 30·1 cm. Formerly Manchu Household Collection.

127 Fan K'uan. *Travelling amid Mountains and Gorges*. Detail of a hanging scroll. Ht 206·3 cm. Taipei.

128 Attributed to Tung Yüan. *Scenery along the Hsiao and Hsiang Rivers*. Detail of a handscroll. Palace Museum, Peking.

129 Chang Tse-tuan. *Life along the River on the Eve of the Ch'ing-ming Festival*. Detail of a handscroll. Ht 25·5 cm. Palace Museum, Peking.

130 Attributed to Su Tung-p'o. *Bare Tree, Bamboo and Rocks*. Handscroll. Ht 23·4 cm. Palace Museum, Peking.

131 Mi Yu-jen. *Misty Landscape*. Hanging scroll. Ht 24·7 cm. Osaka Municipal Museum, Japan (former Abe Collection).

132 Sung Hui-tsung. *The Five-colour Parakeet*. Hanging scroll. Ht 53 cm. Boston.

133 Attributed to Huang Chü-ts'ai. *Pheasant and Sparrows among Rocks and Shrubs*. Hanging scroll. Ht 99 cm. Taipei.

134 Attributed to Li T'ang. *A Myriad Trees on Strange Peaks*. Fan. Ht 24·7 cm. Taipei.

135 Ma Yüan. *On a Mountain Path in Spring*. Album-leaf. Ht 27·4 cm. Taipei.

136 Hsia Kuei. *Pure and Remote View of Hills and Streams*. Detail of a handscroll. Ht 46·5 cm. Taipei.

137 Mu-ch'i. *Evening Glow on a Fishing Village*, one of the 'Eight Views of the Hsiao and Hsiang Rivers'. Detail of a handscroll. Ht 33·2 cm. Nezu Art Museum, Tokyo.

138 Mu-ch'i. *The White-robed Kuanyin*. Hanging scroll. Ht 142 cm. Daitokuji, Kyoto.

139 Ch'en Jung. *The Nine Dragons*. Detail of a handscroll. Ht 46 cm. Boston.

140 Funerary pillow. Ting ware, porcelain. Ht 15·3 cm. Brundage Collection.

141 Mei-p'ing vase. Honan stoneware. Ht 25·4 cm. Mrs Alfred Clark, Fulmer, Buckinghamshire.

142 Bottle with copper-bound rim. Ju ware. Ht 24·8 cm. Percival David.

143 Vase. Northern celadon stoneware. Ht 23·2 cm. Freer Gallery.

144 Jar. Chün stoneware. Ht 12·5 cm. Victoria and Albert Museum, London.

145 Jar. Tz'u-chou stoneware. Ht 20·5 cm. Brundage Collection.

146 Mei-p'ing vase. Tz'u-chou stoneware. Ht 49·5 cm. Brundage Collection.

147 Bowl. Tz'u-chou stoneware. Diam. 9 cm. Brundage Collection.

148 Traveller's flask. Stoneware. Ht 37·5 cm. North China. Private Collection, Japan.

149 Tea-bowl. Fukien *temmoku* stoneware. Diam. 13 cm. Seligman Collection, Arts Council of Great Britain, London.

150 Tripod incense-burner. *Kuan* stoneware. Ht 12·9 cm. Taipei.

151 Vase. *Kinuta*, Lung-ch'üan stoneware. Taipei.

152 Vase. Ch'ing-pai ware, white porcelain. Ht 13 cm. Seligman Collection, Arts Council of Great Britain, London.

153 Aerial view of the heart of Peking. Photograph taken in 1945.

154 Peking: the Forbidden City, looking north from the Wu-men to the T'ai-ho-men. Photograph Hedda Morrison.

155 Ch'ien Hsüan. *The Fourth-century Calligrapher Wang Hsi-chih Watching Geese*. Detail of a handscroll. Ht 23·2 cm. C. C. Wang Collection, New York.

156 Oracle bone, from Anyang. British Museum.

157 *Chuan-shu* script. Rubbing from one of the 'Stone Drums'. Wango H. C. Weng Collection, New York.

158 *Li-shu* script. Rubbing from a stone slab. After Driscoll and Toda.

159 *Ts'ao-shu* script. Ch'en Shun. Part of the inscription on his *Studies from Life*. Handscroll. Taipei.

160 *K'ai-shu* script. The Emperor Hui-tsung. Part of his *Poem on the Peony*, written in the 'thin gold' (shou-chin) style. Handscroll. Taipei.

161 *Hsing-shu* script. Chao Meng-fu. Part of his *Pao-t'u Spring Poem*. Handscroll. Taipei.

162 *K'uang-ts'ao-shu* script. Hsü Wei. Poem. Handscroll. Wango H. C. Weng Collection, New York.

163 Chao Meng-fu. *The Autumn Colours on the Ch'iao and Hua Mountains*. Detail of a handscroll. Ht 28·4 cm. Taipei.

164 Huang Kung-wang. *Living in the Fu-ch'un Mountains*. Detail of a handscroll. Taipei.

165 Ni Tsan. *The Jung-hsi Studio*. Hanging scroll. Ht 73·3 cm. Taipei.

166 Wang Meng. *Thatched Halls on Mount T'ai*. Hanging scroll. Ht 11·4 cm. Taipei.

167 Wu Chen. *Bamboo*. Album-leaf. Ht 42·9 cm. Taipei.

168 Colour woodblock print from the 'Kaempfer series'. British Museum.

169 Colour woodblock print from the *Shih-chu-chai hua-p'u* (*Treatise on the Paintings and Writings of the Ten Bamboo Studio*). British Museum.

170 Lü Chi. *A Pair of Wild Geese on a Snowy Bank*. Hanging scroll. Taipei.

171 Tai Chin. *Fishermen*. Detail of a handscroll. Ht 46 cm. Freer Gallery.

172 Shen Chou. *Landscape in the Manner of Ni Tsan*. Hanging scroll. Ht 140 cm. Nelson Gallery.

173 Shen Chou. *Returning Home from the Land of the Immortals*. Album-leaf mounted as a handscroll. Ht 38·9 cm. Nelson Gallery.

174 Wen Cheng-ming. *The Seven Junipers*. Album-leaf.

175 T'ang Yin. *Gentleman Playing the Lute in a Landscape*. Detail of a handscroll. Ht 27·3 cm. Taipei.

176 Ch'iu Ying. *Spring Dawn in the Han Palace*. Detail of a handscroll. Ht 30·5 cm. Taipei.

177 Tung Ch'i-ch'ang. *Dwelling in the Ch'ing-pien Mountains*. Hanging scroll. Wango H. C. Weng Collection, New York.

178 Wu Pin. Fantastic landscape. Hashimoto Collection, Takatsuki.

179 Yen-lo-wang (Yama). Pottery. Ht 83·8 cm. Royal Ontario Museum, Toronto.

180 *Magician Changing a Bamboo Walking-stick into a Dragon. K'o-ssu* silk tapestry. Taipei.

181 Imperial Dragon robe. Woven silk tapestry. Ht 139·8 cm. Victoria and Albert Museum, London.

182 Vase in the form of a paper-beater. Red lacquer. Ht 17 cm. Taipei.

183 Rectangular dish. Red, greenish-black and yellow lacquer. Taipei.

184 Jar on three lions. Cloisonné enamel. Ht 17 cm. Taipei.

185 Wine vessel, *tsun*, on the back of a phoenix. Cloisonné enamel. Ht 34·9 cm. Taipei.

186 Dish. Porcelain. Diam. 42·9 cm. Percival David.

187 Vase and stand. *Ch'ing-pai* porcelain. Ht 24·1 cm. Brundage Collection.

188 *Bodhisattva. Ch'ing-pai* porcelain. Ht 25 cm. Excavated at Yüan capital, Peking.

189 Wine-jar. White porcelain. Ht 36 cm. Excavated at Pao-ting, Shensi.

190 Temple vases. Porcelain. Ht 63 cm. Percival David.

191 Flask. Porcelain. Ht 47·6 cm. Taipei.

192 Bowl. Porcelain. Diam. 15·5 cm. Percival David.

193 'Monk's hat' jug. Porcelain. Ht 20 cm. Taipei.

194 Kuanyin. Fukien ware; white porcelain. Ht 22 cm University of Sussex, Trustees of the Barlow Collection

195 Vase. Stoneware. Ht 30·7 cm. British Museum.

196 'Fish jar'. Porcelain. Ht 43·1 cm. Brundage Collection.

197 Dish. Porcelain. 'Swatow ware', probably from Shih-ma, Fukien. Diam. 37·2 cm. Brundage Collection.

198 The Po-hai and the Summer Palace, Peking.

199 Peking: the Hall of Annual Prayers, Ch'i-nien-tien, in the Precinct of the Altar of Heaven. Photograph Hedda Morrison.

200 Giuseppe Castiglione. *A Hundred Horses in a Landscape*. Detail of a handscroll. Ht of handscroll 94·5 cm. Taipei.

201 Yüan Chiang. *Gentlemen Conversing in a Landscape*. Hanging scroll. Brundage Collection.

202 Wang Hui. *Landscape in the Manner of Fan K'uan*. Hanging scroll. Huang Pao-hsi Collection, Hong Kong.

203 Wang Yüan-ch'i. *Landscape in the Manner of Ni Tsan*. Hanging scroll. Ht 82 cm. Dr Franco Vannotti Collection, Lugano.

204 Yün Shou-p'ing. *Peony*. Leaf from an album of flower studies. Ht 26·3 cm. Taipei.

205 Wu Li. *White Clouds and Green Mountains*. Detail of a handscroll. Ht 25·9 cm. Taipei.

206 Hung-jen. *The Coming of Autumn*. Hanging scroll. Ht 122 cm. Honolulu Academy of Arts, Honolulu, Hawaii.

207 Kung Hsien. *A Thousand Peaks and A Myriad Rivers*. Hanging scroll. Ht 62·3 cm. Charles A. Drenowatz Collection, Zürich.

208 Hua Yen. Birds, tree and rock. Hanging scroll. Huang Pao-hsi Collection, Hong Kong.

209 Huang Shen. *The Poet T'ao Yüan-ming enjoys the Early Chrysanthemums*. Album-leaf. Ht 28 cm. Stanford Museum of Art, Stanford, California.

210 Chin Nung. Plum blossom. Hanging scroll. Huang Pao-hsi Collection, Hong Kong.

211 Chu Ta (Pa-ta Shan-jen). Landscape in the manner of Tung Yüan. Hanging scroll. Ht 180 cm. Ostasiatiska Museet, Stockholm.

212 Chu Ta. *Two Birds*. Album-leaf. Ht 31·8 cm. Sumitomo Collection, Oiso, Japan.

213 Shih-ch'i (K'un-ts'an). *Autumn Landscape*. Handscroll. Ht 31·5 cm. British Museum.

214 Shih-t'ao. *The Peach Blossom Spring*. Detail of a handscroll. Ht 25 cm. Freer Gallery.

215 Mei-p'ing vase. Porcelain. Ht 19·6 cm. Percival David.

216 Bottle. Porcelain. Ht 43·2 cm. Victoria and Albert Museum, London.

217 Teapot. *Famille verte* porcelain. Ht 12·9 cm. Percival David.

218 Double vase, *t'ao-p'ing*. Porcelain. Ht 38·5 cm. Taipei.

219 Vase. Porcelain. Ht 19 cm. The Mount Trust, England.

220 'Jesuit China' dish. Porcelain. Boston.

221 Ch'en Ming Yüan. Brush-rest. I-hsing ware. Ht 5·75 cm.

222 Carp leaping out of the water. Carved green jade. Ht 16·7 cm. Taipei.

223 Taoist Paradise. Carved red lacquer. L. 110·16 cm.

224 Snuff-bottle. Enamelled glass. Ht (without stopper) 5·8 cm. Percival David.

225 The Great Hall of the People, Peking. 1959.

226 Jen Po-nien. *Pine Tree and Mynah Birds*. Hanging scroll. Tan Tze-chor Collection, Singapore.

227 Wu Ch'ang-shih. *Lychee Nuts*. Hanging scroll. Ht 91·4 cm. Mr and Mrs Allen D. Christensen Collection, Atherton, California.

228 Ch'i Pai-shih. *The Thing for Prolonging Life is Wine!* Hanging scroll. Ht 62·2 cm. Private Collection, Stanford, California.

DIAGRAMS AND MAPS (*numbers refer to pages*)

Index